British Social Attitudes

special international report

D0433129

BEDFORD BOROUGH COUNCIL

WITHDRAWN FOR SALE

Price:

British Social Attitudes

special international report

Edited by
Roger Jowell
Sharon Witherspoon
& Lindsay Brook

Gower

© Social and Community Planning Research, 1989

All rights reserved. No part of this publication may be reproduced, stored in a retrieval system, or transmitted in any form or by any means, electronic, mechanical, photocopying, recording, or otherwise without the prior permission of Gower Publishing Company Limited.

Published by
Gower Publishing Company Limited,
Gower House,
Croft Road,
Aldershot,
Hants GU11 3HR
England

Gower Publishing Company,
Old Post Road,
Brookfield,
Vermont 05036,
USA

5694856

25 APR 1990   BEDFORDSHIRE LEISURE SERVICES COUNTY COUNCIL

British Library Cataloguing in Publication Data

British social attitudes: special international report: the 6th report
   1. Public opinion—Great Britain.
   2. Great Britain—Social conditions—1945-
   I. Jowell, Roger   II. Witherspoon, Sharon   III. Brook, Lindsay
   941.085′8   HD400.P8

R 941.0858
SOC

ISSN 0-267-6869
ISBN 0-566-05821 9 (Hbk)
ISBN 0-566-05824 3 (Pbk)

Typeset in Great Britain by Graham Burn Productions, Leighton Buzzard, Bedfordshire
Printed in Great Britain at the Alden Press, Oxford.

Contents

INTRODUCTION ... ix

CHAPTER 1. MEASURING NATIONAL DIFFERENCES
An introduction to the International Social Survey Programme (ISSP)
by James A. Davis and Roger Jowell 1

What is the ISSP? 2
Difficulties of cross-national measurements 4
Benefits of cross-national data 6
Conclusion 11
Notes 12
References 12
Acknowledgement 13

CHAPTER 2. INTERNATIONAL PATTERNS OF WORK
by David G. Blanchflower and Andrew J. Oswald 15

The value of national comparisons 16
Jobs and joblessness 18
Workforce profiles 18
Unemployment 20
Trade union membership 21
What do people earn? 23
Trade union strength 23
The analysis 24
Factors affecting earnings 24
Unionisation and wages 25
Self-employment 26
Hours of work 27
Conclusions 27

Notes	...	...	...	...	...	...	...	...	...	...	27
References		...	...	...	...	...	...	...	...	...	28
Tables (2.1–2.4)			...	...	...	...	...	...	...	...	30

CHAPTER 3. THE ROLE OF THE STATE
by Peter Taylor-Gooby **35**

Post-war 'welfare capitalism'	...	...	...	...	...	35
The future of welfare capitalism	...	...	...	...	...	36
Government and the economy	...	...	...	...	...	37
Attitudes to state intervention	...	...	...	...	...	37
Expenditure on public enterprise	...	...	...	...	...	39
Government and welfare	...	...	...	...	...	40
Attitudes to state responsibilities	...	...	...	...	...	40
Realities of state spending	...	...	...	...	...	42
Government and family life	...	...	...	...	...	44
Government and citizenship	...	...	...	...	...	46
Passive rights and civil liberties	...	...	...	...	...	46
Active rights and citizen equality	...	...	...	...	...	47
Government intervention: the overall pattern		...	...	...	...	49
State welfare and class solidarity	...	...	...	...	...	49
Conclusion	...	...	...	...	...	...	51
Notes	...	...	...	...	...	...	51
References	...	...	...	...	...	...	52
Tables (3.1–3.5)	...	...	...	...	...	...	53

CHAPTER 4. INEQUALITY AND WELFARE
by Tom W. Smith **59**

Support for welfare programmes	...	...	...	...	...	61
Taxation and redistribution	...	...	...	...	...	63
Sharing the tax burden	...	...	...	...	...	63
Progressive taxation and redistribution	...	...	...	...	64
Perceptions of inequality and social mobility		...	...	...	...	65
Beliefs about opportunity and mobility	...	...	...	...	67
Explanations of inequality	...	...	...	...	...	69
Assessments of social conflict	...	...	...	...	...	71
Inequality and class	...	...	...	...	...	...	72
Conclusions	...	...	...	...	...	...	74
Notes	...	...	...	...	...	...	75
References	...	...	...	...	...	...	76
Acknowledgement	...	...	...	...	...	...	77
Tables (4.1–4.5)	...	...	...	...	...	...	78

CHAPTER 5. KINSHIP AND FRIENDSHIP
by Janet Finch **87**

Contact and support 88
Keeping in touch 89
    Living with relatives 89
    Keeping in contact 91
    Just good friends 94
Helping each other 95
Kin and gender 98
Relatives and friends 100
Conclusions 101
Notes 102
References 102

CHAPTER 6. UNDERSTANDING OF SCIENCE IN BRITAIN AND THE USA
by Geoffrey Evans and John Durant **105**

Public perceptions of science 106
    Public interest 106
    Informedness 107
    How accurate are self-reports? 108
Perceived relevance of science 108
Understanding of science 109
    Scientific knowledge 109
    Knowledge of risks to health 113
Acceptance of scientific theories 114
Public attitudes to science 116
Conclusion 118
Notes 119
References 119
Acknowledgements 119

CHAPTER 7. PRIDE IN ONE'S COUNTRY: BRITAIN AND WEST GERMANY
by Richard Topf, Peter Mohler and Anthony Heath **121**

National pride in liberal democracies 122
    Background evidence 122
    The present study 123
Objects of national pride 125
Cultural homogeneity 128
    British pride in the monarchy 128
    West German pride in the Basic Law 129
    British pride in Parliament 130
    Economic achievements and the welfare state 132
    Who lacks national pride? 132

Attitudes to democracy 133
National pride and political participation 134
Notes 136
References 137
Acknowledgements 138
Tables (7.1–7.4) 139

CHAPTER 8. INTERIM REPORT: THE CHANGING FAMILY
by Stephen Harding **143**

Women at work and at home 144
Attitudes towards children 148
    Family size 148
    Parental duty 149
Divorce 151
Conclusions 153
Notes 154
References 154

APPENDIX I. Technical details of the surveys **157**

ISSP surveys 157
    Britain: British Social Attitudes survey series 157
    United States of America: General Social Survey 159
    Australia: National Social Science Survey 160
    West Germany: ALLBUS 161
    Austria: Sozialer Survey Österreich 162
    Hungary 163
    Italy: Indagine Sociale Italiana 164
    Netherlands 165
    Switzerland 165
    Republic of Ireland 166
Public understanding of science surveys 166
    British survey 166
    American survey 167
Survey of national pride 167
References 169

APPENDIX II. Notes on the tabulations **171**

APPENDIX III. The questionnaires **173**

SUBJECT INDEX **205**

Introduction

This volume, the sixth in the annual *British Social Attitudes* series, assembles and reports on a range of cross-national data, mainly collected as part of the *International Social Survey Programme* (ISSP). In the first chapter, we describe the origins and development of the ISSP. With a membership of 11 nations and with plans for a series of annual surveys extending into the 1990s, the future of this collaborative venture seems assured. However, it was never intended that the ISSP as a body should produce regular reports on the surveys' findings: the funding necessary for such a programme of publications was unlikely to become available. Instead it was left to individual member nations to disseminate the results as opportunities arose; already there is an impressive list of monographs, articles and papers based on ISSP surveys, attesting to the value of the dataset.

This book, as its title indicates, is a special one in the series. As we announced in last year's Report, there was no round of interviewing on British Social Attitudes in 1988. Instead, with the agreement of our core-funders, the Sainsbury Family Charitable Trusts, we brought forward the 1988 survey budget and devoted it to the latest in the series of *British General Election* studies. (The results of the 1987 post-election survey will be published in 1990 by the Pergamon Press, as a sequel to the book *How Britain Votes*.) So this one-year gap in the BSA survey series allowed us to spend time gathering contributions for and editing this international report.

However, fieldwork on the British Social Attitudes survey resumed in 1989. The latest BSA dataset is now being analysed and a selection of the results – together with trends in attitudes since the survey series began in 1983 – will be presented in *The 7th Report,* to be published in autumn 1990. Topics covered in the latest questionnaire include (beside such perennials as economic issues, social policy, health services and public spending) racial prejudice, business and industry, diet and health, and poverty. And as we write, the 1990 *British Social Attitudes* survey is being planned. Thanks to the generosity of our core-funders, the series is now secure until at least 1992.

In *The 5th Report,* we described some of the ways – some planned, others (such as the development of the ISSP) unexpected – in which the BSA survey series has continued to grow. The last 12 months have seen two further developments. First, the Nuffield Foundation and the Policy Planning and Research Unit (PPRU) of the Northern Ireland Office have provided funds for three years to enable us to extend the *British Social Attitudes* survey to Northern Ireland. The two versions of the questionnaire have much in common; but together with colleagues at PPRU and the Policy Research Institute (PRI) of The Queen's University, Belfast and the University of Ulster, we have developed and fielded in 1989 a special series of questions on prejudice and discrimination. This questionnaire module was, of course, fielded alongside standard BSA questions, allowing us to compare the attitudes of the British and the Northern Irish public on a wide range of issues. Preliminary results will be presented and discussed in *The 7th Report.*

Second, the Economic and Social Research Council (ESRC) has provided a grant over a four-year period to SCPR and to Nuffield College, Oxford, to set up a Joint Unit for the Study of Social Trends (JUSST). The Unit's programme has many components, including a large-scale panel study in which respondents from the 1987 *British Social Attitudes* survey will be reinterviewed in 1991; methodological work to develop new measuring instruments of social and political attitudes (also linked to the BSA series); and support for future rounds of the ISSP surveys. The links between SCPR and our colleagues at Nuffield College have already been very fruitful, and we welcome the opportunity provided by the Joint Unit for strengthening them.

As we announced last year, we are also preparing the publication of a cumulative Sourcebook, sponsored by Shell UK Ltd, of *British Social Attitudes* findings. It will be both a companion volume to the annual BSA Report, and a 'stand-alone' reference book with trend data on well over a thousand attitudinal items. The first Sourcebook will now be published (by Gower) in 1990, so that trend information from 1983 to 1989 can be included.

As the survey series develops year by year, we rely more and more on the help of our colleagues within SCPR and on their tolerance of its increasing demands. In particular, we should like to thank Rosemary Peddar and Jude Lewis for their help in organising this year's ISSP conference in London. We are also indebted to the staff of the *ZentralArchiv* in Cologne for their work in preparing the ISSP data and making it available through their Codebooks; and to all our other colleagues in the *International Social Survey Programme* without whose generous co-operation this Report could not have appeared. The responsibility for its contents, however, remains our own.

RMJ
SFW
LLB

1 Measuring national differences

An introduction to the International Social Survey Programme (ISSP)

*James A. Davis and Roger Jowell**

It is said that Britain is a peculiarly class-conscious society, and that statistics prove it. For instance, as many as 56 per cent of British adults agree with the proposition that there are inherent conflicts between workers and management. But is that a high proportion? Is it a *very* high proportion? All we can really say is that it is a narrow majority. Statistics of this sort, even when buttressed by similar findings, tell us very little about any society – not on their own at any rate. They certainly do not tell us whether the British public regards class differences as especially important.

By inserting the word "especially" into that last sentence we have insinuated the notion of relativity. When people casually refer to, say, the Italians as volatile, or the French as stylish, or the British as stand-offish (we have chosen only the most polite national stereotypes here), the word "especially" is implicit in front of each of these adjectives. Italians would not be characterised as being so volatile if, say, the British and others did not see themselves as so phlegmatic. Similarly, when people refer to the Germans as punctilious, they may well be alluding in large part to implicit shortcomings of other European nations.

National stereotypes are, of course, shameless caricatures based partly on observation, partly on hearsay, and partly (perhaps mostly) on prejudice.

*James Davis is Professor of Sociology at Harvard University and Co-director of NORC's General Social Survey. Roger Jowell is Director of SCPR and Co-director of the British Social Atitudes survey series. They co-founded the ISSP in 1983/84, with initial support from The Nuffield Foundation.

They serve to exaggerate rather than to describe differences between countries and, as a by-product, to promote the patently false notion that *nations* vary more in their personalities and attitudes than *individuals* do.

The first modest aim of the International Social Survey Programme is to replace such national stereotypes with well-grounded facts and figures. The second, longer-term and more ambitious aim is to try to make more sense of the differences we do uncover. This book attempts only to begin to fulfil the first aim.

What is the ISSP?

The International Social Survey Programme (ISSP) is a voluntary grouping of study teams in eleven nations (soon to become thirteen or fourteen), each of which undertakes to run a short, annual self-completion survey containing an agreed set of questions asked of a probability-based, nationwide sample of adults. The topics change from year to year by agreement, with a view to replication every five years or so.

The questions themselves are developed by subgroups and then thrashed out at an annual meeting attended by representatives of each national team. At the last meeting in May 1989, in London, there were 29 participants from the 11 national teams, including representatives from the ISSP's 'official' data archive, the ZentralArchiv at the University of Cologne. (Lists of the participating national teams, of the subjects of modules run so far, and of those scheduled until 1991 are given at the end of this chapter.)[1]

A constitution of sorts has now been adopted by members of the ISSP. It contains, for instance, rules of entry for new members and responsibilities of membership,. The primary duty of each member is, of course, to run every annual module (or at least *nearly* every one) in the agreed format. But there are no central funds for the ISSP: each national team covers the costs of its own piloting, fieldwork, data preparation, travel to meetings, and so on.* Since the ISSP has agreed to use one language for drafting and for meetings – (British) English – there are no central translation costs.

Improbable as it may seem, this general formula has worked well so far. The annual questionnaires, for instance (contrary to all advice and experience) have actually been designed for the most part in committee, and though inevitably flawed, are no less successful than most. Admittedly this success owes a lot to careful prior development work by drafting groups and to subsequent adjustments after piloting. In any event, as the following chapters show, fascinating data are already beginning to emerge.

A fuller treatment than is given here, of the results generated so far by the series, is to be provided in the first *ISSP Report,* a book funded by the European Cultural Foundation and due to be published by the Netherlands Social and Cultural Planning Bureau in 1990.

As may by now be apparent, the ISSP has grown and developed

---

*For instance, the National Science Foundation now funds the US part of the programme, and the Economic and Social Research Council now helps to fund the British part.

somewhat haphazardly, and this pattern shows every sign of continuing as long as it seems to work. The ISSP certainly came into being without much serious planning, having emerged as a vague idea during an impromptu meeting between the two of us in 1983 whose purpose was primarily to exchange experiences and explore opportunities for borrowing each other's questions.

At that stage the British Social Attitudes Survey (BSAS) was still in its first year, but had just received news that it was to be given at least a four-year life span through the generosity of the Sainsbury Family Charitable Trusts. The US General Social Survey (GSS), in contrast, was some 12 years old and had already acted as something of a role-model for other national series, including the BSAS itself, the West German ALLBUS (started in 1980) and the Australian National Social Science Survey (NSSS) (which was about to undertake its first fieldwork round).

As is usual at such meetings, we were bemoaning the fact that survey questions are poor travellers, especially across national and cultural boundaries. The BSAS, for instance, despite intentions to the contrary, had managed to transplant only one or two questions directly from the GSS. The West German ALLBUS contained a few more replications as a result of a specific bilateral agreement with the GSS. But a long-standing problem for all national time-series of this sort was, and is, that the concern for year-by-year comparability *within* a country is often in conflict with a concern for comparability *between* countries. Since funding is almost always from national sources, the choice both of topics and of question-wordings tends to reflect national rather than cross-national priorities.

So the conclusion we reached in 1983 was that the ideal way of securing a greater element of cross-national comparability should probably be *via* a standardised bolt-on supplementary questionnaire designed specifically for that purpose. With this in mind, SCPR sought and obtained a small grant from the Nuffield Foundation for convening a meeting (and then another) between representatives of the other three national social attitudes studies with which we already had some contact – those in Australia, West Germany, and the USA. There, the idea of a bolt-on, mutually-designed series of supplementary questionnaires could be aired and, perhaps, taken further.

As it turned out, the idea was warmly received by all four groups, who also decided that these supplements should be in a self-completion format, primarily for reasons of cost and to avoid adding to the already long, personal interviews. At the following meeting, the first bolt-on module, on the role of government, was developed and scheduled for fielding in 1985. It was later translated into American English, Australian English and German to obtain functionally-equivalent rather than identical wordings.

Although we were not quite aware of it at the time, the ISSP had effectively started. Since then, several other modules have been designed and fielded, the membership has grown threefold, and the structure has become a bit more bureaucratic, but not (yet) unduly so.

Difficulties of cross-national measurements

In the USA, cross-national research has been the rage for some time. This
has not been the case in Britain. This could, of course, be because of
British insularity – another national stereotype. But it is more plausibly the
result of rather limited research funds in Britain. Cross-national surveys
tend to be notoriously expensive, and as long as US funds have been
deployed for the purpose, and as long as Britain had been one of the
countries of interest to Americans, perhaps there had been no pressing
need for Britain to get involved. But in these circumstances British
concerns have not very easily got onto the agenda.

On the other hand, when one thinks of the practical and methodological
problems associated with cross-national research, perhaps Britain has been
right to sit largely on the sidelines. There have certainly been some
spectacular failures in ambitious multi-national surveys. And even when
such surveys appear to be relatively problem-free, as in the case (so far) of
the ISSP, it is never altogether clear precisely what is being measured.
Language differences, cultural differences, demographic differences, system
differences, all serve to bedevil strict comparability between one national
finding and another. It is extraordinarily difficult to be sure we are
comparing like with like on almost any social varible. So why bother?

The glib answer to that question is that we cannot learn much about
ourselves as a society unless we compare ourselves with others. We need
data about other countries if only to become better analysts of our own
condition. For instance, how 'redistributive' is our welfare system? How
'punitive' is our legal system? How 'permissive' are our constitutional
freedoms of speech or association? It is well known that these sorts of
questions are extremely difficult to answer, even when concrete facts and
figures can be compared. That being so, it is doubly difficult to address
more abstract questions about the attitudes of various nations, such as how
tolerant they are, how democratic, how religious, how class-conscious, how
left-wing. And these are, of course, primarily the sorts of questions with
which the ISSP deals.

It would be comforting to believe that all we had to do was look at the
ISSP data to see whether or not there were statistically significant
differences and, if so, grasp them as conclusive evidence of 'real'
differences between nations. In reality, however, every difference thrown up
by the survey, however large, has to be viewed initially with considerable
suspicion. Might it be the language factor at work? Might it be the result of
some esoteric cultural or historical cue? Moreover, the individual data
analyst might not be the most appropriate person to answer these sorts of
questions.

Naturally, it helps a good deal to have an international team to devise
the questions and comment critically on interpretations of the findings. But
even close scrutiny by eminent scholars is far from infallible. For example,
when the questionnaire employs a phrase such as "slightly agree", does it
have the same connotation to British and American respondents, let alone,
when translated, to Hungarian respondents? Who knows? But if we were to
let fundamental difficulties like these get in the way, we would not embark
on comparative social science measurements in the first place.

What we try to do in each module is to ensure that all questions are as culturally-neutral as possible. A large amount of time is therefore given to adjusting and fine-tuning each word and phrase so that it seems to have the greatest chance of being translated into the various languages and transplanted into the various cultures without changing its original meaning. Great attention to detail and often fine judgements are required. Even so, there are simply no sure-fire tests of whether these judgements are correct. Careful piloting helps but often fails to uncover nuances.

So we are certainly not going to try to persuade sceptics to accept the findings in this book as conclusive evidence of cross-national differences on any subject. The only claim we make for the survey results that follow is that they are a great deal more scientific and well-grounded than the national stereotypes they seek to replace.

Nor can we pretend that, in forming the ISSP, we have taken care to select countries which together represent a balanced range of world views. As we have noted, membership has depended largely on the availability in a country of a compatible team willing and able to conduct a collectively-designed national survey to a certain standard, each year. For reasons of cost, this has meant in most cases that countries have been unable to join unless they had some existing time-series, or one in prospect, capable of accommodating an ISSP module of questions. It has also meant that membership so far has been concentrated in richer countries.*

As a result of different joining dates and different start-up speeds, not all member countries have contributed data to the chapters that follow. Although one of the rules of ISSP membership is speedy archiving, Israel and Norway, for instance, have only just joined, and have not yet had time to collect data. The other nine member countries are all represented in one or more of the chapters according to the availability of their data for each module at the time of writing.

Despite the fact that recruitment to ISSP membership has been based primarily on factors such as availability and compatibility, there are nonetheless a number of interesting ways in which the member nations may be grouped for purpose of analysis. Among the eleven current members[2] are, for instance, seven Western European social democracies (Austria, Britain, Holland, Ireland, Italy, Norway and West Germany), plus Israel; there are two countries that may be classified as free-market democracies (Australia and the USA); and there is Hungary as the sole representative, for the time being, of Eastern Europe. This sort of broad three-way grouping is helpful for certain analytic purposes, as Tom W. Smith demonstrates in Chapter 4.

A second way of grouping countries is by system: citizens within federal systems represented, for instance, by the USA, Australia and West Germany, may differ on certain variables from those within unitary systems such as Britain. A third grouping may be by cultural origin: English-speaking countries with Anglo-Saxon/Celtic origins (Australia, Britain, the Republic of Ireland and the USA) may differ in some respects

---

*We are pleased, however, that a team in the Philippines – the Manila-based research institute, Social Weather Stations Inc. – will be joining the ISSP in 1990.

from, say, the countries of continental Europe. On other issues, as Stephen Harding demonstrates in Chapter 8, it is the predominant religion of a country that seems to provide the most interesting insights.

None of these dimensions can, of course, be isolated adequately without more thorough multivariate analyses than any of the authors have been able to undertake so far. With more time for analysis and more fieldwork rounds to provide supporting evidence, we may well become less diffident in future in attributing particular national differences to a country's religion, class-structure, political system, history, language or whatever. For the moment, however, we are content to describe differences and to offer a number of competing explanations for each of them *including* the possibility of artefactual differences caused by measurement errors.

In addition to meticulous questionnaire design, careful piloting and sound sampling practices, an effective way of reducing the likely influence of artefactual results is to include several questions on each topic or sub-topic covered. It is always unwise to rely on any single survey question for evidence. Questionnaires should ideally be made up of *groups* of questions, each group designed to cover a single dimension. This is just a similar sort of precaution to that taken by insurance companies when they re-insure, or by bookies when they lay off bets. Any single question – however careful the design process has been – may in the end turn out to be fatally flawed. We need some way of discerning such flaws, particularly when cross-national comparisons are the object of the exercise.

Answers to groups of questions on a single dimension should form a pattern. If they do not, there are then only two possible reasons: either there is in fact no single dimension, or the questions selected have failed to capture it. Individual questions whose answers do not conform to the pattern are regarded as suspect. In any event, since survey analysis consists largely of trying to decipher and make sense of patterns, it depends heavily on multiple measures. That is probably why virtually all influential survey results tend to travel in convoy. Moreover, when, as in the case of some of the findings on social networks reported by Janet Finch in Chapter 5, the results travel in *multinational* convoy, that is even more reassuring.

The questionnaires for each of the four modules fielded between 1985 and 1988 are included in Appendix III.*

Benefits of cross-national data

Analysis of ISSP data is still in its infancy. Even so, the early results demonstrate amply that nations are not as strikingly different in the way they view things as their stereotypes imply. Some images will doubtless be confirmed, since most stereotypes, like the best lies, tend to be based on half-truths. But in general the patterns we uncover are far too complex to

---

*We have not reproduced the questionnaires for the two studies reported in Chapters 6 and 7. They are, respectively, the British-USA comparative study on the public's understanding of science, and the British-West German comparative study on patriotism. The relevant questions on which comparisons have been based are, however, included in the text of the two chapters.

be encapsulated in a catchy phrase or telling anecdote.

One of the great values of social science research (as opposed to casual, or even close, observation) is that in addressing questions such as whether a society is "class-bound", or "open" or "libertarian", or "permissive", the researcher's first task is to break down those fuzzy images into testable specifics. While journalists, for instance, may get away with broad, plausible generalisations, *particularly* about societies other than their own, social scientists are not (or should not be) allowed to. They are expected to be more rigorous and to produce evidence rather than assertions. After all, they have recourse not only to more 'scientific' approaches to measurement but also to representative samples of the population. That, of course, is a mixed blessing: subgroups in a population have an infuriating habit of disagreeing with each other on many issues, causing a potentially simple story to become overcomplicated.

At the risk of overstretching this point, we are going to look at a few recent observations by eminent journalists in our respective countries to see how their view of some aspects of society compares with a data-based view. (This exercise is one in which selective examples will have to do. It is certainly not 'evidence'.) Our aim is not to disparage journalists (particularly not the ones we have chosen to quote) but to argue the case for cross-national research as an adjunct to, not as a substitute for, other methods of comparing societies. We grant that social research could never do the sort of job that foreign correspondents do in building up public knowledge and understanding of how particular societies work. Still, the best journalists – and even the best novelists – tend to be brilliant observers of perhaps one or two societies, or segments of them. They cannot be expected to have such an intimate knowledge of the way people in a wide range of societies view themselves and their worlds. For this, we suggest, everyone has to rely on comparative social statistics of one sort or another, if only to avoid being beguiled by the insights and impressions of cab-drivers and other such omniscient social commentators.

But, in case it still needs emphasising, we must beware of beguiling statistics too. Here is an extract from a book by *New York Times* journalist, Flora Lewis (1987) which examines and contrasts European nations on a number of variables, of which religion is one. She says:

> The overwhelming majority (in Britain) is Protestant, and large numbers regularly go to church. *The Times* (London) discovered, to its surprise, that more people go to church on Sunday than to football matches on Saturday. . . .(p.51)

This is an interesting use of comparative statistics, but is the comparison telling? To begin with, soccer spectators are overwhelmingly male, so half of the population is left out of the equation. Furthermore, virtually every British community has a church, while professional soccer grounds are concentrated in the bigger towns and cities. So, even if Lewis's purpose had been to compare one British pastime with another, the comparison she chose would have been unhelpful. But given that her actual purpose was to make a statement about how relatively religious the British are as a nation, the comparison that matters is between the British and other nationalities. The ISSP data allow us to make just that comparison, and they certainly do not support the impression that Lewis, via *The Times,* seeks to give.

True, among British Christians, the overwhelming majority (82%) do describe themselves as Protestant as opposed to Catholic. And true, large numbers (one in five) of people in Britain do go to church (or mosque, or synagogue, or temple) fairly regularly. But the proportion of regular churchgoers in Britain is actually smaller than that in seven of the eight ISSP countries below. Only Hungary has a (much) smaller proportion than Britain's, as the figures show:

Regular attendance at church, etc
(monthly or more often) (1987)

%

USA	54
Italy	45
Austria	39
West Germany	29
Netherlands	28
Australia	25
Britain	20
Hungary	7*
Average (mean)	31

Note. *Hungarian data are from 1986.

Moreover, an obvious indicator of the cultural importance of religion in a society is the proportion of people who profess *no* religion at all. On this measure, Britain appears to be very indifferent to religion, surpassed only by the Netherlands. Over one in three Britons say they have no religion, against a maximum of one in ten, for five of the other six countries for which we have data. (Hungarian data are missing here because they ask about baptism rather than belief.)

Proportion saying "no religion"

%

Netherlands	54
Britain	34
Australia	11
Austria	9
West Germany	8
USA	6
Italy	4
Average (mean)	11

Moving from religion to another subject on which we have cross-national data, we are able once again to compare conventional wisdom with survey findings. Here we cite an article by American journalist James Atlas, writing in the influential Sunday magazine of the *New York Times* (Atlas, 1989). Discussing attacks on free speech in Britain, the tone of the article is conveyed by its title, 'Thatcher puts a lid on'. A key point in the article is that the British public, unlike the American public, does not care much about freedom of speech. To buttress this point, Atlas quotes a former London correspondent of the *New York Times,* as follows:

> Listening to speech after speech in the drafty hall (in London) I remembered something the American columnist Anthony Lewis had told me before I left: 'The issues that make us rise in passion don't move the English'. Which doesn't make them any less important, I thought.

This view seems uncontroversial enough until one examines the available data. The ISSP 1985 survey contained six items which specifically 'tested' people's commitment to civil liberties in circumstances where there was an element of tension between the right to free expression and the possible need for restraint. We show below the basic proportions in Britain and the USA who would allow each form of free expression. The ordering of the items – in terms of how libertarian our respondents were – was the same in the two countries, and we present them in descending order of 'libertarianism'.

	1985	
People who would defend the right . . .	**Britain** %	**USA** %
. . . of people to publish pamphlets to protest against a government action they strongly oppose	86	68
. . . of people to organise protest marches and demonstrations against a government action they strongly oppose	70	66
. . . of a newspaper to publish confidential government papers about the government's economic plans	63	61
. . . of people who believe that whites are racially superior to other races to hold public meetings to express their views	40	57
. . . of people to organise a nationwide strike of all workers to protest against a government action they strongly oppose	29	20
. . . of a newspaper to publish confidential government papers about the government's defence plans	25	17

So, on five of the six items the British appear, after all, to be more 'passionate' than the Americans in their defence of free speech. And on the sixth item – defending the right of racists to hold public meetings to express their views – it is far from clear on which side a 'liberal' would actually come to rest. Again, it seems a representative dataset based on multiple items within more than one country serves to throw doubt on conventional wisdom about national attributes.

Of course we realise that different questions would have come up with different results and, for that matter, that different journalists would have come to different conclusions (see, for instance, Lewis, 1987 p.40). But no matter: all we are trying to emphasise is that the picture across nations is always a great deal more complicated than either the most plausible anecdote or the single poll question might suggest.

We could be accused of having chosen two subjects for these arguments on which we knew we were on strong ground. (In fact we chose two subjects which were not covered elsewhere in this book.) But let us nonetheless touch on a third and final subject on which, surely, conventional wisdom and systematic data coincide: the unique, class-bound character of British attitudes and behaviour. Take Anthony Sampson for instance, writing about the effect of the British education system which, he says,

> reinforces and perpetuates a class system whose divisions run through all British institutions, separating language, attitude and motivations (Sampson, 1982).

The same sort of point is made by Sampson's *Observer* colleague, Robert Chesshyre (1988) and by numerous others. At its simplest, everyone agrees that the British class system is almost uniquely powerful (and bad) in contrast with, say, the American one which is almost invisible (and good). But what exactly do these sorts of blanket comparisons imply? They could mean one or more of the following possibilities, each of which could be tested against data:

- that the British social structure is much like everyone else's (see Erikson *et al,* 1982), but that the British are more aware of it. (It is said that Eskimos have forty different words for snow.)

- that the British social structure is different. Britain has social divisions other countries do not have.

- that the British social structure overall is much like everyone else's but that mobility within it is less frequent or more difficult than in other countries.

- that one's social class in Britain influences one's attitudes and behaviour more than it does in other countries (see Vanneman and Cannon (1987) for instance, on the strong links between class and party affiliation in Britain in comparison with those in other countries, especially the USA.)

Chapter 4 reports on aspects of these issues, so we will not rehearse these details here. Suffice to say that Britain does not come out especially high as a class-conscious or class-bound society, at least not consistently so, in comparison with the other ISSP nations. In fact in most respects, Britain is somewhere in the middle of the league, not very different from the USA.

Even as far as social mobility is concerned, Britain is nowhere near the extreme, but somewhere around the average of the ISSP nations. The ISSP 1987 module contained a number of questions to find out about intergenerational mobility, using both 'objective' and 'subjective' measures. But there are other data available on this subject too. The reality is, first, that national variation in upward mobility is small; second, that Britain is in the middle of the 'league table'; third, the USA has only slightly greater upward mobility between generations than Britain does (see also

Ganzeboom *et al*, 1988). Americans (and Australians) do seem to be more optimistic than others about their chance for upward mobility, but it is their optimism, not the reality, which distinguishes them in our data.

These results may seem surprising, but similar conclusions have been reported in the technical and scholarly literature for some time. Intergenerational occupational mobility patterns in industrial societies are remarkably similar. But there remains a disconcerting gap between these well-established findings of contemporary social science and public discussion – even 'informed' public discussion – of the issue.

In summary, when we examine whether or not the British class system is unique, and when we base such an examination on multiple measures within several countries, the answer we get is emphatic. Although there are *aspects* of the British class structure – for instance the abiding relationship between social class and political party – which set it aside from most (but by no means all) other countries, there are not that many. Such differences as there are have been talked up, as much by British observers as by anyone else.

Conclusion

Public attitudes are as much a part of social reality as are behaviour patterns, social conditions or demographic characteristics. Some social attitudes are also no less slow to change. Yet their rigorous measurement, particularly across nations, has never been accorded a very high priority.* The ISSP is, we hope, helping to rectify this omission.

No attempt is made in any of the chapters that follow to provide anything approaching an exhaustive analysis of the data available. They contain only a first glance at a large and complicated dataset. As we have said, a second glance – via the Dutch Social and Cultural Planning Bureau – is expected soon, and the data themselves have been deposited in archives for others to quarry.

At a minimum the guided tour that follows, based as it is on random sampling and careful data collection, should provide sounder and subtler insights into the attitudes of different nations, including one's own than the classical grand tour could ever do. On the other hand, to the extent that most of us seem to cherish our myths and stereotypes about other nations, it could prove to be an uncomfortable journey.

---

*Although principally about contrasting social attitudes, the dataset also contains numerous background details about people's characteristics and behaviour in order to place attitudes within a wider social context. Where possible we try to standardise those details between countries, but there are inevitable difficulties especially in measures of social class.

Notes

1.   Currently, national teams participating in ISSP are:

Australia: Department of Sociology, Research School of Social Sciences, The Australian National University, Canberra.

Austria: Sozialer Survey Österreich, Institut für Soziologie der Universität Graz, Graz.

Britain: Social and Community Planning Research (SCPR), London.

Hungary: Társadalomkutatási Informatikai Egyesülés (TARKI), Budapest.

Ireland: Department of Social Sciences, University College, Dublin.

Israel: Department of Sociology and Anthropology, Tel Aviv University, Tel Aviv.

Italy: EURISKO Ricerca Sociale e di Marketing, Milan.

Netherlands: Sociaal en Cultureel Planbureau (SCP), Risjwijk.

Norway: National Committee for Survey Resarch, and the Norsk Samfunnsvitenskapelig Datatjeneste (NSD), Bergen.

USA: National Opinion Research Center (NORC), University of Chicago, Chicago.

West Germany: Zentrum für Umfragen, Methoden und Analysen (ZUMA), Mannheim.

The ISSP is administered through its secretariat at SCPR in London. All enquiries may be addressed there.

The ISSP's archive and computing adviser is the ZentralArchiv für Empirische Sozialforschung (ZA) at the University of Cologne. For further details, see Appendix I.

Five modules have been fielded so far (though not by all the countries listed above, and not always in the calendar year for which the module was designed.

1985 : The role of government
1986 : Family networks and support systems
1987 : Social inequality
1988 : Women and the family
1989 : Work orientations

In 1990, the group plans to repeat a subset of items from the "role of government" module. In 1991, it plans to field a module on religion and religious belief.

2.   In Chapter 2, Swiss data have also been included, even though Switzerland is not one of the ISSP member nations. In 1987 the Soziologisches Institut der Universität Zurich fielded a questionnaire replicating the 1987 ISSP module on social inequality. See Appendix I for full details.

References

ATLAS, J., 'Thatcher Puts a Lid On: Censorship in Britain', *New York Times Magazine,* March 5, (1989), p.97.
CHESSHYRE, R., *The Return of a Native Reporter,* Penguin Books, London (1988), p.14.
ERIKSON, R., GOLDTHORPE, J.H. and PORTOCARERO, L., 'Social Fluidity in Industrial Nations', *British Journal of Sociology,* vol.33 (1982), pp.1–34.

GANZEBOOM, H.B.J., LUIJKX, R., and TREIMAN, D.J., *International Class Mobility in Comparative Perspective,* Paper presented to the American Sociological Association, Atlanta (1988).
LEWIS, F., *Europe: A Tapestry of Nations,* Simon & Schuster, New York (1987), pp.40, 51.
SAMPSON, A., *The Changing Anatomy of Britain,* Coronet Books, London (1982), pp.145–146.
VANNEMAN, R, and CANNON, L.W., *The American Perception of Class,* Temple University Press, Philadelphia (1987).

Acknowledgement

We are extremely grateful to Caroline Cross for typing and correcting, more than once, not only this chapter, but almost all the other chapters too.

2 International patterns of work

David G. Blanchflower and Andrew J. Oswald*

Work matters. Psychologists see it as 'crucial to self-esteem, well-being and both physical and mental health' (Warr, 1985). Economists and industrial relations specialists define modern industrial societies according to the way they organise work; sociologists view work as one of the most important aspects of modern life. People may or may not enjoy their jobs, but in market societies they cannot do without them – either psychologically or practically.

This chapter, based on ISSP (International Social Survey Programme) data collected between 1985 and 1987, reports findings about working life and employment in eight industrialised countries. Some of the findings reveal things that were previously unknown, and so are particularly interesting; others simply confirm what has long been suspected. Their particular strength is that they are based on eight nearly identical surveys. Usually with survey data on employment, definitions are necessarily based on those prevailing in each country. For example, unemployment may have to be defined with reference to job search activities, to benefit eligibility, and so on. Thus the comparisons that can be made between countries are always bedevilled by whether like is really being compared with like. The ISSP surveys have perforce to leave many of these definitional issues to respondents themselves – for instance by asking them if they are unemployed. But while there may be cultural differences in the answers, we are still much closer than is usual to having truly equivalent data from all the countries.

---

*David Blanchflower and Andrew Oswald are Professors in the Department of Economics, Dartmouth College, New Hampshire, USA; Research Associates at the National Bureau of Economic Research, USA; and members of the Centre for Labour Economics, London School of Economics.

The dataset therefore offers an unusual opportunity to social scientists who are interested in work. Some of the simple, descriptive 'facts' we look at will also be of much wider interest. Among the questions we tackle in this chapter are:

- How can internationally comparable survey data best be used to shed light on the nature and characteristics of work?

- Can internationally consistent unemployment rates be calculated? And if so, what do they show?

- How do union membership, self-employment and employment vary across countries?

- What forces seem to shape earnings levels? And are the mechanisms the same – qualitatively or quantitatively – across nations?

- In which countries are trade unions the strongest?

In investigating this last point, we cover new and exciting ground. Using multiple regression analysis (a form of analysis which can look at several variables at once) we study the effects of trade union membership on overall wage rates in the different countries, and come to some surprising conclusions.

The value of national comparisons

There are many reasons why comparing countries on issues such as these is of interest. The most important, of course, is that work-related issues shed light on the overall efficiency of an economy and on the material well-being of a society. Unemployment, for example, worries both politicians and citizens because it represents an obvious waste of resources and is typically spread unevenly across a nation. If countries have rather different levels of unemployment – and they do – this offers the investigator the chance to isolate what it is that shapes unemployment rates. What secret do the Swiss, with their very low unemployment rates, possess and could Britain, with its much higher numbers of unemployed, learn from them?

Moreover, the structural characteristics of economies – in terms of employment and unemployment, pay and so on – are inherently worth studying. A government wishing to introduce new forms of income tax, or to subsidise a particular sector of industry, or to change the legislative framework of industrial relations, should know (or want to know) something about economic life in other countries, if only to measure its economic performance against that of its main trading competitors. International comparisons, such as those from the ISSP data, allow us to see just where different countries stand on a host of variables. And, in turn, background and behavioural data such as these can serve to illuminate attitudes towards work and leisure – topics specifically addressed by the ISSP nations in their 1989 surveys and to be reported on in a later volume.

Figures on the extent of self-employment and unionisation are especially interesting because they may relate to how well economies are performing. For example, almost all citizens of Western countries work in a job which they personally did not create – but rather in a post made for them by the actions of an entrepreneur somewhere. 'Job makers' are rare; but they are an essential, if often little considered, component of a capitalist society. Indeed, this is a point often made by the present British government in its desire to create a more entrepreneurial economy. Comparative statistics on self-employment offer an insight into the number and characteristics of the self-employed in the various countries we have examined.

We also discuss the price of labour – that is, wages and salaries – and the factors which determine it. The wage rate is, simultaneously, a measure of general economic well-being, a factor shaping how hard and how long and where individual employees work, and an important influence on the number of available jobs in society. Wage levels affect everyone. They mould the distribution of individual income and so, in the long run, the distribution of national wealth.

Finally, we look at trade unions, the main organisations by which individual employees band together. They matter for political as well as economic reasons and they often arouse strong emotions. Although it is often asserted that this or that country has unusually powerful trade unions, and this or that country has especially quiescent or impotent ones, it is not always clear what such statements mean. We examine just one definition of trade union strength – indeed, one of the few objective criteria we *can* use – the power of unions to influence wage rates.

These are the main issues that we cover. Much of the chapter is, of course, purely descriptive. To widen the scope and look for detailed explanations of the findings would mean filling in the historical background to the labour markets in each country, and looking at its social structure. Bruno and Sachs (1985), for example, have argued – in the context of the oil shock of the mid-1970s – that the behaviour of different economies depends upon the form of their labour markets.

> It would seem only natural that a theory for a country's (or several countries') response can only be formulated if one takes its specific institutional or structural features into consideration. (p.274)

Newell and Symons (1987) and Calmfors and Driffill (1988) argue similarly. In particular, the latter claim that poor economic performance stems in part from a labour market with neither very high *nor* very low levels of unionisation – that is, countries with medium levels of unionisation perform worse than countries at either of the two extremes.

An especially interesting point to an economist is that – despite each country's own particular history and own distinctive institutions – many of the features we describe seem to show overarching similarities between the market economies of all eight nations. This structural similarity is, we think, one of the most striking aspects of our analysis.

Jobs and joblessness

The countries examined in this chapter are Australia[1], Austria, West Germany, Britain, Hungary, Italy, Switzerland,[2] and the USA. The survey data for most countries were collected in each of three years, from 1985 to 1987. Amalgamating datasets in this way means that we have relatively large numbers of respondents for our analyses. For some countries, for instance Switzerland and Hungary, we have data for only one or two years and the numbers are accordingly reduced. Details about the sample in each country are provided in Appendix I.

Workforce profiles

As a background, and using data mainly from 1985 and 1986, we show below for each country eight measures of the composition of the workforce. Already we can see some striking differences.

Workforce characteristics

	Austria	West Germany	Britain	Hungary	Italy	USA	Switzer-land
% of employees who are:							
Working part-time	2%	3%	13%	n/a	7%	6%	2%
Men	—	—	2%	n/a	4%	3%	—
Women	4%	7%	26%	n/a	14%	8%	5%
Women	39%	35%	45%	49%	32%	47%	31%
In manual occupations	41%	29%	45%	52%	52%	29%	n/a
In manufacturing industry	19%	33%	27%	29%	n/a	21%	n/a
In public service occupations	n/a	31%	34%	n/a	20%	30%	28%
Supervisors	n/a	n/a	38%	21%	16%	31%	43%

Notes. The percentage bases are employees only; Hungarian data are for 1986 only and Swiss data for 1987 only.
n/a = not available.

For instance, we can see that in Austria only two per cent of the employed labour force as a whole work part-time, whereas in Britain part-time working is disproportionately common, with more than one in eight employees working under 20 hours a week. Looking along the third row of the table, we see that this is because so many British women work part-time. Indeed, they are nearly twice as likely as women in any other of the nations we examined to work part-time. We know too from other sources (for example, Dex and Shaw, 1986) that women part-timers in Britain work shorter hours on average than do their American and mainland European counterparts. This is partly because national insurance thresholds make part-time working economically efficient from the employer's point of view, but in any case the British profile in this respect is very distinct.

In all of the nations, women account for between one third and one half of all employees. Much wider differences are apparent in other respects. Only 13 per cent of Americans claim to supervise others, compared with 43 per cent of the Swiss. Given the comparatively similar cultural and technological characteristics of these two nations, it is hard to know how to interpret this evidence. Either working arrangements are much less hierarchical in the USA, or Americans simply perceive them as such.

In Britain as many as one third of employees work in the public sector. At the other end of the spectrum, the figure for Italy is one in five. Manual work is, however, especially important in Italy and Hungary (with just over half of employees in manual occupations), only a little less so in Britain (45 per cent) and least prevalent in West Germany and the USA (29 per cent). Employees in manufacturing industry are most common in West Germany where they make up a third of the workforce. But despite all these differences, perhaps the main feature of the table above is the broad similarity between these seven countries. This will be a recurrent theme throughout the chapter.

Next we examine workforce participation rates, sometime known as economic activity rates. In particular, what proportion of adults under 'retirement age' is active in the labour market, either with a job or looking for one? And how many of those over 'retirement age' (65 and over) continue to work?*

Workforce participation rates

	Austria	West Germany	Britain	Hungary	Italy	USA	Switzer- land
All aged under 65	66%	62%	76%	71%	60%	76%	79%
Men aged under 65	82%	82%	94%	81%	82%	90%	92%
Women aged under 65	51%	43%	61%	63%	38%	64%	59%
Married women, aged under 65	46%	37%	58%	63%	33%	59%	39%
Women aged 65+	1%	2%	1%	—	4%	8%	*
Men aged 65+	1%	4%	8%	2%	8%	18%	*

Notes. Again the data are from 1985 and 1986, except for Hungary (1986 only) and Switzerland (1987 only). The percentage bases are all those employed or seeking work, in the relevant age range. * = less than 0.5%.

As we see, the proportion of men aged under 65 who either have a job or want one ranges from about eight in ten (in Austria, West Germany, Hungary and Switzerland) to around nine in ten (in Britain, the USA and Switzerland). So we find high male participation rates in all seven countries. But we see rather greater differences between countries when we look at *women's* economic activity rates. Only 38 per cent of Italian women are active in the labour market; in Austria, which is in the middle of the 'league', the figure is 51 per cent; but the highest female participation rates are found in Switzerland, Britain, Hungary and the USA, where approaching two thirds of women have taken up or are seeking paid work.

Another striking cross-national difference is the varying proportion of the over-65s who continue to be active in the labour market. Whereas very

---

*The workforce is defined as the employed (employees *and* self-employed) and the unemployed. 'Adults' comprise those aged 16 and over in Austria, 17 and over in Switzerland and 18 and over in the other five countries under examination. The Italian sample did not include those aged 75 and over; the Austrian sample did not include those aged 70 and over.

few older women (except perhaps in the USA) participate in the labour market, in Britain and Italy about one in twelve older men remain economically active; and in the United States, a remarkable 18 per cent of men – nearly one in five – stay in the workforce after they have reached the age of 65.

Unemployment

We turn now to unemployment – an issue of great social, political and economic importance, especially in Europe where historically high rates of unemployment have been reached over the past ten years. Although it is known that different countries have suffered to different degrees, it has not been easy to make precise measurements. This is because each nation tends to have its own way of calculating its unemployment rates. For instance, they may be defined according to prevailing criteria of eligibility for social benefits, or according to particular job search activities in a given period of time. So the ISSP data are of some interest, for they allow us to compare unemployment rates using a common definition. In each of the countries, respondents were asked whether they considered themselves unemployed.* Of course, there may be cultural differences which predispose respondents in different countries to answer differently; we also know that respondent self-reporting of unemployment generally produces higher unemployment rates than those which result from applying official definitions. But our method, whatever its flaws, has the merit of providing *comparable* measures of joblessness for each nation. Three main points stand out, as the table below shows (again the data are mainly from the 1985 and 1986 surveys):

Unemployment rates

	Austria	West Germany	Britain	Italy	USA	Switzer- land
Men	3.9%	4.5%	12.7%	4.7%	3.9%	0.4%
Women	6.5%	6.3%	11.9%	6.9%	3.7%	2.0%
Aged under 25	6.7%	7.1%	21.7%	17.8%	5.9%	4.3%
Aged 25-44	4.4%	6.0%	9.9%	4.6%	3.2%	0.3%
Aged 45+	4.3%	3.3%	10.7%	1.4%	4.5%	0.4%
All	4.9%	5.1%	12.4%	5.4%	3.8%	0.9%

Notes. The percentage bases are all those who defined themselves as 'in paid work' or 'unemployed'. Swiss data are from 1987.

First, looking at male unemployment rates in the mid-1980s, the figure for Britain at nearly 13 per cent was more than twice as high as that for any other nation. At the opposite end of the spectrum is Switzerland where less

---

*This question was not asked in Hungary because of difficulties over the definition of 'unemployed'.

than one per cent of men aged under 65 reported being unemployed. Britain's unemployment rate has risen dramatically over the past decade (though it is now declining); these data make explicit the fact that British male unemployment has been not only high historically, but also high by international standards. For instance, on our figures, Austria, West Germany, Italy and the USA all showed a similar rate of around four per cent.

Second, the female unemployment rate was, except in the USA and Britain, higher than the male unemployment rate. This may be of less social consequence: many of the women who said they are unemployed and would like a job have husbands in paid work, so they may not be living in households where there was no earned income coming in. Nonetheless, our data have uncovered a measure of frustrated demand for paid work among women living in several of the Western European industrialised nations. Even in Britain and the USA, women were about as likely as men to say they are unemployed.

Third, unemployment was consistently higher among the young. In the mid-1980s, in both Britain and Italy, about one in five young people aged under 25 said that they were unemployed. This is likely to have serious social and economic repercussions. Even in Switzerland, with its low overall rate of unemployment, we see that four per cent of young adults (under 25) said that they were unemployed, a ratio of over 10:1 compared with their older counterparts.

Trade union membership

The ISSP datasets also yield information about whether respondents are members of trade unions.* Such data are seldom collected on large-scale, government-sponsored surveys, since they are often seen as politically sensitive. So these results are of great interest. And, as the table below shows, the proportion of the labour force belonging to a trade union differs a great deal from country to country.

Around a third of Swiss and West German employees, and around a half of Britons and Austrians, are members. But in the USA we find that less than one in five of all employees – even male employees – belong to trade unions. The highest level of unionisation is found, unsurprisingly perhaps, in Hungary where seven out of ten employees are union members. Given the relationship between the Communist Party and the trade unions in Eastern European nations, it is likely that union membership has a very different meaning in Hungary from that in Western market economies; in the latter, unions are of course essentially voluntary associations.

It is also unsurprising that (except in Hungary) women are less likely – usually *much* less likely – to be unionised than are men, and that manual workers are more highly unionised than non-manual workers. Typically, across all the Western industrialised nations, we can see that union

---

*Except for Italy, where this question was not asked.

% Trade union members

	Austria	West Germany	Britain	Hungary	USA	Switzer-land
All	52%	32%	47%	71%	17%	36%
Men	58%	39%	51%	62%	21%	42%
Women	40%	20%	41%	81%	12%	24%
Aged under 25	39%	23%	35%	71%	8%	28%
Aged 25-44	54%	32%	47%	70%	17%	36%
Aged 45+	60%	37%	53%	73%	20%	41%
Working full-time	52%	33%	49%	n/a	17%	36%
Working part-time	12%	6%	27%	n/a	10%	*
In manual occupations	61%	44%	53%	61%	28%	n/a
In non-manual occupations	45%	27%	42%	82%	12%	n/a

Notes. The percentage bases are employees only: Hungarian data are for 1986 only and Swiss data for 1987 only. n/a = not available.

members are male, blue-collar workers in full-time jobs. Only in Britain, it seems, have the trade unions managed to make much of an inroad – albeit still a modest one – into the part-time labour market. But in common with Austria, with its strong corporatist institutions favouring union membership, the British trade union movement seems to have been relatively successful in recruiting women.

It is also worth noting that, in Britain, the unionisation rate in the public sector (at 75 per cent, exceptionally high) is more than double that in the private sector.

% Trade union members

	Austria	West Germany	Britain	Hungary	USA	Switzer-land
All	52%	32%	47%	71%	17%	36%
In manufacturing industries	57%	35%	48%	79%	21%	n/a
In service occupations	50%	31%	46%	68%	15%	n/a
Public sector	n/a	47%†	75%	n/a	20%	62%
Private sector	n/a	30%†	32%	n/a	15%	26%

Notes. The percentage bases are employees only. The data are from 1985 and 1986 except for Hungary (1986 only) and Switzerland (1987 only). † = 1985 data only. n/a = not available.

In addition – and contrary to commonly-held beliefs – employees in service occupations are only a little less likely to be unionised than those in manufacturing. Probably this can be explained, in part at least, by the high unionisation levels in the public sector, where nearly all the jobs are service ones.

What do people earn?

We can also use the ISSP data to examine the distribution of earnings. How far are they equally or unequally distributed among the workforces of the various nations? A simple measure of income inequality can be calculated by deriving, for each of the countries, the coefficient of variation of individuals' earnings.* This coefficient measures the *spread* of a distribution. So the higher the coefficient the greater is the variation from average earnings, and the lower the coefficient the smaller is the variation. Using the data from the 1986 surveys, we find wide cross-national differences:

	Coefficient of earnings variation
Italy	104.20
USA	79.14
Switzerland	76.90
Britain	66.60
West Germany	58.46
Hungary	56.02
Austria	55.75

Table 2.1 provides more details.

For three countries – Hungary, Austria and West Germany – we find low coefficients – that is, earnings in each are relatively evenly distributed. The case of Hungary – our only non-capitalist country – is particularly interesting, since its coefficient is almost identical to that of two of its near neighbours, West Germany and Austria, and not that dissimilar to that of the other countries. This accords with the observations of Sir Henry Phelps-Brown (1977):

> the most remarkable feature of the comparison between the Soviet-type and Western pay structures is the extent of their similarity. This will surprise those who expected the Soviet-type economies to have achieved a much greater equality. In fact ... the dispersion of individual earned incomes is lower in these economies than in some, if not all, of the Western economies. But it is no part of the Soviet philosophy of pay under socialism to give equal pay for unequal work. (p.43)

Italy appears as the outlier, with the greatest inequality in earnings of the seven nations, followed by the USA and Switzerland. Britain is in the middle of the range.

Trade union strength

People may mean many things when they speak of 'strong' trade unions. They may be referring, for instance, to the institutional links between unions and political parties, or to the muscle that such links allow them to show. But a more objective way in which union strength can be assessed is by measuring the effect that (all other things being equal – to the extent

---

*The coefficient of variation is defined as the standard deviation divided by the arithmetic mean $\times$ 100.

they can be controlled for) unions have on the wage levels of their members, in relation to those of non-unionised workers. After all, improved pay bargaining power is one of the important attractions that trade unions hold for the individual employee.

The analysis

Economists have a standard method for examining the effect of union membership on wage rates.[3] They use multiple regression analysis to identify the main factors which determine wages, and use union membership as one of the possible explanations of variations in wage levels. Other variables are also included, to control for the many other things that typically influence a person's earned income: these include age, years of schooling, sex, marital status, and the characteristics of the work done. The statistical correlations are used to look at whether union members are better paid than non-union members, once other influences are held constant.

The standard literature, surveyed in Lewis (1986), Blanchflower (1984), Freeman and Medoff (1984) and Hirsch and Addison (1986), typically estimates the so-called union/non-union wage differential at around 10 to 15 per cent. In other words, by these calculations unionisation increases wages by a little more than one tenth. So the prediction would be that a non-union worker would raise his or her pay by that amount at a union workplace. To date, almost all the statistical studies have looked at the USA, Canada and Britain. One exception is Mulvey (1986): using Australian cross-sectional data, he found that the effect of union membership is to raise pay by an average of nine per cent.

So ISSP data provide an opportunity, for the first time as far as we know, to make international comparisons of union strength across a wider range of nations. Our analysis assumes that employees' earnings depend on six main factors: age, years of education, sex, marital status, full- or part-time working, as well as membership or non-membership of a union.[4] The results, which pool the 1985, 1986 and 1987 samples, are given in **Table 2.2**. This table shows not only the size of the effect of each factor but also the statistical significance of the relationship (a measure of its reliability). An important point to note is the extent to which our formula succeeds in explaining variations in earnings levels across the different countries – that is, its predictive strength. For example, we find that it explains about 60 per cent of the variance of employees' pay in Britain, but only about 38 per cent of the variance in the USA. So, using this formula, we can predict much more accurately the level of pay of a British respondent than we can for an American respondent.

Factors affecting earnings

Table 2.2 provides a lot of information. For instance, as would be expected, in every country wages rise with age: on average, older workers are paid more than younger ones. But it is not a straightforward linear relationship: each extra year older a person becomes means that his or her pay increases become smaller and smaller.* All else being equal, the difference in pay between a 20-year-old and a 30-year-old will thus be more than the difference between a 30-year-old and a 40-year-old and so on.

We can also look at the effect of education on people's incomes. Here we find more marked cross-national differences. In the USA and Britain, there is noticeably more variation in wage rates according to a person's years in formal education than in the other six countries. To an economist, this means that the British and American labour markets reward a person's investment in education more highly than do those of other countries; each extra year of schooling brings relatively higher pay. Yet income differentials due to education are smallest in just those countries – Switzerland and West Germany – where proportionally more young people stay on at school past the minimum school-leaving age. So, although Britain and the USA are the countries where individuals get the highest return from their investment in education, this does not necessarily mean that these economies have the most productive education system from the point of view of the economy as a whole.

In which countries are women most strongly 'discriminated' against in terms of pay? According to our analysis, the answer is Britain, followed by the USA and Germany. Indeed, in the USA and Britain men earn roughly half as much again as their female counterparts. Discrimination appears to be least marked in Austria. Of course, pay differentials may not be simply a measure of discrimination: they may reflect the extent to which women are segregated in different sorts of occupations from men. Nonetheless, a woman seems to be at a significant disadvantage when it comes to earning power. Moreover, this is true even if one takes into account the obvious fact that people who work part-time (predominantly women) earn less on average than those who work full-time. This earnings gap is most pronounced in the USA and Britain.

Unionisation and wages

When we turn to the effect of trade union membership on wage levels, as **Table 2.2** shows, the coefficient for union membership varies markedly across nations, from a low of 0.04 for Switzerland to a high of 0.23 for the USA. This indicates that, after controlling for all the other factors, being a union member can add on average from four per cent to nearly 25 per cent extra to an employee's earnings according to the country he or she lives in.[5] The 'league table' is as follows:

---

*This is the meaning of the negative and significant coefficients for the age-squared variable.

	Estimates of % extra earnings attributable to union membership
USA	26%
Australia	13%
Britain	8%
Hungary	8%
West Germany	7%
Austria	6%
Switzerland	4%*

Note. *This figure is not statistically significant.

The estimates for Britain, Australia and the USA are broadly comparable to those reported elsewhere (see, for example, Mulvey (1986) for Australia, Freeman and Medoff (1984) for the USA and Blanchflower and Oswald (forthcoming) for Britain). We can therefore have some confidence in the other figures which are, as far as we are aware, the first published estimates of union impact on wages in West Germany, Switzerland, Austria and Hungary. On these figures, British trade unions have much the same impact on wages as do their counterparts in mainland Western Europe. Proponents of the thesis that unions in Britain have more muscle than most cannot use these figures to substantiate their claim.

Self-employment

Most workers in industrialised countries are not self-employed. They work in jobs made for them by someone else, though they may not have thought about it in such terms. But some, more entrepreneurial, individuals create jobs for themselves. In the table below, we show the proportions of those in self-employment across seven of the ISSP nations.

	% self-employed*
Italy	29%
Switzerland	23%
USA	16%
Austria	15%
West Germany	12%
Britain	10%
Hungary	4%

Note. *Based on all those in work in each country.

A detailed breakdown of self-employment rates in each country by sex, age, sector and so on will be found in **Table 2.3**. As might be expected, Hungary, the only communist country, has the smallest proportion of self-employed. Italy is at the other extreme: approaching a third of Italians work for themselves. Britain, despite the rise in the numbers of self-employed in the past decade, is near the bottom of the European 'league'.

Hours of work

Do people in different countries work noticeably different numbers of hours a week? In fact, the average working week appears to differ only slightly in all the countries studied.* Switzerland comes top of the league with an average of nearly 46 hours; Italy is at the bottom at around 38 hours. Women tend to work fewer hours than men, especially in Britain and Italy. Predictably, perhaps, the self-employed generally work much longer hours than employees (except in the USA, where both groups average just over 40 hours a week). In Western Europe, self-employed people typically put in an *extra* seven to twelve hours per week compared with their employed counterparts. **Table 2.4** gives full details.

Conclusions

The eight ISSP nations under study are in many respects quite different from one another. They range from capitalist to communist, from rich to comparatively poor, from ex-colonial Old World powers to confident New World nations. Yet their heterogeneity is not, in this chapter, their most obvious characteristic. Patterns of working life turn out to be fairly similar across the various countries. Hours of work and labour force participation rates are almost the same in the eight nations; only the USA has a markedly low, and Hungary a markedly high, level of unionisation; only Britain has an exceptional unemployment rate; all but Italy and Switzerland have fairly low levels of self-employment.

One example of cross-national similarities is revealed in **Table 2.2**, which shows that people's earnings across different countries are explained by almost identical factors. If one wishes to guess the earnings of a particular Hungarian, or of a particular American, one needs to know that individual's age, years of schooling, and gender, and whether he or she belongs to a union.[6] Then a broadly common algebraic formula allows approximate earnings to be estimated. Why this formula – one which dates back to the work of Jacob Mincer (1958) – performs so well is still not clearly understood. Whatever the exact interpretation, however, it seems that employees in our different countries have their rates of pay shaped by universal forces.

Notes

1. We have some concerns about the Australian sample, and so we have presented only the results of the multiple regression analysis for that country, as this type of analysis is robust with regard to assumptions of randomness.
2. Data on Switzerland are available only for 1987 and so sampling errors will be larger than for other countries. Switzerland is not one of the countries participating in the ISSP, but a team at the Soziologisches Institut der Universität Zurich has replicated the 1987 module and kindly provided us with the data.

*Unfortunately, these data are not available for Hungary where we know that a large proportion of the population has second jobs.

3. The idea of using econometric methods to estimate the effects of trade union membership stretches back at least to Lewis (1963). An authoritative informal explanation of methods and results can be found in Freeman and Medoff (1984).

4. The definitions of the variables used in the multiple regression analyses are as follows:

Dependent variables

(i)   West Germany: natural logarithm of net monthly income *after* deduction of income tax and national insurance.

(ii) Austria: natural logarithm of *net* income per month.

(iii) Australia: natural logarithm of *gross* income over preceding 12 months.

(iv) USA: natural logarithm of *gross* annual earnings over preceding 12 months.

(v)   Britain: natural logarithm of gross annual earnings *before* deduction of income tax and national insurance.

(vi) Hungary: natural logarithm of monthly earnings.

(vii) Switzerland: natural logarithm of monthly earnings.

Independent variables

(i)   Age (Age^2): age of respondent.

(ii)   Education: years of schooling.

(iii) Male: (1, 0) dummy variable if male.

(iv)   Union: (1, 0) dummy variable if union member.

(v)   Married: (1, 0) dummy variable if married or living as married.

(vi)   Part-time: (1, 0) dummy variable if employed for up to 20 hours per week.

(vii) 1986 dummy: (1, 0) dummy for 1986.

(viii) 1987 dummy: (1, 0) dummy for 1987.

5. Because the earnings variable is measured in natural logarithms, these estimates are obtained by taking the (natural) anti-logarithm of the coefficient, deducting one and multiplying by 100 per cent. That is, if **M** is the coefficient, calculate

$$100(e^M - 1)$$

For further details of this procedure, see Blanchflower (1984).

6. Some economists (particularly Richard Freeman) have pointed out to us that the equations' *coefficients,* and therefore the *size* of the relationships, are not identical across nations, and of course that is true. We merely wish to claim that the same pressures seem to be at work across the countries, and that some of these can be captured by an equation. Many economists take this for granted, but other social scientists may not.

References

BLANCHFLOWER, D., 'Union Relative Wage Effects: A Cross-Section Analysis Using Establishment Data', *British Journal of Industrial Relations,* vol. 22 (1984), pp311-332.

BLANCHFLOWER, D. and OSWALD, A., 'The Wage Curve', *Scandinavian Journal of Economics* (forthcoming).

BRUNO, M. and SACHS, J., *Economics of Worldwide Stagflation,* Basil Blackwell, Oxford (1985).

CALMFORS, L. and DRIFFILL, J., 'Bargaining Structure, Corporatism and Macroeconomic Performance', *Economic Policy,* vol. 6 (1988), pp13-62.

DEX, S. and SHAW, L., *British and American Women at Work: Do Equal Opportunities Policies Matter?* Macmillan, London (1986).

FREEMAN, R. and MEDOFF, J., *What Do Unions Want?,* Basic Books, New York (1984).

HIRSCH, B. and ADDISON, J., *The Economic Analysis of Unions: New Approaches and Evidence,* Allen and Unwin, Boston (1986).

LEWIS, H.G., *Unionism and Relative Wages in the United States,* University of Chicago Press, Chicago (1963).

LEWIS, H.G., *Union Relative Wage Effects: A Survey,* University of Chicago Press, Chicago (1986).

MINCER, J., 'Investment in Human Capital and Personal Income Distribution', *Journal of Political Economy,* vol. 66 (1958), pp281-302.

MULVEY, C., 'Wage Levels: Do Unions Make a Difference?', in Nilard, J. (ed.), *Wage Fixation in Australia,* Allen and Unwin, Sydney (1986).

NEWELL, A. and SYMONS, J., *Mid-1980s Unemployment,* mimeo, Centre for Labour Economics, London School of Economics, London (1987).

PHELPS-BROWN, H., *The Inequality of Pay,* Oxford University Press, Oxford (1977).

WARR, P., *Psychology at Work,* Penguin Books, Harmondsworth (1985).

2.1 EARNINGS DISTRIBUTIONS OF EMPLOYEES, 1986
by country

Britain

	GROSS ANNUAL INCOME		RESPONDENTS	
			No	%
1.	Under	£2000	52	7.7
2.	£2000 -	£2999	66	9.7
3.	£3000 -	£3999	49	7.2
4.	£4000 -	£4999	67	9.9
5.	£5000 -	£5999	61	9.0
6.	£6000 -	£6999	64	9.4
7.	£7000 -	£7999	45	6.6
8.	£8000 -	£9999	84	12.4
9.	£10000 -	£11999	86	12.7
10.	£12000 -	£14999	55	8.1
11.	£15000 -	£17999	21	3.1
12.	£18000 -	£19999	6	0.9
13.	£20000 and more		22	3.2

Mean   = £7736

Standard Deviation   = £5153

Coefficient of Variation =   £66.60

BASE: 678

USA

	GROSS ANNUAL INCOME		RESPONDENTS	
			No	%
1.	Under	$1000	20	2.9
2.	$1000 -	$2999	30	4.4
3.	$3000 -	$3999	26	3.8
4.	$4000 -	$4999	23	3.4
5.	$5000 -	$5999	23	3.4
6.	$6000 -	$6999	17	2.5
7.	$7000 -	$7999	23	3.4
8.	$8000 -	$9999	32	4.7
9.	$10000 -	$12499	62	9.1
10.	$12500 -	$14999	72	10.6
11.	$15000 -	$17499	50	7.3
12.	$17500 -	$19999	46	6.7
13.	$20000 -	$22499	45	6.6
14.	$22500 -	$24999	34	5.0
15.	$25000 -	$29999	51	7.5
16.	$30000 -	$34999	46	6.7
17.	$35000 -	$39999	34	5.0
18.	$40000 -	$49999	24	3.5
19.	$50000 -	$59999	14	2.1
20.	$60000 and more		10	1.5

Mean   = $19077

Standard Deviation   = $15099

Coefficient of Variation = $79.14

BASE: 678

Hungary

	GROSS MONTHLY INCOME		RESPONDENTS	
			No	%
1.	Up to -	1.999 Forint	5	0.9
2.	2.000 -	2.999 Forint	26	4.7
3.	3.000 -	3.999 Forint	86	15.4
4.	4.000 -	4.999 Forint	104	18.7
5.	5.000 -	5.999 Forint	83	14.9
6.	6.000 -	6.999 Forint	65	11.7
7.	7.000 -	7.999 Forint	36	6.5
8.	8.000 -	8.999 Forint	40	7.2
9.	9.000 -	9.999 Forint	20	3.6
10.	10.000 -	12.499 Forint	36	6.4
11.	12.500 -	14.999 Forint	17	3.1
12.	15.000 -	19.999 Forint	19	3.4
13.	20.000 -	39.999 Forint	20	3.6
14.	40.000 Forint and more		-	-

Mean   = 6585 Forint

Standard Deviation   = 3689 Forint

Coefficient of Variation =   56.02 Forint

BASE: 557

Italy

	GROSS MONTHLY INCOME		RESPONDENTS	
			No	%
1.	Up to	149.999 Lire	9	2.8
2.	150.000 -	199.999 Lire	11	3.4
3.	200.000 -	299.999 Lire	62	19.0
4.	300.000 -	399.999 Lire	77	23.5
5.	400.000 -	499.999 Lire	41	12.5
6.	500.000 -	599.999 Lire	58	17.7
7.	600.000 -	699.999 Lire	22	6.7
8.	700.000 -	799.999 Lire	6	1.8
9.	800.000 -	899.999 Lire	17	5.2
10.	900.000 -	1,099.999 Lire	9	2.8
11.	1,100.000 -	1,999.999 Lire	3	0.9
12.	2,000.000 -	2,999.999 Lire	6	1.8
13.	3,000.000 Lire and more		6	1.8

Mean   = 51551 Lire

Standard Deviation   = 53718 Lire

Coefficient of Variance =   104.200 Lire

BASE: 327

2.1 (continued) EARNINGS DISTRIBUTIONS OF EMPLOYEES, 1986
by country

West Germany

	NET MONTHLY INCOME		RESPONDENTS	
			No	%
1.		Under DM 400	11	1.1
2.	DM 400 - under	600	58	5.9
3.	DM 600 - under	800	43	4.4
4.	DM 800 - under	1.000	28	2.9
5.	DM 1.000 - under	1.250	81	8.3
6.	DM 1.250 - under	1.500	64	6.5
7.	DM 1.500 - under	1.750	126	12.8
8.	DM 1.750 - under	2.000	115	11.7
9.	DM 2.000 - under	2.250	125	12.7
10.	DM 2,250 - under	2.500	46	4.7
11.	DM 2.500 - under	2.750	70	7.1
12.	DM 2.750 - under	3.000	33	3.4
13.	DM 3.000 - under	3.500	60	6.1
14.	DM 3.500 - under	4.000	43	4.4
15.	DM 4.000 - under	4.500	27	2.8
16.	DM 4.500 - under	5.000	22	2.2
17.	DM 5.000 - under	5.500	10	1.0
18.	DM 5.500 - under	6.000	12	1.2
19.	DM 6.000 - under	8.000	2	0.2
20.	DM 8.000 - under	10.000	1	0.1
21.	DM 10.000 - under	15.000	4	0.4
22.	DM 15.000 and more		-	-

Mean   = DM 1992

Standard Deviation   = DM 1165

Coefficient of Variation =   DM 58.46

BASE: 981

Austria

	NET MONTHLY INCOME		RESPONDENTS	
			No	%
1.	Under	4.000 S	22	5.7
2.	4.000 -	5.999 S	39	10.1
3.	6.000 -	7.999 S	53	13.7
4.	8.000 -	9.999 S	75	19.4
5.	10.000 -	11.999 S	65	16.8
6.	12.000 -	13.999 S	59	15.3
7.	14.000 -	15.999 S	33	8.5
8.	16.000 -	17.999 S	13	3.4
9.	18.000 -	19.999 S	4	1.0
10.	20.000 -	21.999 S	6	1.6
11.	22.000 -	23.999 S	5	1.3
12.	24.000 -	25.999 S	4	1.0
13.	26.000 -	27.999 S	1	0.3
14.	28.000 -	29.999 S	1	0.3
15.	30.000 -	31.999 S	2	0.5
16.	32.000 -	33.999 S	-	-
17.	34.000 -	35.999 S	-	-
18.	36.000 -	37.999 S	1	0.3
19.	38.000 -	39.999 S	1	0.3
20.	40.000 S and more		2	0.5

Mean   = 10901 S

Standard Deviation   = 6078 S

Coefficient of Variation =   55.75 S

BASE: 386

Switzerland *

	GROSS MONTHLY INCOME		RESPONDENTS	
			No	%
1.	Under	500 SFR	24	4.2
2.	500 -	1000 SFR	34	6.0
3.	1000 -	1500 SFR	29	5.1
4.	1500 -	2000 SFR	54	9.5
5.	2000 -	2500 SFR	59	10.4
6.	2500 -	3000 SFR	84	14.8
7.	3000 -	4000 SFR	117	20.6
8.	4000 -	5000 SFR	85	15.0
9.	5000 -	6000 SFR	33	5.8
10.	6000 -	10000 SFR	40	7.1
11.	10000 -	20000 SFR	5	1.1
12.	20000 SFR and more		3	0.5

Mean   = 3473.5 SFR

Standard Deviation   = 2670.6 SFR

Coefficient of Variance =   76.9 SFR

BASE: 567

*1987 data

2.2 FACTORS AFFECTING EMPLOYEES' EARNINGS (COEFFICIENTS), 1985–87 by country

EXPLANATORY VARIABLES (see note 4 at the end of this chapter)	Britain	USA	Australia	West Germany	Austria	Hungary *	Switzerland **
Age (t - statistic)	.047 (7.79)	.1013 (10.22)	.0336 (4.52)	.0773 (12.41)	.0836 (10.39)	.0465 (9.98)	.0626 (8.83)
Age² (t - statistic)	-.0005 (7.04)	-.0010 (8.44)	-.0003 (3.55)	-.0008 (10.43)	-.0009 (8.83)	-.0005 (8.39)	-.0005 (7.87)
Years of education (t - statistic)	.1339 (16.55)	.0918 (13.74)	.0282 (7.49)	.0306 (10.03)	.0647 (9.77)	.0433 (18.55)	.0105 (2.89)
Sex (male) (t - statistic)	.5630 (23.75)	.5108 (13.53)	.4264 (14.47)	.4578 (20.07)	.3491 (12.53)	.4176 (28.29)	.4068 (7.10)
Union membership (t - statistic)	.0805 (3.57)	.2314 (4.78)	.1213 (4.51)	.0683 (2.99)	.0719 (2.60)	.0778 (4.67)	.0399 (0.79)
Marital status (t - statistic)	.0859 (2.96)	.0764 (1.95)	-.0132 (0.43)	-.0081 (0.33)	-.0264 (0.80)	.0294 (1.58)	-.0064 (0.10)
Working part-time (t - statistic)	-1.2071 (30.39)	-1.2806 (16.80)	-.7364 (14.85)	-.6347 (10.74)	-.6916 (9.02)	+	-.5873 (3.26)
1986 dummy (t - statistic)	.1362 (5.14)	.0228 (0.43)	-.3474 (10.59)	.1217 (4.75)	.0195 (0.59)	+	+
1987 dummy (t - statistic)	.1930 (7.15)	.1096 (0.14)	-.1529 (4.75)	.2261 (7.14)	.2525 (7.28)	-.0369 (2.44)	+
Constant (t - statistic)	5.8177 (39.50)	5.6879 (26.70)	1.5393 (10.46)	5.1347 (42.40)	6.5296 (42.64)	6.9305 (81.15)	6.0508 (37.48)
Adjusted R² (= % of variance of pay accounted for by the model)	.5982 = 60%	.3845 = 38%	.344 = 34%	.411 = 41%	.408 = 41%	.3556 = 36%	.3577 = 36%
N=	1884	1853	1946	1855	1047	2688	451
F=	312.5	127.9	112.9	144.5	79.3	212.9	39.2

BASE: *all employees*

* = 1986 and 1987 only; ** = 1987 only; + = no data available

Notes:

For each country, a multiple regression cross-section equation was estimated. The dependent variable in each case was the natural logarithm of people's earnings, and the explanatory variables were the nine listed in the left-hand column above.

The coefficient for each variable in the above table is an estimate of the size of the relationship between that variable and the independent variable, in this case, earnings. Individual coefficients may be positive (in which case the variable is positively associated with the independent variable, here, earnings), or negative (in which case the variable is negatively associated with the independent variable). We do not understand why the coefficient on the variable "1986 dummy" in the Australian equation enters with a negative sign.

The t-statistic tests the statistical significance of the estimates of each individual coefficient in the regression model. In general, the larger the statistic, the less likely it is that the estimate of the individual coefficient has arisen purely as result of random variation, and the more likely it is that there is a relationship between the dependent variable and the independent variable (in this case, earnings).

The F-statistic serves to test how well the regression model as a whole fits the data. In general, the greater the F statistic, the less likely it is that the total variance explained, R², is the result of random, or chance, variation.

2.3 SELF-EMPLOYMENT RATES, 1985–86 by country

		Britain	USA	Australia	West Germany	Austria	Hungary *	Italy	Switzerland **
SEX	Male	14%	19%	15%	14%	14%	5%	28%	26%
	Female	4%	13%	8%	10%	17%	3%	31%	19%
AGE	Under 25	7%	7%	4%	2%	3%	1%	33%	6%
	25–44	11%	15%	12%	12%	15%	6%	28%	22%
	45+	11%	22%	16%	16%	26%	2%	31%	31%
WORKING	Full-time	12%	15%	12%	12%	15%	+	29%	23%
	Part-time	*	27%	14%	7%	19%	+	30%	31%
OCCUPATION	Non-manual	11%	16%	12%	13%	21%	4%	28%	+
	Manual	10%	16%	13%	9%	6%	3%	8%	
SECTOR	Manufacturing	6%	6%	8%	8%	12%	1%	+	+
	Service	12%	18%	13%	14%	16%	5%		
	Private	15%	18%	19%	17%	+	+	33%	28%
	Public	-	11%	-	3%			-	9%
ALL		10%	16%	12%	12%	15%	4%	29%	23%
		2457	1308	1641	1849	1037	562	1252	775

BASE: *all in employment*

* = 1986 only; ** = 1987 only; + = no data available

Note: 'Self-employment rate' is the number who claimed to be self-employed expressed as a percentage of all those who claimed to be in full- or part-time paid employment

2.4 AVERAGE LENGTH OF WORKING WEEK, 1985-86 by country

	Britain	USA	Australia	West Germany	Austria	Italy *	Switzerland *
	hrs	hrs	hrs	hrs	hrs	hrs	hrs
SEX							
Male	44.4	44.6	43.5	45.4	46.5	41.4	48.0
Female	31.0	37.9	32.0	36.9	40.6	32.2	40.7
AGE							
Under 25	40.0	35.5	38.4	42.7	42.7	37.1	44.0
25-44	38.6	42.6	39.5	44.1	44.1	38.5	45.3
45+	38.2	41.1	39.1	45.6	45.6	38.6	47.4
UNION MEMBERSHIP							
Member	38.8	42.7	38.7	41.8	41.8	+	46.8
Not a member	38.7	41.3	39.7	46.2	46.2		45.4
WORKING							
Full-time	42.0	43.6	41.9	44.9	44.9	42.4	46.5
Part-time	15.7	10.9	11.2	14.4	10.4	18.2	n/c
OCCUPATION							
Non-manual	38.8	41.1	39.0	42.4	44.9	35.3	+
Manual	38.6	42.4	39.8	42.8	43.0	41.1	
EMPLOYMENT STATUS							
Employee	37.5	41.2	38.2	41.1	41.0	36.0	44.0
Self-employed	49.5	42.8	46.9	53.4	62.3	43.8	52.5
ALL	38.7	41.5	39.3	42.6	44.2	38.3	45.9
BASE: all in employment (full- or part-time)	2457	1308	1641	1849	1037	1252	775

* = 1986 only; ** = 1987 only; n/c = not calculated (percentage base too small);
+ = data not available

Note.　No data are available for Hungary

3 The role of the state

*Peter Taylor-Gooby**

The first ISSP (International Social Survey Programme) questionnaire, fielded in six countries in 1985 (Australia, Austria, Britain, Italy, the USA and West Germany), probed attitudes towards the role of government. It investigated views on a wide range of issues, including state intervention in the economy, support for welfare programmes, the freedom allowed to political protest and governmental obligations *versus* parental rights. Preliminary results, based only on British and American data, have already been reported by Davis (1986). In Chapter 4 of this Report, Tom W. Smith discusses attitudes towards the role of government in protecting the vulnerable, tackling poverty and reducing inequality. Here our task is twofold. First, we review briefly the arguments that have developed over recent years as to the proper function of the state. We then go on to examine the extent to which the public in each of these six Western industrialised nations support or oppose any 'rolling-back' of the government economic and social intervention which has tended to typify the social and liberal democracies in the post-war era.

Post-war 'welfare capitalism'

The role of government in the Western democracies has tended to develop according to a common pattern over the post-war period. During the three decades of steady economic growth since 1945, successive governments deployed an increasing proportion of national resources, the greater part of which were allocated to social welfare programmes rather than to direct intervention in the economy. State ownership of industry remained at a low

*Reader in Social Policy, University of Kent at Canterbury.

level, and economic policies were aimed more at the regulation of market activity. State intervention in family life was – by and large – strictly limited.

Inherent in what we call 'welfare capitalism' is a conflict between political equality and class inequality. Governments of the Western democracies have – almost without exception – shied away from any 'positive' notion of individual economic rights which demands far-reaching state intervention to reduce class inequality and poverty. Instead they have tended to adopt a liberal model which restricts encroachments upon citizens' freedom to those necessary to encourage equality of opportunity and to ensure equal legal and political rights through a parliamentary system of government.

However, the faltering of economic growth, sparked by the oil crisis of the mid-1970s, called the post-war settlement into question. In most of the countries reviewed, the rate of increase in state spending fell back sharply. Annual increases in welfare spending in Western countries fell from an average of 6.5 per cent of GDP in the 1960s to 2.6 per cent by the mid-1980s (OECD, 1988a). Other developments, such as the growth of the women's movement, also challenged some of the hitherto unquestioned assumptions underlying social policies. Even the commitment to protecting the civil liberties of the individual citizen – although still widely accepted in principle – began to come under pressure with increases in violent political protest and 'terrorist' actions. In what directions has public opinion moved in these changed circumstances?

The future of welfare capitalism

Economic uncertainty and social changes are likely to exacerbate conflicts between different interest groups, and undermine the broad consensus in support of the welfare state. The growth of unemployment, for instance, has increased the number of households without market incomes, while demographic changes have led to a rapid growth in the proportions of retired people and single-parent families. As a result of these developments, income levels have tended to become more polarised. As a result, it might be predicted that the increasingly affluent majority – feeling relatively well insulated – will become less inclined to provide for the needs of the disadvantaged minority with which it no longer empathises.

Evidence for the beginnings of attitudinal shifts such as these may perhaps be reflected in recent political changes in the six nations we are examining. Certainly, the electorate has moved to the right in Britain, the USA, West Germany and – until recently, anyway – Australia. Right-wing movements are also growing in importance in Italy and Austria. It should, however, be noted that – in Britain at least – there is scant support for a wholesale dismemberment of the welfare state (Taylor-Gooby, 1987) and, indeed, a growing concern about the condition of its most cherished institution, the NHS (National Health Service) (Bosanquet, 1988).

Yet while the post-war tradition still has strong advocates in the political centre, which propose 'social democratic' or 'mixed economy' solutions, new models of the proper role of government have been developed by

those on the right. Some propose a lessening of intervention on all fronts –
the so-called 'rolling back of the state'; others recognise that state action is
essential to preserve the freedom of markets against the self-interested
activities of monopolists, trade unions, professional groups, cartels,
lobbyists and pork-barrelling politicians. So a reduction in social and
economic intervention may go hand-in-hand with restrictions on freedom
of association and on civil liberties (and, conceivably, greater intervention
in family life to protect the vulnerable) – the model of 'free market and
strong state'. (For a review of the arguments, see Dunleavy and O'Leary,
1987.)

On the political left, many recent writers have recognised the difficulties
faced by centrally-planned economies – for example, in fulfilling the
aspirations of their citizens and in ensuring individual rights. In place of
support for high levels of intervention across the board, the emphasis is
now on decentralising state power, modifying the control exercised by
parliament: over any interventionist programmes, increasing individual
participation and supporting a more positive interpretation of citizens'
rights – 'civil society socialism' as opposed to 'democratic centralism' (see
Keane, 1988).

How far do models such as these – proposed from the centre, right and
left – find sympathy with the citizens of our six nations? In stable
democracies, public attitudes are likely to be important in determining any
new – or modified – settlement between government and the market, the
family and the citizen. Many of the questions asked in 1985 are to be
repeated in 1990 – next time in at least eleven countries – so we shall then
have the opportunity to see a moving picture instead of a snapshot.

Government and the economy

Attitudes to state intervention

In the countries under review, post-war policy has been broadly guided by
neo-Keynesian principles – state intervention to try to secure economic and
social stability and to influence (but not control) equality of outcomes,
within a largely private sector capitalist system. The proper sphere of
government has traditionally included the manipulation of interest rates,
some control over the availability of resources, influence (mainly, but not
always, indirect) on prices and wages and the management of relations
with other national economies.

As noted, direct state ownership of industry has generally been eschewed.
As the table below shows, there is indeed little popular enthusiasm for
direct state ownership of a range of important manufacturing and service
sector industries. There is, however, a much higher level of support for
government intervention in controlling their prices and profits:

% favouring for ... electricity	Britain	USA	Australia	West Germany	Austria	Italy
government ownership	27%	6%	37%	19%	28%	36%
government control	46%	62%	44%	64%	62%	60%
(either)	(73%)	(68%)	(81%)	(83%)	(96%)	(96%)
... local public transport						
government ownership	19%	11%	30%	25%	33%	32%
government control	39%	47%	41%	56%	53%	63%
(either)	(58%)	(58%)	(71%)	(81%)	(86%)	(95%)
... steel industry						
government ownership	18%	3%	5%	9%	25%	23%
government control	34%	35%	34%	46%	49%	66%
(either)	(52%)	(38%)	(40%)	(55%)	(75%)	(89%)
... banking and insurance						
government ownership	9%	3%	5%	5%	17%	25%
government control	34%	49%	39%	55%	55%	65%
(either)	(43%)	(52%)	(45%)	(60%)	(72%)	(90%)
... car industry						
government ownership	9%	2%	3%	2%	9%	15%
government control	32%	36%	29%	42%	46%	69%
(either)	(41%)	(38%)	(32%)	(44%)	(55%)	(84%)

In Italy, Austria and West Germany, there are majorities in favour of state control over prices and profits in most of the industries covered, as there are for electricity and public transport in Australia, Britain and the USA. Everywhere except in Italy and Austria people are content to leave the car industry to the private sector. In most countries there is substantial support for state regulation of banking and insurance. The Italians emerge as the most interventionist and Americans as the least. Broadly, then, the pattern of attitudes corresponds to the realities of post-war interventionism, with the emphasis on regulation rather than on state ownership.

The issue of government responsibility is also addressed when we ask about the provision of jobs, price regulation and help for industry.

It is definitely the government's responsibility to...	Britain	USA	Australia	West Germany	Austria	Italy
... provide a job for everyone who wants one	38%	14%	20%	35%	47%	52%
... keep prices under control	61%	31%	51%	25%	50%	76%
... provide industry with the help it needs to grow	54%	17%	30%	11%	23%	34%

Here three distinctive patterns emerge. Italians, and to a lesser extent Britons, are inclined to regard these areas as the responsibility of government. (It is perhaps interesting that the countries with the worst post-war inflation rates are most in favour of price controls.) Corporatist

Austria agrees on the matter of jobs and prices, but not on direct industrial aid. The remaining three countries favour lower levels of interventionism (although a bare majority of Australians sees price control as within the government's sphere).

A similar pattern appears in answers to a series of questions on specific policies or "things the government might do to help the economy", where the issues of job creation, price control and aid for industry are joined by those of wage control, support for new technologies, reductions in the working week, government spending cuts and business deregulation. Figures for all six countries are shown in **Table 3.1**.

Prevailing policies and economic conditions exert strong influences upon responses. For example, the low level of unemployment in Austria probably accounts for the lack of support for job creation policies there. The British lack of enthusiasm for wage control may reflect in part the perceived strength of trade unions in this country (but see Chapter 2). The relatively low level of support among Britons for controls on prices (only one in five were strongly in favour) may have something to do with the rapid decline in the rate of inflation in the early 1980s (and to the fact that the government of the day has firmly rejected this strategy).*

% strongly in favour/in favour of...	Britain	USA	Australia	West Germany	Austria	Italy
... government financing of projects to create new jobs	88%	69%	77%	71%	72%	91%
... control of wages by legislation	33%	23%	54%	28%	58%	73%
... control of prices by legislation	60%	38%	69%	56%	86%	91%

The complete set of responses to this question will be found in **Table 3.1**.

To summarise, attitudes to economic intervention indicate that, with some national variations, public preferences correspond more or less to the policies of the mixed economies of the post-war period. Even in highly interventionist Italy, majorities do not support nationalisation of any of the industries covered. Even in the *laissez-faire* USA, majorities do not regard price control or help for industry as outside the sphere of government responsibility.

Expenditure on public enterprise

As a postscript to this discussion, we look at the percentage of each nation's Gross Domestic Product (GDP) accounted for by 'public enterprise': this gives a measure, albeit crude, of the significance of state ownership of industry in each country's economy.

British Social Attitudes data for the years since 1985 show a continuing trend against laws to control both wages and prices.

	State spending on public enterprise (as % of GDP)
Austria	5.3%
Australia	4.3%
Italy	3.3%
Britain	2.9%
West Germany	2.7%
USA	0.9%

Source: OECD (1985).

The role of the US government as an 'owner' of industry is negligible. Differences between the other five Western nations, though real, are small.

By and large, the variations between the countries mirror attitudes towards government intervention in industry: the less significant the role of the public sector, the less enthusiasm for its retention or expansion. Only in Britain and Australia is there a lower degree of public support for state ownership than their positions in the 'league table' above would suggest. This may indicate why in Britain anyway, the privatisation policies of the present government have, so far at least, enjoyed some popularity.

Government and welfare

Attitudes to state responsibilities

Cross-national attitudes to government responsibilities for its citizens' welfare fall into a pattern familiar from single-nation studies. Universal services, such as health care and pensions, are seen as state responsibilities by majorities in all countries except the USA; provision for unemployed people, and policies to reduce income differences, receive rather less support. Overall, support is highest in Britain and Italy and lowest in the USA and (to a lesser extent) in West Germany.* In Australia, there is little enthusiasm either for provision for the unemployed or for redistributive policies.

As the table below shows, the traditional welfare state programme of helping the majority, but providing a heavily regulated and parsimonious règime for less deserving minorities, is widely endorsed in most of the countries. As we will see in Chapter 4 however, social engineering policies, designed to redistribute income between those who are better and worse off, attract rather less support. Indeed, in the USA, Australia and West Germany, it is clear that welfare interventions are supported only insofar as they do not threaten the prevailing class order of society. In Austria, Italy and Britain, on the other hand, approaching one half of the population believes that one of the responsibilities of government is to reduce the extremes of income inequality.

---

*As Davis (1986) noted, "Britons and Americans have essentially similar relative *priorities* for 'welfare state' activities, but Britons are much more enthusiastic about every one of them." (p.103)

It is definitely the government's responsibility to. . .	Britain	USA	Australia	West Germany	Austria	Italy
. . . provide health care for the sick	86%	36%	60%	54%	66%	87%
. . . provide a decent standard of living for old people	79%	43%	62%	56%	64%	82%
. . . provide a decent standard of living for unemployed people	45%	16%	15%	24%	16%	40%
. . . reduce income differences between rich and poor people	48%	17%	24%	28%	41%	48%

A further series of questions asked whether or not state spending should be increased in a range of areas, from health to the environment, from old age pensions to culture and the arts. In general, the pattern of responses corresponds to that already noted: enthusiasm for extra spending on universal services, even if (as we reminded respondents) "it might require a tax increase to pay for it", and much more muted support when it comes to unemployment benefits and 'non-welfare' items:

% wanting much more/more state spending on	Britain	USA	Australia	West Germany	Austria	Italy
Health	88%	60%	62%	52%	61%	81%
Old age pensions	75%	44%	55%	46%	50%	76%
Education	75%	66%	64%	40%	38%	63%
Unemployment benefits	41%	25%	13%	35%	16%	57%
Police and law enforcement	40%	51%	67%	30%	23%	48%
The environment	37%	43%	32%	83%	74%	61%
The military and defence	17%	20%	46%	6%	13%	12%
Culture and the arts	10%	16%	10%	14%	12%	33%

We should note especially the very wide popularity of mass welfare provision programmes in both Britain and Italy. Could it be that, in these two countries, they are seen as under particular threat – in contrast, perhaps, to the recent increase in affluence of the private sector? This seems particularly likely in respect of British views on health care. West Germans and Austrians are alone in expressing relative satisfaction with their (already high) levels of expenditure on education; Australians in their keenness for extra money for law enforcement; Italians in their support for culture and the arts. In passing we should also note that in 1985 only West Germans saw the environment as in great need of additional spending: 43 per cent of German respondents wanted *much more* government spending in this area. We await with some interest the responses among the ISSP nations when we repeat this question in 1990.

Our cross-national data on attitudes to welfare lead us to three main conclusions. First, respondents make clear distinctions between different types of social welfare programme, strongly endorsing some and showing much less enthusiasm for others. Second, the national patterns of enthusiasm for state involvement in such programmes correspond roughly to the patterns of enthusiasm for economic intervention. Third, there are similar variations in attitudes across nations towards provision for unemployed people; whereas job creation is fairly popular, the provision of benefits is not regarded by many as a priority for extra government spending. It appears therefore that although most people believe that the state has a duty to provide a decent standard of living for those without jobs, they feel its primary duty is to facilitate the creation of jobs themselves, rather than to compensate people for being out of work.

Realities of state spending

We conclude this section by looking at the available data, gleaned from OECD published statistics, on the extent to which the governments of our six nations intervene to provide financially for the welfare needs of their citizens. In this way, we may be able to see if the substantial variations in attitudes already revealed can be explained – to some extent, at least – by the different routes the various countries may have taken. As we have seen, the range is wide – from the strong interventionism of Austria and Italy to the rejection of any threat to individual market freedoms that characterise Australia and the USA.

We look first at total state spending and at social spending, both expressed as percentages of each nation's GDP:

	Britain	USA	Australia	West Germany	Austria	Italy
Total state spending as % of GDP	47%	37%	39%	47%	52%	51%
Total *social* spending as % of GDP	19%	17%	17%	24%	25%	28%

Source: OECD (1988a).

In terms of total state spending, the ISSP countries fall into two distinct groups: the European social democracies on the one hand, and the USA and Australia on the other. The role of the state is more powerful, then, in those countries that are inclined to grant it greatest legitimacy. But if we look at the second row of figures, we see that on *social spending* Britain is closer to anti-interventionist USA and Australia than to her social democratic near-neighbours. Could this perhaps help to explain the conflicting attitudes of the British towards welfare provision, captured in successive *British Social Attitudes* surveys? The British public strongly supports extra spending on, for example, health care and pensions (even if this entails tax increases), while at the same time being strongly and increasingly critical of many state-provided services. Public opinion therefore seems to support an increase in the relatively low proportion of state resources devoted to social spending – low that is, relative to West Germany and to several other (non-ISSP) European social democracies:

	Britain	USA	Australia	West Germany	Austria	Italy
State health spending as % of GDP*	5.2%	4.4%	4.9%	6.4%	5.3%	5.4%
Private health spending as % of GDP	0.9%	6.3%	1.9%	1.8%	2.9%	1.3%
(Age weighted) pension provision as % of GDP†	0.4%	0.6%	0.4%	0.8%	0.8%	0.7%

Source: OECD (1988a).

† A provision index has been computed for state pension provision.[1] Health care spending varies so widely between different social groups in the various countries that a comparable index cannot reliably be calculated.

In passing, we should note that, in the USA, total health spending is nearly 11 per cent of GDP, well over half of which is accounted for by the private sector. In no other country studied here does the private sector play so large a role.

In the arena of social intervention, we can trace a crude correspondence between attitudes to state responsibility for health care provision and the proportion of resources devoted to private medicine. There is, however, little relation between existing levels of state health spending and support for an increase. When public and private spending are combined, there is a rough correspondence between low levels of total spending and support for an increase (except in the case of Austria, a high spender which wants more).*

Support for more spending on pensions is associated more with attitudes to state responsibility for pensions rather than with actual spending levels,** perhaps because occupational and private pension provision is an important component in the incomes of many retired people in countries such as Britain, the USA and Australia. (Comparable data are not conveniently available on 'non-state' pensions.)

	Britain	USA	Australia	West Germany	Austria	Italy
Unemployment benefit spending as % of GDP	1.8 %	0.4 %	1.3 %	1.5 %	0.8 %	0.8 %
% of labour force unemployed	11.2 %	7.1 %	8.2 %	7.2 %	3.6 %	10.5 %
% of GDP spent on unemployment benefits weighted by % of population entitled	0.16%	0.06%	0.16%	0.21%	0.22%	0.08%

Source: OECD (1988b).

---

* A possible contributory factor may be that Austrians come lower in both infant mortality and life expectancy league tables than do the inhabitants of any other OECD country, except Portugal, Greece and Turkey (OECD, 1988a, Tables 14 and 15).
**This is so even when spending levels are used to generate a relative measure – our 'provision index' – which takes into account cross-national differences in demography and retirement age (see note 1 at the end of this chapter).

Support for the view that benefits for unemployed people are a state responsibility, and support for increased spending on them, appear to follow the contours of each country's unemployment *rates* rather than the current levels of state spending on unemployment benefits. Using the 'provision index' to adjust spending on benefits to reflect differences in unemployment rates does not produce higher correlations with attitudes towards unemployment benefits. Thus, although West German and American unemployment rates are similar, West Germany spends about three times as much as the USA on benefits for each unemployed person; yet one third of West Germans favour *more* state spending on unemployment benefits, compared with about one quarter of Americans.

Our attempts to use OECD data to point out cross-national differences in welfare provision, and relate them to levels of need, are necessarily imperfect. More detailed and laborious work would be needed to improve on them. But our findings do indicate that there are real (though weak) relationships between attitudes, levels of social spending and need.

Government and family life

Parents are expected to play an important part in the emotional, social, moral and cultural development of their children, providing a framework of motives and rewards in preparation for adult life. But the family is also expected to protect and care for its vulnerable members, such as children and the elderly, and to look after them if they are sick or disabled. A series of the questions in the 1985 ISSP survey asks about the circumstances in which public authorities should be permitted to intervene for the sake of a child's welfare. For each of eight different 'problems', respondents were asked to choose between three options: the authorities should (a) take no action, (b) give warnings or counselling, or (c) take the child from its parents. In each case, the hypothetical child is ten years old. The answers show broad cross-national agreement as to the circumstances in which no intervention is necessary, in which counselling should be offered and in which a child should be removed from its parents.

The table below shows the proportions in each country supporting the most drastic option of separating the child from its parents in each of the following circumstances:

	Britain	USA	Australia	West Germany	Austria	Italy
Parents regularly beat the child	87%	84%	85%	74%	77%	57%
Parents do not provide proper food and clothing	56%	57%	67%	41%	57%	32%
Parents refuse essential medical treatment because of religious beliefs	47%	56%	59%	61%	n/a	65%
Child takes drugs and parents don't do anything about it	38%	26%	41%	30%	31%	59%
Child regularly stays out late and parents don't know where it is	13%	13%	16%	6%	n/a	7%
Parents allow child to watch violent or pornographic films	12%	12%	11%	12%	n/a	6%
Parents refuse to send child to school	5%	14%	9%	18%	n/a	16%
Child frequently skips school and parents do nothing	5%	8%	7%	4%	7%	11%

Note. n/a = not asked

Some three-quarters or more of respondents (except in Italy) endorse removal in the case of regular beatings, between half and two-thirds for neglect or denial of essential medical treatment, and between a quarter and nearly half for drug abuse (again except in Italy). The remaining problems attract less drastic remedies. Only Italians deviate from this pattern, being much *less* in favour of intervention to prevent beatings or neglect and strikingly *more* so in the case of drug abuse. The English-speaking nations display the most concern about violence. Americans (perhaps surprisingly) appeared in 1985 to be the least concerned about drugs.

The overall pattern of response suggests that state intervention is more acceptable when the family fails to provide physical care than when it fails to provide a proper moral and cultural framework. This corresponds, perhaps, to the democratic liberal maxim of restricting individual freedom only when it interferes directly with the freedom of others. So parental freedom is endorsed, except where its exercise may lead to a serious threat to the child's health or well-being.

The distinctive pattern emerging from the Italian survey diminishes somewhat when we look at the regional pattern *within* Italy. The views of Italians living in the more heavily industrialised north-east are closer to those of other mainland Europeans than to their compatriots elsewhere. But this can be only part of the explanation of Italian differences. The issue clearly requires further investigation. In most countries, however, the boundaries between family and state in the sphere of parental responsibility are clearly drawn, with majorities granting the state a final responsibility for care and protection but wanting the family to play the principal role in moral and social guidance.

Government and citizenship

Discussions of the concept of citizenship usually distinguish between two different notions of freedom. The first stresses freedom from coercion by the state, which is fundamental to the unfettered exercise of political rights in a representative parliamentary democracy. For instance, citizens must be free to join or form parties and express choices periodically through the ballot box. The second notion stresses, in addition, the state's role in securing a degree of substantive equality for its citizens, as a precondition of equal opportunity to achieve individual goals in life. This calls for a higher degree of state intervention, extending beyond the civic and political sphere into social, economic and family life. We shall call these notions of freedom 'passive' and 'active' rights.

Passive rights and civil liberties

Political freedom, including the right of protest, is an integral feature of Western democracies. As the table below shows, there is majority support in all six countries for the right to protest against the government by holding public meetings, by publishing pamphlets and (except in West Germany and Austria) by demonstrating.* The right to organise nationwide protest strikes is supported by a majority only in Italy, and direct action through occupying or damaging a government building receives little support in any of the six countries.

% saying it should 'definitely' or 'probably' be allowed	Britain	USA	Australia	West Germany	Austria	Italy
Protest meetings	89%	78%	91%	91%	86%	79%
Protest pamphlets	86%	69%	87%	73%	68%	79%
Marches and demonstrations	70%	66%	69%	31%	33%	67%
Nationwide strike	30%	20%	22%	42%	39%	59%
Occupy government offices	12%	9%	9%	6%	12%	12%
Damage government buildings	1%	3%	1%	*	*	2%

Note * = less than 0.5%.

So while the citizens of these parliamentary democracies see a place for orderly protest against the government of the day, they firmly draw the line at any action that could lead to violence.

The principle that individual conscience should on exceptional occasions stand above the law is approved by decisive majorities (most strikingly in West Germany; unfortunately this question was not asked in Austria). Even the right of newspapers to publish confidential government economic plans is defended by moderate majorities. However the disclosure of secret *defence* plans is widely condemned in all countries (most emphatically in Australia and the USA).

---

*To Germans and Austrians, 'marches and demonstrations' may well be a chilling reminder of the rallies of the Third Reich.

	Britain	USA	Australia	West Germany	Austria	Italy
% agreeing that						
Conscience should come before breaking the law	61%	56%	68%	88%	n/a	60%
Newspapers should be allowed to publish confidential...						
...economic plans	63%	61%	60%	63%	56%	64%
...defence plans	26%	17%	16%	23%	30%	24%

Note. n/a = not asked

Majorities of respondents in all countries also place limits – some of them quite strict – on the rights of *others* who might threaten the liberal democratic settlement: they are not prepared to tolerate racists or revolutionaries as teachers in secondary schools, and in Britain, Australia and Italy, they also reject the right of racists to hold public meetings or (Britain excepted) to publish books expressing their views. In West Germany, America and Austria opinion on the rights of racists is much more evenly divided. (See **Tables 3.2** and **3.3** for detailed figures.)

The pattern of answers shows few cross-national variations, and suggests strong support for what we have called 'passive' citizen rights. Individual conscience is defended in extreme circumstances, and pamphleteering and public meetings are regarded as legitimate forms of protest. Those who threaten the rights of other citizens – for instance, racists – receive short shrift, as do parents who threaten the basic rights of children; yet those who threaten the system as a whole – revolutionaries – find a greater measure of tolerance.

Alongside these views, however, there is strong support for a range of state powers. Censorship is seen as necessary over defence matters (but not over economic plans). Protest by means of direct action is not supported as a legitimate civil liberty. The idea of extending democracy to encompass greater civil liberties of these kinds fails to strike chords in popular sentiment – just as right-wing aspirations to strengthen state power and to extend the free market also fail to command much support.

Active rights and citizen equality

When we begin to consider state intervention to secure 'active' rights to equal participation in society, the picture becomes more confused. The relevant questions cover policies intended to achieve equal treatment for women and men in work and in education, and to reduce inequalities of social class and wealth.*

There is a clear belief in every country (except Italy) that women have fewer opportunities than men and suffer discrimination in employment.

*We did not ask about race inequalities because each of the participating nations has a somewhat different position in respect of ethnic minorities. The presence in some countries of immigrants without permanent rights of residence further confuses the situation.

Educational opportunities for women are seen as more equally available. People in West Germany, Austria and the USA are most strongly aware of inequalities, followed by those in Britain, Australia and Italy (where the view that men and women receive equal pay is widespread). **Table 3.4** gives full details.

Policies to improve women's chances in education and at the workplace are supported within each country roughly in proportion to the strength of belief that gender discrimination actually exists. But when positive discrimination – preferential treatment for women to help redress the balance – is mooted, support declines abruptly. Such an approach might achieve equal outcomes but only at the expense of men, who would find the state intervening to curb their current privileges.

	Britain	USA	Australia	West Germany	Austria	Italy
% strongly in favour/in favour of government policies to...						
...increase opportunities for women in business and industry	56%	49%	47%	72%	76%	52%
...increase opportunities for women to go to university	45%	44%	39%	42%	50%	38%
...give women preferential treatment for jobs and promotions	7%	14%	6%	10%	20%	21%

Turning to class inequality, we see that respondents in all countries acknowledge the privilege enjoyed by those with a wealthy background. To an extent too, the children of professionals are generally seen as having superior life-chances (see **Table 3.5**). We did not ask a direct question on how class inequalities might be mitigated. However attitudes to the redistribution of wealth (see the table below) show substantial cross-national variations, with strong support in Italy and Austria, more moderate attitudes in West Germany, Britain and Australia, and opposition by a substantial majority of Americans (see also Chapter 4). Moreover, even those who recognise the existence of inequality in their society do not necessarily think it is the job of government to do something about it. We looked for associations between people's perceptions of the amount of inequality with their support for policies designed to mitigate it; on the whole, relationships were weak. Thus, large majorities of Austrians and Italians, almost irrespective of their perceptions of privilege, want something done. The majorities for action are smaller in West Germany and Britain, while Australians are divided equally. The legitimacy of bought privilege in the USA is indicated by the fact that only a third, even of those who recognise it, want policies to reduce it.

The overall pattern of attitudes to citizenship is one in which class issues appear more intransigent than inequalities of gender. There are clear limits to support for redistribution of wealth and strong national variations. In many of the countries, the reduction of inequality is seen as part of the role of government. The strongest support goes to the liberal ideal of equality of opportunity, with its corollary of unequal outcomes. People appear to be more willing to support programmes that promote equality of the sexes than those aimed at tackling class differences. Such a strategy might, of course, have the effect of assimilating women into the prevailing structure of social class inequalities, thus strengthening rather than threatening that structure.

Government intervention: the overall pattern

As noted earlier, the post-war tradition of democratic welfare capitalism has been pursued with different degrees of vigour in the six countries. This tradition is characterised by a moderate level of economic regulation rather than ownership, a high degree of social intervention in defined areas of mass needs – minority needs being carefully curtailed by the demands of the capitalist economic system – a rigid distinction between spheres of family and public life, and little impingement upon the political rights of the individual citizen. The problem of integrating democratic political equality with class inequality is resolved by emphasising 'passive' rights to freedom from interference, more strongly than 'positive' rights to more equal outcomes. This notion has come under challenge from both left and right.

In general, the attitudes of the citizens of the six nations correspond more closely to the traditional post-war settlement than they reveal any enthusiasm for change, although within this framework there are substantial national variations. There is little support for state ownership of industry, but a considerable measure of approval for economic interventions within the general structure of a privately dominated market-economic system. Social welfare that provides for mass needs is warmly endorsed, but provision for minorities, whose interests challenge the work ethic, receives meagre approval. Direct social engineering to advance equality of outcomes is not endorsed.

By and large, the family remains a separate sphere but one in which the state may intervene to protect a child's physical well-being. The political rights appropriate to a representative democracy are supported, but a decentralisation of power to a 'civil society' is not. There is support for the reduction, but not for the eradication, of inequalities, but such support is weakest in the English-speaking countries. Positive notions of citizenship receive more support when gender equality rather than class inequality (implicit in the structure of capitalist work incentives) is at stake.

State welfare and class solidarity

Finally, we investigate a specific issue raised by the earlier discussion of possible shifts in people's ideas about the proper role of government. How far is the pattern of support for state welfare spending changing? It has been suggested that the combination of rising average incomes and increasing inequality divides the interests of the middle classes from those of the poor (see, for example, Halsey, 1988, pp.29–33). For this analysis, we divided respondents into four more or less equal groups, according to their level of household income.* Income has been used as a proxy for class, since a common class schema cannot yet be easily applied to the ISSP data. On the table below, we show figures only for the poorest and wealthiest quartiles in the six countries[2].

% favouring. . .	Britain	USA	Australia	West Germany	Austria	Italy
. . .more spending on health care:						
Poorest quartile	90%	66%	69%	54%	73%	82%
Wealthiest quartile	84%	54%	55%	33%	59%	78%
. . .more spending on pensions:						
Poorest quartile	87%	60%	63%	51%	61%	79%
Wealthiest quartile	63%	37%	45%	32%	50%	75%
. . .more spending on unemployment benefits:						
Poorest quartile	59%	47%	19%	41%	27%	63%
Wealthiest quartile	25%	14%	7%	19%	13%	52%
Government should reduce income differences between those with high and low incomes:						
Poorest quartile	58%	49%	51%	63%	70%	79%
Wealthiest quartile	37%	22%	30%	52%	62%	64%

As already noted, there are substantial national variations in overall levels of support, associated to an extent with national differences in provision and need. But within each country there are also differences between those with higher and lower family incomes. In general, respondents in the top quartile are less likely to favour state spending than are the poorest in the bottom quartile. But in some cases the differences are very small. So, for instance, in Britain 90 per cent of the poorest quartile favour more health spending, but so do 84 per cent of the wealthiest quartile. This must testify to public concern about levels of spending on the NHS. On other items of state spending, Britons are much more divided in their views, depending on how well-off they are. The USA shows similar differences between the richest and the poorest, though with less overall enthusiasm for state spending than in Britain. In the other countries, the gap between those at the top and the bottom of the income divide is somewhat less marked.

On the issue of redistribution, however, a clear divide *is* apparent. In the USA, Australia and Britain, substantial majorities of the most affluent are opposed to government measures to reduce income differences between the rich and poor. In West Germany, Austria and Italy, nations more in favour of redistribution anyway, these divisions are not nearly so marked. In some

---

*One exception is West Germany, where respondents were not asked to give their household income: we used respondents' own earnings instead. Note also that in the USA, the top household income category coded comprises about 40 per cent of respondents, and hence does not really approximate to income 'quartiles'.

ways, then, the social democratic consensus is less strong in Britain than elsewhere in Western Europe, though British support for particular items of state spending seems to reflect concern – not felt to the same degree in any of the other five countries – about inadequacies in current welfare provision.

Conclusion

Public opinion within the six advanced Western countries covered is at once supportive and critical of welfare capitalism. It supports a mixed economy, strong welfare services and the preservation of a democratic order. It criticises the failure of the system to provide more generously for some of its most vulnerable groups, to make the reduction of unemployment more of a priority and to reduce inequalities, particularly in respect of women's rights. But public opinion does not necessarily support equalisation of incomes or higher levels of benefits: rather it wants more equal access to jobs and universal benefits.

So the pattern of attitudes charted by our survey conforms more to the post-war democratic welfare capitalist tradition than to the radical proposals from right or left. Public opinion in all the countries seems opposed to 'rolling back the state', or to a 'free economy and strong state', or to a highly interventionist 'democratic centralism' or to a large extension of civil liberties. Social circumstances have recently undergone fundamental change, and new theories may be developing as to the proper role of government. But reformers, whether of the left or of the right, seem to have some way to go before they win over the majority of citizens.

Notes

1. The numbers of people receiving state pensions and unemployment benefit vary widely between different countries; this variation should therefore be taken into account in assessing national variations in spending on these benefits. 'Provision indices' were computed by dividing the percentage of GDP spent on relevant benefit by the percentage of the population over minimum state pension age (in the case of pensions) and the percentage unemployed (in the case of unemployment benefit). The resulting statistics do not take into account *actual* take-up of the benefits among the relevant population groups. However, they do give a better idea of how differences in spending relate to differences in need than do the spending figures alone.
2. The income bands used in the analysis in this chapter were as follows. All except those for West Germany represent gross household income when the fieldwork was conducted.

    Britain (annual)   USA (annual)
    1. Up to £3,999   1. Up to $9,999
    2. £4,000 – £7,999   2. $10,000 – $19,999
    3. £8,000 – £11,999   3. $20,000 – $34,999
    4. £12,000 and over   4. $35,000 and over

Australia (annual)
1. Up to $A15,499
2. $A15,500 – $A25,499
3. $A25,500 – $A35,499
4. $A35,500 and over

West Germany (respondents' monthly earnings)
1. Up to DM1,000
2. DM1,000 – DM1,999
3. DM2,000 – DM2,999
4. DM3,000 and over

Austria (monthly)
1. Up to 9,999S
2. 10,000S – 15,999S
3. 16,000S – 21,999S
4. 22,000S and over

Italy (monthly)
1. Up to 900,000 lire
2. 900,001 lire – 1,200,000 lire
3. 1,200,001 lire – 1,800,000 lire
4. 1,800,001 lire and over

References

BOSANQUET, N., 'An ailing state of National Health', in Jowell, R., Witherspoon, S., and Brook, L., (eds), *British Social Attitudes: the 5th Report,* Gower, Aldershot (1988).

DAVIS, J.A., 'British and American attitudes: similarities and contrasts', in Jowell, R., Witherspoon, S., and Brook, L., (eds), *British Social Attitudes: the 1986 Report,* Gower, Aldershot (1986).

DUNLEAVY, P. and O'LEARY, B., *Theories of the State,* Macmillan, London (1987).

HALSEY, A.H., (ed.) *British Social Trends since 1900,* Macmillan, London (1988).

KEANE, J., *Democracy and Civil Society,* Verso, London (1988).

OECD (Organisation for Economic Co-operation and Development), *The Public Sector,* Economic Studies, OECD, Paris (Spring, 1985).

OECD (Organisation for Economic Co-operation and Development), *The Future of Social Protection,* OECD, Paris (1988a).

OECD (Organisation for Economic Co-operation and Development), *Economic Outlook,* OECD, Paris (December, 1988b).

TAYLOR-GOOBY, P., 'Citizenship and welfare', in Jowell, R., Witherspoon, S., and Brook, L. (eds) *British Social Attitudes: the 1987 Report,* Gower, Aldershot (1987).

3.1 GOVERNMENT INTERVENTION TO HELP THE ECONOMY (1985: Q221a–d) by country

	Britain	USA	Australia	West Germany	Austria	Italy
	%	%	%	%	%	%
WHICH ACTIONS ARE YOU IN FAVOUR OF AND WHICH ARE YOU AGAINST?						
Control of wages by legislation						
Strongly in favour	10	9	14	11	26	31
In favour	22	14	39	17	33	42
Neither in favour or against	21	23	17	20	23	15
Against	36	38	21	22	12	11
Strongly against	12	16	8	31	7	2
Control of prices by legislation						
Strongly in favour	20	8	24	28	55	54
In favour	40	30	45	28	31	37
Neither in favour or against	16	22	12	10	7	5
Against	20	30	15	17	5	4
Strongly against	4	10	4	18	2	1
Cuts in government spending						
Strongly in favour	11	41	33	40	52	35
In favour	27	39	42	37	29	34
Neither in favour or against	25	12	13	15	15	20
Against	29	7	10	6	3	11
Strongly against	9	2	1	3	1	1
Government financing of project to create new jobs						
Strongly in favour	37	28	25	30	28	56
In favour	50	42	52	41	44	36
Neither in favour or against	8	16	11	15	23	6
Against	4	11	9	9	5	2
Strongly against		4	3	5	1	*
Unweighted BASE:	1530	677	1528	1048	987	1580

3.1 (continued) GOVERNMENT INTERVENTION TO HELP THE ECONOMY (1985: Q221e-h) by country

	Britain %	USA %	Australia %	West Germany %	Austria %	Italy %
WHICH ACTIONS ARE YOU IN FAVOUR OF AND WHICH ARE YOU AGAINST?						
Less government regulation of business						
Strongly in favour	13	15	19	14	18	12
In favour	42	34	42	28	27	30
Neither in favour or against	34	32	24	32	39	38
Against	10	33	13	19	13	18
Strongly against	2	16	2	8	3	3
Support for industry to develop new products and new technology						
Strongly in favour	37	22	38	31	30	27
In favour	53	49	54	44	37	48
Neither in favour or against	7	20	6	18	25	18
Against	2	9	1	5	7	7
Strongly against	*	2	*	2	2	1
Supporting declining industries to protect jobs						
Strongly in favour	19	17	15	25	19	35
In favour	31	34	34	33	28	41
Neither in favour or against	21	24	22	14	24	13
Against	25	20	24	17	20	10
Strongly against	4	5	6	11	10	1
Reducing the working week to create more jobs						
Strongly in favour	16	6	7	22	14	28
In favour	34	20	18	29	23	37
Neither in favour or against	23	28	20	20	22	20
Against	24	34	38	16	26	13
Strongly against	4	12	16	14	16	3
BASE: *Unweighted*	*1530*	*677*	*1628*	*1048*	*987*	*1580*

3.2 RIGHTS OF REVOLUTIONARIES (1985: Q204a)
by country

THERE ARE SOME PEOPLE WHOSE VIEWS ARE CONSIDERED EXTREME BY THE
MAJORITY. FIRST, ... PEOPLE WHO WANT TO OVERTHROW THE GOVERNMENT
BY REVOLUTION. DO YOU THINK THAT SUCH PEOPLE SHOULD BE ALLOWED TO ...

	Britain	USA	Australia	West Germany	Austria	Italy
	%	%	%	%	%	%
... Hold public meetings to express their views						
Definitely	28	29	27	37	33	24
Probably	26	26	24	40	38	18
Probably not	11	12	15	11	15	18
Definitely not	35	33	35	12	15	40
... Teach 15 year olds in schools						
Definitely	5	9	5	5	6	9
Probably	8	12	8	14	15	11
Probably not	19	22	19	31	33	23
Definitely not	68	58	68	50	46	57
... Publish books expressing their views						
Definitely	29	27	28	27	21	27
Probably	39	30	33	47	46	26
Probably not	12	14	16	16	17	17
Definitely not	21	28	22	10	16	31
Unweighted	*1528*	*677*	*1528*	*1048*	*987*	*1580*

BASE:

3.3 RIGHTS OF RACISTS (1985: Q 204b)
by country

THESE ARE SOME PEOPLE WHOSE VIEWS ARE CONSIDERED EXTREME BY THE MAJORITY. SECOND, ... PEOPLE WHO BELIEVE THAT WHITES ARE RACIALLY SUPERIOR TO ALL OTHER RACES. DO YOU THINK THAT SUCH PEOPLE SHOULD BE ALLOWED TO ...

	Britain	USA	Australia	West Germany	Austria	Italy
	%	%	%	%	%	%
... Hold public meetings to express their views						
Definitely	20	29	19	20	17	13
Probably	20	30	20	30	32	15
Probably not	19	15	18	21	24	21
Definitely not	42	27	43	29	27	51
... Teach 15 year olds in schools						
Definitely	5	9	4	5	6	6
Probably	8	15	7	11	17	11
Probably not	19	22	18	27	29	22
Definitely not	68	54	57	68	47	61
... Publish books expressing their views						
Definitely	22	28	22	16	15	17
Probably	31	30	27	37	37	22
Probably not	15	16	17	21	19	19
Definitely not	32	26	34	26	28	42
Unweighted	*1528*	*677*	*1528*	*1048*	*987*	*1580*

BASE:

3.4 OPPORTUNITIES FOR AND DISCRIMINATION AGAINST WOMEN (1985: Qs 211–213) by country

	Britain	USA	Australia	West Germany	Austria	Italy
	%	%	%	%	%	%
Opportunities for university education are in general ...						
Much better for women	1	2	2	1	N/A	1
Better for women	2	7	3	2		4
No difference	78	79	82	77		85
Worse for women	17	11	13	19		9
Much worse for women	2	1	1	2		1
Job opportunities, compared with those for men with similar education and experience are, in general ...						
Much better for women	2	3	2	*	N/A	1
Better for women	5	7	4	1		7
No difference	39	33	48	12		49
Worse for women	49	52	43	59		41
Much worse for women	5	5	3	28		2
Compared with men who have similar education and jobs, in general ...						
Women are paid much better	1	1	1	-	*	*
Women are paid better	2	2	2	1	*	2
No difference	33	21	50	12	12	74
Women are paid worse	60	69	45	66	65	23
Women are paid much worse	5	8	3	22	23	1
BASE: Unweighted	1528	677	1528	1048	987	1580

3.5 CLASS INEQUALITY (1985: Q210 a–c)
by country

	Britain	USA	Australia	West Germany	Austria	Italy
	%	%	%	%	%	%
A person whose parents are rich has a better chance of earning a lot of money than a person whose parents are poor						
Agree strongly	29	30	28	23	41	36
Agree	43	37	40	47	33	36
Neither agree nor disagree	13	12	12	18	15	13
Disagree	13	17	16	10	9	11
Disagree strongly	2	3	4	3	3	4
A person whose father is a professional person has a better chance of earning a lot of money than a person whose parents are poor						
Agree strongly	22	19	25	18	40	34
Agree	46	33	39	45	34	37
Neither agree nor disagree	16	19	13	19	13	13
Disagree	14	25	19	14	10	12
Disagree strongly	2	4	5	4	3	5
In [country] what you achieve in life depends largely on your family background						
Agree strongly	17	11	9	8	21	22
Agree	36	20	27	27	30	41
Neither agree nor disagree	18	20	20	29	26	21
Disagree	26	41	35	28	19	13
Disagree strongly	4	8	10	7	3	3
BASE: _Unweighted_	_1528_	_677_	_1528_	_1048_	_987_	_1580_

4 Inequality and welfare

*Tom W. Smith**

This chapter explores comparative attitudes to inequality and to the related issue of what sorts of measures should be adopted to protect the most vulnerable in society. Some forms of vulnerability are universal: for instance, no-one is immune from illness, and none can escape old age. So an element of self-interest certainly exists when it comes to supporting policies and programmes that provide basic health care for the sick and a decent standard of living for the elderly.

But support for welfare provision in general may also have much to do with perceptions of – and attitudes towards – inequality. Even to someone who is reasonably well-off, concern for the fact that many others live in poverty may lead that person to support redistributive policies. The greater the concern, perhaps, the stronger will be the support for such policies. Conversely, someone who is unaware of or indifferent to inequality, or feels that the poor have only themselves to blame, may be predisposed against any state intervention that aimed to redistribute wealth. The 1987 ISSP (International Social Survey Programme) questionnaire module was designed explicitly to address these sorts of issues.

All the countries we investigate – indeed all industrialised nations – have a number of government programmes intended to protect their citizens from the difficulties caused by, for example, illness and unemployment. Indeed this protection has come to be regarded as a fundamental right of citizenship – an entitlement that society owes to all its members (Marshall, 1963; Mann, 1986). Nonetheless, nations differ greatly not only in the way they structure and administer their welfare programmes, but also in the

*Co-director of the General Social Survey, National Opinion Research Center (NORC), University of Chicago.

breadth and generosity of their provision. For example, whereas in the mid-1980s Italy devoted 28 per cent of its GDP to such programmes, the equivalent figure for Australia and the USA was only 17 per cent.[1] To simplify an exceedingly complex picture, we shall divide our seven nations into three groups according to their political structures. The first, represented only by Hungary, is communist or state socialist. The second, represented by Britain, Italy, the Netherlands and West Germany (all countries with mixed economies and developed welfare programmes), can be called social democracies. The third, consisting of Australia and the USA, both of which have much more limited state welfare provision, we label capitalist (sometimes called liberal) democracies.

Communist countries exercise centralised governmental control over their economies, and most people are employed by state-owned industries. Through government programmes and through benefits provided by public employers, communist states have created comprehensive welfare systems which have placed such services as health care and education entirely within the public sector. While the social democracies of Western Europe also have wide-ranging 'cradle-to-grave' welfare systems that cover many aspects of life, most jobs remain in the private sector and the public sector does not monopolise all social services. Finally, in the capitalist democracies of the USA and Australia, almost all industrial and commercial employment is in the private sector and its citizens' welfare is served by a combination of private and public programmes.[2]

These different economic models have developed for a complex set of historical reasons (Flora and Heidenheimer, 1981; Mommsen, 1981; Tomasson, 1983; Jansson, 1988). Our two capitalist democracies are both new nations, former frontier societies peopled by a diverse mix of immigrants. Although they are extensions of Western society in general and British society in particular, the USA and Australia also represent new beginnings – self-made nations that 'grew up' democratic and capitalist. They have been less constrained by the monarchical and feudal traditions of Europe than their mother countries of the Old World. The social democracies of Western Europe developed not from the middle classes, as the capitalist democracies did, but from the top and bottom. In part the welfare state came from the top – both from a feudalistic sense of *noblesse oblige* and from a *real-politik* attempt to bribe the working class, and from the bottom, as the working class organised itself into labour movements and socialist parties, which challenged both the landed classes and emergent industrialists for political and economic power. They pressed for the welfare state both to secure material protection and benefits for their class and to promote their sense of a just society. In contrast, communist nations developed from the bottom, the top having been overthrown by social revolutions or military occupations and then eliminated by redistributive and collectivist policies and stringent, centralised party control.

These different political economies have developed from different historical dynamics. Nonetheless, they exhibit themselves today through differences in the policy preferences and ideologies of their citizens.[3] In part this is because the system that evolved in each country reflects the wishes of its citizens. In part, citizens in each system have come to expect, and accept as natural, the welfare programmes offered.

So in the first part of this chapter we examine similarities and differences between countries in their public attitudes towards the welfare state, focusing first on the level of public sympathy for social welfare benefits. Then we assess the public's willingness to finance such welfare benefits through taxation, asking how far taxation itself is seen as an appropriate instrument for achieving greater redistribution. We look at possible reasons for differences between nations in support for the welfare state. Are they associated with the degree of perceived inequality, with perceptions of one's own social mobility, or perhaps with optimism about one's own economic prospects? Do beliefs about 'getting ahead in life' help to explain attitudes towards the welfare state? In particular, do people in some nations believe that opportunities depend primarily on family and class origins, while those in other countries believe they depend primarily on individual initiative? And are some concerned more about inequality of outcomes than about equality of opportunity?

In the second part of this chapter, we concentrate on the theme of social inequality. Is it seen as serving a useful purpose (as perhaps spurring on individual effort or as a prerequisite of general prosperity), or is it merely a product of the prevailing class or economic system? We also discover whether or not perceived levels of class conflict vary between nations. Finally, we examine the relationship between class (income level, occupational status and education) and a broad range of attitudes (for instance, towards welfare programmes, taxation and redistribution, opportunities for getting ahead, and class conflict) and consider whether cross-national differences in these relationships help to explain cross-national differences in general beliefs about social inequality.

Support for welfare programmes

The five questions we asked on this theme covered a range of welfare policies, from providing a decent standard of living for the unemployed to the more general issue of whether more should be spent on benefits for the poor. The picture is clear. Public support for welfare spending is highest among the Hungarians (average of nearly 80 per cent), followed closely by the Italians and – rather less enthusiastically – by the citizens of the other three social democracies of West Germany, Britain and the Netherlands. But as the summary table below shows, it is the gap between the social democracies and those countries we have termed capitalist democracies that is the widest. In general, these differences in preferences match the actual levels of social welfare benefits and programmes provided in each nation. Intriguingly then, support for welfare provision in the European social democracies is much closer to that in Hungary than to that in the culturally similar nations of Australia and the USA.

| | Average over five 'welfarist' items* | Strongly agree/agree that the government should . . . | |
		. . . provide everyone with a guaranteed basic income	. . . spend more on benefits for the poor
Hungary	79%	78%	72%
Italy	76%	67%	83%
West Germany	64%	51%	80%
Britain	63%	59%	82%
Netherlands	60%	48%	55%
Australia	42%	36%	59%
USA	38%	20%	58%

Note. *The five items were 'reduce differences in income between people with high incomes and those with low incomes'; 'provide a job for everyone who wants one'; 'spend less on benefits for the poor' (strongly *dis*agree/*dis*agree); 'provide a decent standard of living for the unemployed'; and 'provide everyone with a guaranteed basic income'.

Full details are given in **Table 4.1**.

Differences are greatest for the 'levelling' items (income redistribution and a guaranteed income or wage). For example, while nearly 80 per cent of Hungarians support a minimum income for all, this is favoured by only 20 per cent of Americans. The European social democratic norm is around 50 per cent. Differences, while still marked, tend to be smaller for items to do with government action to help the needy or dependent. So spending more on benefits for the poor is supported by over 80 per cent of Italians and around 60 per cent of Americans and Australians. Naturally, support will depend in part on what is already provided in each country. This may explain why the Dutch are the least supportive of more spending on the poor and why it is also the least popular of the five items among the Hungarians: government expenditure on the poor is already rather high in both these countries.

In brief, the tripartite division into communist, social democratic and capitalist democratic nations explains many of the cross-national differences in preferences for the welfare state. Nations with the strongest public demand for various social welfare programmes are the most likely to have such programmes. Partly this indicates that people tend to accept the types of governmental measures they already have, but we feel it also indicates that where social welfare measures exist, they do so because of public demand.

On one aspect of egalitarianism, however, there is something close to a consensus across the seven nations (see also Haller, Moshammer and Raubel, 1987). This is the issue of government support for children from poor families to go on to higher education. As the table below shows, people in different nations certainly differ somewhat in the *strength* of their support, but few in any country disagree with the proposition. The percentage favouring such a policy ranges from around 70 per cent (Australia) to nearly 90 per cent (Italy).

	The government should provide more chances for children from poor families to go to university
% strongly agreeing/agreeing	
Italy	89%
West Germany	84%
Netherlands	84%
Britain	83%
USA	75%
Hungary	72%
Australia	71%

Moreover the expected ordering of countries (communist, social democratic and capitalist democratic) does not conform on the issue of educational opportunity as it did on the other items. The USA is close to the middle of the range and Hungary is towards the lower end. Indeed, Americans and Australians are more supportive of government action for educational opportunity than they are for any of the other welfare measures and by a much wider margin (on average +38 percentage points in the USA and +29 percentage points in Australia), than in the social democracies (+13 to +24 percentage points) or in our lone communist state (−7 percentage points).

Why should this be so? A likely explanation is the existence of what has been called the 'opportunity ideology' in the USA (Smith, 1987). Educational programmes are, *par excellence,* a means of promoting equality of *opportunity* rather than equality of *outcomes.* Education is a route to upward mobility, not a means of redistribution. Indeed over a range of issues, many Americans believe not only that equality means equal opportunity, but also that attempts to eliminate (or even reduce) inequalities in living standards are themselves inequitable (Rasinski, 1987).

Taxation and redistribution

Sharing the tax burden

We then went on to ask about attitudes to the levels of taxation necessary to finance government welfare programmes (although the question wording did not explicitly link the one concept with the other). Here too we found cross-national variations, but not nearly as marked as when we asked about welfare policies. On average, across the seven countries, the proportion of people saying that the taxes of those with high, middle, and low incomes are too high is about the same. (The exception is Hungary where direct taxation is a fairly recent phenomenon and still low by Western standards.) In none of the countries does more than about one in three feel that the rich are too highly taxed; indeed, except in Australia, fewer than a quarter are of this opinion.

Taxation is much too high/too high for those . . .

	a . . . with high incomes	b . . . with middle incomes	c . . . with low incomes	Difference c − b
West Germany	12%	49%	80%	31%
Hungary	17%	34%	53%	19%
USA	17%	68%	67%	−1%
Italy	18%	61%	84%	23%
Britain	24%	40%	85%	45%
Netherlands	25%	57%	76%	19%
Australia	34%	59%	69%	10%

Similarly, a majority in each country agrees that those with low incomes are paying too much in taxes. When comparing the public's perceptions of the tax burden of those with high and low incomes, all nations appear to be rather progressive and pro-levelling, although the percentage believing that the poor bear a greater tax burden than the rich ranges from +68 percentage points in West Germany to +35 percentage points in Australia. This also suggests widespread support across all the nations for a 'soak-the-rich' taxation strategy to finance desired welfare programmes.

Examination of the figures on taxing the middle class shows however that there are strong national differences that are related to political system. America emerges as especially concerned about the tax burden of the middle class. Only in America are the taxes of those with middle incomes rated as more burdensome than the taxes of those with high incomes. The Australians alone come close to sharing this belief. Davis (1986) noted that "America is a pious middle-class nation, while Britain is a secular working-class one". To some extent this characterisation of the British applies to the other European social democracies too. There is little evidence of a widespread middle-class tax revolt that might jeopardise the sorts of government welfare programmes that have been seen to command widespread support among the citizens of the social democracies. In Britain concern about the direct tax burden shouldered by the middle income groups is notably muted in comparison both with the (relatively) low-taxed Americans and with their more highly-taxed Western European neighbours (Taylor-Gooby, 1987). On the other hand, the present British government has recently lowered tax rates for the well-off and public opinion can hardly have failed to notice.

There is however further evidence to suggest that – to a greater or lesser extent – people in all seven countries believe that high earners can and should bear more of the tax burden. A certain measure of self-interest is at play here: higher taxes for those on high incomes can lead to lower taxes for the rest, although in practice the extent to which taxing high earners more would reduce the burden on others is, of course, strictly limited.

Progressive taxation and redistribution

Respondents were asked whether "people with high incomes should pay a larger share of their income in taxes than those with low incomes, the same share or a smaller share". A second question invited them to agree or disagree that "it is the responsibility of the government to reduce the differences in income between people with high incomes and those with low incomes".

In contrast to responses to the question about taxation *levels*, there seems to be something approaching a consensus when we asked specifically about *progressive* taxation. About two-thirds to three-quarters of respondents in all nations agreed that high income earners should be taxed more heavily than those on low incomes. Support is a bit weaker in the capitalist democracies, but not markedly so (about ten percentage points lower). The sharp differences that appear over support for welfare measures among the capitalist democratic, social democratic and communist nations are muted on the issue of progressive taxation, but they re-emerge over the question of income *redistribution*.

	Supports progressive taxation	Favours government action to reduce income differences
Italy	77%	81%
Britain	75%	63%
West Germany	73%	56%
Netherlands	70%	64%
Hungary	69%	77%
USA	64%	28%
Australia	63%	42%

Where people in the capitalist democracies differ from their counterparts in Western Europe (and in Hungary) is apparently on the desirability of using the taxes of the rich explicitly to redistribute income. Yet again Americans and Australians emerge as notably more hostile to government programmes designed to promote greater equality of outcomes. And on these figures, yet again Britain remains firmly within the Western European social democratic 'camp' – despite the ideology of Britain's current governing party.

Perceptions of inequality and social mobility

One of the reasons that people in the capitalist democracies of the USA and Australia are less enamoured of welfare programmes is that they see current conditions as being already more equitable than do the citizens of other countries. While around three in five Americans and Australians agree that income differences are too large, this belief is shared by many more of those living in the social democracies and in Hungary.

	Strongly agree/agree that income differences are too large
Italy	86%
Britain	75%
Hungary	74%
West Germany	72%
Netherlands	66%
Australia	58%
USA	56%

Moreover, individual Americans (and, to a lesser extent, Australians) are rather more inclined to rate themselves as near the top of the social structure than are individuals in other countries. Respondents in all seven nations were asked to place themselves on one of ten 'rungs of a ladder' representing different positions in the social structure. While 18 per cent of Americans see themselves as on one of the top three rungs, 10 per cent or fewer of people in the West European democracies rank themselves thus.[4] The differences are, however, less marked than many discussed in this chapter.

		Top three rungs	Fourth to seventh rung	Eighth to tenth rung
USA	%	18	72	10
Australia	%	10	84	6
Italy	%	10	84	7
West Germany	%	10	81	9
Britain	%	8	75	17
Hungary	%	3	74	24

It may not be surprising that such a high proportion of the British place themselves near the bottom of the social structure, compared with their more prosperous Western European neighbours. Only Hungarians are less likely than the British to place themselves at the top and more likely to place themselves at the bottom.

Citizens of the USA and Australia are also much more optimistic about their *own* chances of becoming more prosperous than are those of any other nationality. Americans are considerably out in front with 71 per cent agreeing that "people like me and my family have a good chance of improving our standard of living". Only Australians even begin to approach the American figure, while the Europeans (conspicuously the Dutch) are markedly less confident (see the table below). While responses may partly reflect the short-term economic prospects in each country, this question probably also taps deeper and more enduring feelings about personal opportunity – a throwback perhaps to the frontier spirit, the popular notion of the USA as the 'land of opportunity'.

But the optimism of the Americans and (to a lesser extent) of the Australians does not seem to be based on past experience of greater upward mobility: the proportion of Americans and Australians reporting that their own job is better than their father's does not differ much from that of citizens of other countries.

	Strongly agree/agree that people like me have good chance of improving standard of living	Level of own job much higher/ higher than father's
USA	71%	47%
Australia	58%	46%
Italy	43%	37%
West Germany	36%	25%
Britain	36%	47%
Hungary	33%	57%
Netherlands	23%	43%

As we can see, five of the seven countries report an 'upward mobility rate' in the range of 37 to 47 per cent; only the West Germans and the Hungarians deviate from the norm. This finding echoes those of many more detailed studies of actual (as opposed to reported) comparative mobility (for example, Erikson, Goldthorpe and Portocarero, 1982; Ganzeboom, Luijkx and Treiman, 1988). In particular, the oft-told tale of American fluidity and British rigidity appears to be fiction rather than fact. So it seems we cannot look to differences in levels of intergenerational mobility as an explanation for the greater opposition in the capitalist democracies to egalitarianism and social welfare policies.

Beliefs about opportunity and mobility

Do cross-national differences in what we have called the 'ideology of opportunity' help to explain support for – or hostility towards – welfare programmes? In particular, do *beliefs* about the kinds of opportunities that society provides for self-advancement, and the factors influencing these opportunities, differ across nations even if the perceived *degree* of opportunity does not? Other studies have indicated that Americans are less likely to see intergenerational mobility as dependent upon family background than are the British, West Germans, Austrians or Italians (Haller and Hoellinger, 1986; Smith, 1987). Do Americans therefore regard their own upward mobility as stemming from the greater openness of their society, while Europeans believe that success in life is in some degree influenced by a person's class origins?

However, as the table below shows, people in all countries tend to agree on which factors are most important for "getting ahead in life". Moreover, such differences as do occur do not generally follow the communist/social democratic/capitalist democratic pattern observed so far.

Factors influencing "getting ahead in life" (rank orders)

	Britain	USA	Australia	West Germany	Netherlands	Italy	Hungary
Hard work	1	1	2	4	2	4	3
Ambition	3	2	1	2	3	6	1
Good education	2	3	3	1	1	1	5
Natural ability	4	4	4	5	4	3	2
Knowing right people	5	5	5	3	5	2	4
Well-educated parents	6	6	6	6	6	7	8
Wealthy family	7	7	7	7	7	8	6
Political connections	11	8	8	9	8	5	7
Race	8	9	9	8	9	13	n/a
Gender	9	10	10	10	11	11	10
Religion	12	11	11	12	10	10	11
Political beliefs	13	12	13	11	12	9	9
Part of the country	10	13	12	13	13	12	12

Notes. Percentages for each country are shown in **Table 4.2**. Race was not asked about on the Hungarian questionnaire.

People in all seven industrial nations tend to rank personal characteristics such as hard work, ambition, natural ability and education as the most important. Next, typically, comes "knowing the right people". This is usually followed by parentally-transmitted characteristics of wealth and education. Rated least important (usually) are ascribed characteristics such as race, sex, religion, and region of origin and political factors (connections and beliefs).

The English-speaking nations (Britain, the USA and Australia) are especially close in their ranking of achievement factors, with only minor differences in both ranking and absolute levels. West Germany and the Netherlands also closely resemble one another and differ from the English-speaking nations primarily in ranking one's education a little higher than personality attributes. It may be that, in West Germany and the Netherlands, education is seen as certifying one's personal ability, or that it is viewed as the mechanism through which individuals turn their personal ability into achievement. Italy differs in giving more weight to connections: "knowing the right people" (ranked second) and to political connections (ranked fifth) than does any of the other nations, while the personal characteristics of hard work and ambition are seen as less important. Hungary is distinguished by the relatively low emphasis on education (Braun and Kolosi, 1988).*

Likewise, while the *relative* ranking of political connections and political beliefs is only a bit higher in Hungary, their *absolute* levels are well above those of other nations (see **Table 4.2**). This would seem to reflect the pervasive role of the Communist Party (at least in 1987 when we asked the questions) in social and economic life.

---

*However this is far from saying that Hungarians disparage education *per se:* we have already seen that over 70 per cent support greater opportunities for children of poor parents to go on to higher education.

While the Hungarian pattern shows the importance of a country's political system in shaping beliefs about opportunity, overall cross-national differences in beliefs about opportunity and mobility are small, and appear to be governed more by cultural patterns than by government structure and political ideology.

Explanations of inequality

Similarities between the nations are even greater when we asked respondents to agree or disagree with various possible justifications of inequality. They were asked to agree or disagree with eight possible explanations, which we subsequently grouped and labelled as 'financial incentives', 'class conflict' and 'promotion of general prosperity'. As a convenient way of summarising the data, average percentages were calculated for each of the three groups.

First, we found that there is a majority belief in all countries bar one that pay inequalities serve an important purpose in that, without rewards, people would neither work so hard nor acquire the skills and education needed for technical and professional occupations. As the table below shows, on average, between around 60 and 80 per cent of the public in six of the seven countries believes consistently that at least some pay differences are needed to stimulate the development of human capital, hard work and the assumption of responsibilities.

		Strongly agree/agree that financial incentives are needed if people are . . .			
	Average	. . . to work hard	. . . to take extra responsibility	. . . to get skills and qualifications	. . . to study for a vocation
Australia	79%	72%	82%	81%	81%
West Germany	73%	69%	64%	74%	85%
Britain	70%	61%	82%	69%	69%
Italy	68%	54%	77%	73%	67%
USA	66%	68%	70%	57%	68%
Hungary	62%	70%	60%	61%	55%
Netherlands	46%	36%	64%	43%	42%

Only the Netherlands is a notable outlier, its citizens being much less likely to believe that pay differentials are a necessary incentive to work and to get ahead.

In order to explore further how different nations explained their inequalities, we asked about the role of class and vested interests in perpetuating inequality. We find that, of the three explanations of social inequality, class conflict is next most popular. These are the responses to two propositions that we put to respondents:

| | Average | Strongly agree/agree that inequality continues to exist because . . . | |
		. . . it benefits the rich and powerful	. . . ordinary people don't join together to get rid of it
Italy	67%	74%	61%
West Germany	52%	63%	40%
Netherlands	51%	58%	45%
Britain	49%	59%	40%
USA	44%	46%	42%
Australia	44%	55%	32%
Hungary	32%	36%	28%

In most countries, an average of between 44–52 per cent agree that inequality is perpetuated because it benefits the rich and powerful and because ordinary people have not organised to eliminate it. The outliers are Hungary and Italy, Hungarians being the least likely to see class conflict as an explanation for inequality and the Italians the most likely to express this belief. The other Western European social democracies cluster closely together, their averages ranging between 49 per cent and 52 per cent. And the Dutch agree with the class interest explanation more than with the personal incentive explanation (at 51 per cent *versus* 46 per cent respectively). Predictably (in view of our previous findings) a majority of Americans rejects the two propositions. But perhaps among the most surprising of our findings are the answers given to these questions in Hungary. Both statements are, after all, predicated on a 'Marxist' view of the world, and both are decisively rejected.

We also wanted to discover whether a measure of economic inequality within society was seen as necessary for promoting *general,* as opposed to individual, economic success. The results are shown in the table below.

| | Average | Strongly agree/agree that . . . | |
		. . . large differences in income are necessary for national prosperity	. . . allowing businesses to make good profits is best way to improve everyone's standard of living
Australia	41%	28%	53%
Britain	40%	26%	53%
USA	39%	31%	46%
Hungary	39%	25%	54%
Italy	37%	18%	57%
West Germany	32%	24%	40%
Netherlands	24%	16%	31%

So, of the three general explanations of inequality (incentives, class conflict and the promotion of economic prosperity) the latter is clearly the least popular, with typically an average of only 33–41 per cent endorsing the two propositions which come under this heading. Once again the Dutch are outliers, being less likely to endorse this factor than citizens of the other six countries. However, the Netherlands does follow most other nations in endorsing general prosperity less frequently than financial incentives and class conflicts. The Hungarians alone endorse the general economic good more frequently than class interests as an explanation for the existence of inequality.

It may be of interest that decisive majorities in five of the seven countries fail to support the view that *large* differences in income are necessary for national prosperity. (It may well be that the word 'large' put people off.) And Hungary is the most enthusiastic about business profits, with Britain not far behind. For full details, see **Table 4.3**.

As in the earlier examination of the factors that are most important for getting ahead in life, there is more agreement than disagreement among the nations on the reasons for inequality. This suggests that beliefs about inequality are to a large degree shaped by pan-cultural forces. Among these forces the two most likely are their common Western cultural heritage and their status as industrialised nations. Moreover, the national differences that do emerge do not closely follow communist, social democratic and capitalist democratic lines. Instead they seem to reflect individual national variations, resulting from either particular historical developments or differences in current economic and social conditions.

Assessments of social conflict

To what extent are social divisions seen as serious conflicts within each of the seven nations? We asked about five pairs of social groups: poor people and rich people; the working class and the middle class; the unemployed and people with jobs*; management and workers; farmers and city people. We were interested in the extent to which views on income inequality were related to perceived conflict between structured social groups; and also in whether support for a stronger government role in combatting inequality was associated with feelings that there was a collective dimension to social conflict.

Perceiving very strong/strong conflicts between . . .

	Average	...poor and rich	...management and workers	...unemployed and people with jobs	...farmers and city people	...working class and middle class
Netherlands	49%	77%	68%	48%	32%	22%
Italy	47%	59%	51%	57%	24%	45%
USA	43%	59%	53%	46%	36%	20%
Australia	40%	43%	51%	46%	42%	18%
Hungary	40% †	54%	41%	n/a	26%	37%
Britain	38%	52%	54%	39%	26%	20%
West Germany	30%	36%	52%	36%	11%	13%

Note. † Excluding '...unemployed and people with jobs'.

*This question was omitted on the Hungarian questionnaire since unemployment does not exist in the same form as in the other nations.

Full details are given in **Table 4.4**.

Once again we find that there is more cross-national agreement than disagreement, in that the seven nations generally report similar levels of social conflict overall. The West Germans are the least likely to perceive divisions, the Italians and Dutch the most likely, but these differences are not great.

Moreover, with few exceptions, such conflicts as *are* thought to exist are not perceived as strong. Even so, very few citizens of any country believe that *no* divisions exist between the groups we nominated. The pattern that emerges is that people across the nations perceive greater conflict between economic groups than between explicitly mentioned social classes or between farmers and city dwellers. The conflicts between the poor and the rich, and between management and workers, are seen to be the strongest, those between the unemployed and people with jobs come second or third, while class and rural/urban conflicts come fourth or fifth (again see **Table 4.4**).

However, the perception of greater conflict between income groups and work hierarchies than between classes probably does not indicate that these are more important or salient social dividers than class. It may merely reflect the fact that the social distance between the former two groups (rich *versus* poor and managers *versus* employees) is seen as greater than the distance between the middle and working classes. If the class terms had been widened (for example, upper *versus* lower class) or if the economic terms had been narrowed (for example, average income *versus* lower than average income), we suspect that the levels of perceived conflict would have been similar for class and economic groups.

There are a few notable differences between countries. For instance, the West Germans are conspicuous in denying class conflicts; the Dutch are particularly likely to see conflicts between the poor and the rich; the Italians are especially prone to see poverty and unemployment as divisive. And there are some cross-national differences in perceptions of conflict between farmers and city-dwellers, an issue that may become more salient with the growth of 'green' movements worldwide.

In any event there seems to be no general pattern which explains the country-by-country differences in rankings of conflict. But these differences are not great and, where they exist, they may well merely reflect the particular socio-economic conditions in each nation, such as the level of unemployment, the size and condition of the farm sector, and so on.

Inequality and class

Having examined how the nations differ on attitudes towards the welfare state and social inequality, we next consider the class basis for these attitudes within each nation. We took three measures of socio-economic status (household income, occupation and education) and looked at the extent to which they were associated with attitudes. (We shall use the term 'class' loosely to cover these measures.) Detailed figures are shown in **Table 4.5**.

Overall, we see that in all countries class *is* related to support for the welfare state and to beliefs about equality. Of the 126 associations measured, all but three are positive. Moreover, in just over three quarters of the cases, the relationships are statistically significant. On the other hand, except for a few variables and a few countries, the relationships are not particularly strong. So we find that class is consistently related to attitudes towards social welfare and inequality, but that the relationship is generally modest.

The associations with social class tend to be strongest in relation to support for social welfare policies and levelling, and weakest for helping the poor to go to university and for progressive taxation. As a general rule, the association with class tends to be greater for variables that showed the larger cross-national differences in terms of the various countries' prevailing political ideologies (for example, social welfare programmes and income redistribution) and the degree of perceived income inequality in each. It tends to be lower for those variables that showed a greater measure of cross-national agreement (for example, progressive taxation and helping the poor to attend university). On these issues, not only does a degree of *cross-national* consensus exist, but also there is a fair degree of interclass consensus *within nations.*

Modest to moderate differences also appear when we look at associations between class and explanations for existing social inequality. Those in the lower classes are more likely than those in the upper classes to attribute inequality to class divisions. These differences are, however, altogether less striking than the ones noted earlier (again see **Table 4.5**).

To summarise, class differences appear on a number of social welfare and social inequality items. As the table below shows, on average these differences are quite similar across nations both in terms of their absolute values and in the pattern of associations across variables.[6]

	Average degree of association (gamma)*
Netherlands	+.201
Britain	+.193
United States	+.175
Australia	+.150
Italy	+.147
West Germany	+.133

Notes. * .000 indicates no relationship; 1.00 indicates a perfect relationship. An explanation of this measure of association is given in note 7 at the end of this chapter.

These averages are rather close to one another. Moreover, they do not differ much according to the political system operating in each country. Cross-national variations are not explained by the different class structures of the various countries. In particular, the greater support in the social democracies than in the capitalist democracies for more benefits and redistribution is not the result of a radicalised working class in the former which demands more than a passive working class does in the latter. True, the working classes in the social democracies *are* more in favour of such

measures than their counterparts in the capitalist democracies. But it is
also the case that the *middle classes* in the social democracies are more
supportive of welfare and egalitarian measures than are the middle classes
in the capitalist democracies, and that this 'class gap' is virtually identical
under both political systems. There are indeed differences *within* nations,
but these tend to be fairly constant in size; variations *between* nations seem
to be related to something other than the 'objective' class structure. So class
differences between nations are not a likely explanation for cross-national
variations in attitudes towards the welfare state and social inequality.

Conclusions

We have found that cross-national differences in popular preferences for
welfare policies in general, and levelling programmes in particular, are
large. Respondents in the study's one communist nation, Hungary,
overwhelmingly favour the full gamut of welfare policies. Support in the
social democracies of Western Europe is lower, but still substantial. In the
capitalist (or liberal) democracies of the USA and Australia, support is
lower still, with majorities failing to endorse programmes such as these.
Part of the explanation is that people in the capitalist democracies are
more inclined to believe that income gaps in their nations are smaller, that
their own relative social position is higher, and that their chances for
future advancement are greater than do citizens of the social democracies
and of Hungary. However, this egalitarian optimism does not (as has often
been suggested) appear to result from higher rates of individual upward
mobility in the recent past. Rather it is the *evaluation* of inequality – how
unfair it is felt to be and whether government is seen as an appropriate
redistributive agent – that varies enormously between nations.

Moreover, the lower level of support among Americans for redistributive
measures, and the relatively greater enthusiasm for measures that allow
scope for individual opportunity, suggest that an ideology of opportunity
plays a key role. Australians also (to a slightly smaller degree) appear to
conform to this pattern. Given their similarities as 'pioneering' and
'immigrant' nations, one might wonder whether the experience of nation-
building, or the influx of immigrants in search of a better life (or both),
might have helped to create an enduring ethos of 'individualism'. In
contrast, citizens of Hungary and of the European social democracies are
more supportive of an egalitarian ideology, and of government programmes
designed to lessen inequality and provide for some at least of the citizen's
basic needs. Not surprisingly, we have also found that those nations with
well-established welfare states are more in favour of welfare state provision.
In that sense we are all products of our experience.

Despite their decidedly different stances on welfare policies, the citizens
of the seven nations have very similar *perceptions* of social inequality. Such
national differences as do exist are not strongly related to the various
countries' political systems. Personal qualities such as hard work, rather
than family position or ascribed attributes, are widely seen as important for
personal advancement – although Hungarians and Italians (the latter the
most pro-welfare in the social democracies) both give relatively greater

weight to personal and political connections than do people in the other nations.

Similar proportions of respondents in most countries also endorse the various *explanations* of social inequality. Majorities in each believe that incentives are needed to stimulate human capital development and personal productivity; substantial numbers in each believe that the 'haves' are keen to maintain the differences that operate to their advantage; there is, however, less support for the proposition that overall economic prosperity depends on these differences.

Finally, the perceived level of conflict between social groups is also similar across nations. There are clear nation-specific variations, but they do not follow the general pattern evident in respect of welfare policies. The results suggest that the seven nations, while sharing many beliefs about the nature of society and of human behaviour and motives, differ nonetheless in the value their citizens attach to equality of opportunity and outcome, and in their beliefs about how governments might best achieve these goals.

Notes

1. The detailed figures for the seven nations discussed in this chapter are:

Netherlands	27.6%	Hungary	16.2%
Italy	28.0%	Australia	17.0%
West Germany	24.0%	USA	17.0%
Britain	19.0%		

    Source: OECD, 1988

2. For example, in the USA health and medical care for the poor is covered by Medicaid, for the elderly by Medicare and for most employed people by private health care. For some employed people no collective protection exists.

3. As Cameron (1978) and Hicks and Swank (1984) have demonstrated, the comprehensiveness of a country's welfare provision varies inversely with the electoral strength of its right-wing political party (or parties).

4. At 37 per cent the Dutch are much more heavily represented in the bottom three levels of the social standing scale than are the other six nations. This is probably because they used a ladder with a widening base, clearly suggesting that more people were on the bottom rungs than in the rest of the scale. In the other countries the vertical scale was uniform throughout its length.

5. We have not included Hungary in this discussion. Hungarian data were not available for the social welfare policy and class conflict scales because one of the constituent questions was not asked. Moreover, occupational details were not collected in the same format as in the other countries.

6. The numbers in **Table 4.5** are a measure of association called gamma. It can range from a low of .000, indicating no relationship between two variables to a high of +1.00, indicating a perfect relationship. Here a positive relationship means that those with lower income, lower status occupations and less schooling are more in favour of the welfare state and levelling policies, and see more inequality and class conflict than do those with higher incomes, higher occupational status, and greater education. As a rule of thumb, social scientists might consider gammas below 0.2 as weak, even if they are significant. Gammas in the range 0.2–0.3 can be considered moderate, and over 0.3 they begin to become strong.

References

BRAUN, M. and KOLOSI, T., *Attitudes towards Social Inequality in Hungary, the Federal Republic of Germany and the United States of America,* (unpublished paper, 1988).

CAMERON, D.R., 'The Expansion of the Public Economy: a Comparative Analysis', *American Political Science Review,* no. 72 (1978), pp.1243-61.

DAVIS, J.A., 'British and American Attitudes: Similarities and Contrasts' in Jowell, R., Witherspoon, S. and Brook, L. (eds), *British Social Attitudes: the 1986 Report,* Gower, Aldershot (1986).

DAVIS, J.A., *Bee-tas and Bay-tas: how Social Structure Shapes Attitudes in Britain and the United States,* Paper presented to the American Sociological Association, Chicago (1987).

ERIKSON, R., GOLDTHORPE, J.H. and PORTOCARERO, L., 'Social Fluidity in Industrial Nations', *British Journal of Sociology,* vol. 33 (1982), pp. 1–34.

FLORA, P. and HEIDENHEIMER, A.J. (eds), *The Development of Welfare States in Europe and America,* Transaction Books, New Brunswick NJ (1981).

GANZEBOOM, H.B.J., LUIJKX, R. and TREIMAN, D.J., *International Class Mobility in Comparative Perspective,* Paper presented to the American Sociological Association, Atlanta (1988).

HALLER, M. and HOELLINGER, F., *Perceptions and Ideologies of Inequality in Advanced Capitalist Societies: a Comparison of Attitudes in Western Germany and the United States,* Paper presented to the Research Committee on Social Stratification, International Sociological Association, Rome (1986)

HALLER, M., MOSHAMMER, G. and RAUBEL, O., *Leviathan or Welfare State: Attitudes toward the Role of Government in Five Advanced Western Nations,* Paper presented to the American Sociological Association, Chicago (1987).

HICKS, A. and SWANK, D.H., 'Government Redistribution in Rich Capitalist Democracies', *Policy Studies Journal,* no. 13, (1984), pp.265-86.

JANSSON, B.S., *The Reluctant Welfare State: a History of American Social Welfare Policies,* Wadsworth, Belmont CA. (1988).

MANN, M., 'Work and the Work Ethic' in Jowell, R., Witherspoon, S. and Brook, L. (eds), *British Social Attitudes: the 1986 Report,* Gower, Aldershot (1986).

MARSHALL, T.H., *Sociology at the Crossroads and Other Issues,* Heinemann, London (1963).

MOMMSEN, W.J. (ed.), *The Emergence of the Welfare State in Britain and Germany,* Croom Helm, London (1981).

OECD (Organisation for Economic Cooperation and Development), *The Future of Social Protection,* OECD, Paris (1988).

RASINSKI, K.A., 'What's Fair is Fair – or Is It? Value Differences Underlying Public Views about Social Justice', *Journal of Personality and Social Psychology,* no. 53 (1987), pp.201-11.

SMITH, T.W., 'In Search of House Effects: a Comparison of Responses to Various Questions by Different Survey Organizations', *Public Opinion Quarterly,* vol. 42, no. 4 (1978), pp.443-63.

SMITH, T.W., 'House Effects and the Reproductibility of Survey Measurements: a Comparison of the 1980 General Social Survey and the 1980 American National Election Study', *Public Opinion Quarterly,* vol. 46, no. 1 (1982), pp.54-68.

SMITH, T.W., 'The Polls: the Welfare State in Cross-national Perspective', *Public Opinion Quarterly,* vol. 51, no. 3 (1987), pp.404-21.

TAYLOR-GOOBY, P., 'Citizenship and Welfare', in Jowell, R., Witherspoon, S., and Brook, L., (eds), *British Social Attitudes: the 1987 Report,* Gower, Aldershot (1987).

TOMASSON, R.F., 'The Welfare State', *Comparative Social Research,* vol. 6, no. 1 (1983), pp.1-378.

Acknowledgement

Funding for the General Social Survey project, on which the 1987 questions on inequality were asked, came from the National Science Foundation, Grant No. SES8747227.

4.1 SUPPORT FOR WELFARE PROGRAMMES (1987: B207b,d,e)
by country

	Britain	USA	Australia	West Germany	Netherlands	Italy	Hungary
	%	%	%	%	%	%	%
IT IS THE RESPONSIBILITY OF THE GOVERNMENT TO REDUCE THE DIFFERENCE IN INCOME BETWEEN PEOPLE WITH HIGH INCOMES AND THOSE WITH LOW INCOMES.							
Strongly agree	21	7	9	17	16	35	31
Agree	42	21	33	39	48	46	46
Neither agree nor disagree	12	24	20	15	11	9	11
Disagree	19	34	26	14	18	7	7
Strongly disagree	3	12	6	8	6	2	2
Can't choose	3	3	6	8	2	1	3
THE GOVERNMENT SHOULD PROVIDE A JOB FOR EVERYONE WHO WANTS ONE.							
Strongly agree	23	14	10	35	23	44	45
Agree	35	30	28	39	51	38	45
Neither agree nor disagree	17	20	24	13	16	9	5
Disagree	20	25	27	6	8	7	3
Strongly disagree	3	9	6	3	1	1	1
Can't choose	3	1	5	5	1	1	2
THE GOVERNMENT SHOULD SPEND LESS ON BENEFITS FOR THE POOR.							
Strongly agree	1	3	2	1	4	2	3
Agree	4	14	12	4	17	5	7
Neither agree nor disagree	12	22	22	11	22	6	15
Disagree	53	43	47	32	39	34	47
Strongly disagree	29	15	12	48	16	49	25
Can't choose	1	2	5	3	3	4	3
BASE: Unweighted	*1212*	*1564*	*1574*	*1397*	*1638*	*1027*	*2606*

4.1 (continued) SUPPORT FOR WELFARE PROGRAMMES (1987: B207f,g) by country

	Britain %	USA %	Australia %	West Germany %	Netherlands %	Italy %	Hungary %
THE GOVERNMENT SHOULD PROVIDE A DECENT STANDARD OF LIVING FOR THE UNEMPLOYED							
Strongly agree	17	6	5	16	10	22	n/a *
Agree	47	30	30	47	49	46	
Neither agree nor disagree	18	26	30	21	23	16	
Disagree	13	30	25	8	13	11	
Strongly disagree	3	6	5	4	2	3	
Can't choose	2	3	5	6	2	2	
THE GOVERNMENT SHOULD PROVIDE EVERYONE WITH A GUARANTEED BASIC INCOME							
Strongly agree	20	6	7	16	10	26	39
Agree	40	15	30	35	38	41	39
Neither agree nor disagree	13	20	21	17	18	11	11
Disagree	22	40	30	15	23	13	7
Strongly disagree	4	17	8	9	8	8	2
Can't choose	2	3	5	9	4	2	2
BASE: Unweighted	1212	1564	1574	1397	1368	1027	2606

* This item was not asked in Hungary

4.2 FACTORS INFLUENCING GETTING AHEAD IN LIFE (1987: B207a–g)
by country

HOW IMPORTANT FOR GETTING AHEAD IN LIFE IS ... ?	Britain	USA	Australia	West Germany	Netherlands	Italy	Hungary
	%	%	%	%	%	%	%
... COMING FROM A WEALTHY FAMILY							
Essential	4	4	4	7	1	6	16
Very important	17	16	14	17	10	34	18
Not important at all	14	18	16	15	22	16	13
... HAVING WELL–EDUCATED PARENTS							
Essential	3	6	4	8	1	7	10
Very important	24	33	16	30	25	38	16
Not important at all	7	5	12	6	7	6	12
... HAVING A GOOD EDUCATION YOURSELF							
Essential	24	35	22	38	14	29	13
Very important	49	49	46	48	60	50	25
Not important at all	1	*	1	*	1	1	7
... AMBITION							
Essential	38	42	40	20	20	17	28
Very important	42	45	44	47	47	31	44
Not important at all	1	*	*	1	1	7	1
... NATURAL ABILITY							
Essential	14	13	19	16	7	26	28
Very important	43	46	48	41	44	49	42
Not important at all	1	*	*	1	1	1	1
... HARD WORK							
Essential	36	37	33	20	18	18	25
Very important	48	52	49	39	49	39	36
Not important at all	1	*	*	2	1	4	2
... KNOWING THE RIGHT PEOPLE							
Essential	13	8	11	18	7	28	15
Very important	27	32	21	42	36	48	26
Not important at all	3	2	6	3	2	1	5
BASE: *Unweighted*	*1212*	*1564*	*1574*	*1397*	*1638*	*1027*	*2606*

Note: the answer categories 'fairly important', 'not very important' and 'can't choose' have been omitted from this table

4.2 (continued) FACTORS INFLUENCING GETTING AHEAD IN LIFE (1987: B207h–m) by country

4.2 (continued) FACTORS INFLUENCING GETTING AHEAD IN LIFE (1987: B207h–m) by country

HOW IMPORTANT FOR GETTING AHEAD IN LIFE IS ... ?	Britain %	USA %	Australia %	West Germany %	Netherlands %	Italy %	Hungary %
... HAVING POLITICAL CONNECTIONS							
Essential	2	3	5	6	1	22	12
Very important	5	13	9	16	5	33	17
Not important at all	28	14	23	18	31	10	11
... A PERSON'S RACE *							
Essential	3	2	4	7	1	2	
Very important	14	12	10	15	6	8	n/a
Not important at all	18	23	27	30	35	52	
... A PERSON'S RELIGION							
Essential	2	4	2	4	1	3	2
Very important	3	10	3	7	3	11	3
Not important at all	45	35	47	47	50	44	58
... THE PART OF THE COUNTRY A PERSON COMES FROM							
Essential	1	1	1	2	*	2	1
Very important	6	6	4	5	2	10	2
Not important at all	30	38	47	48	48	41	58
... BEING BORN A MAN OR A WOMAN							
Essential	2	3	2	6	*	2	4
Very important	10	12	7	15	3	12	8
Not important at all	30	27	43	31	45	38	32
... A PERSON'S POLITICAL BELIEFS							
Essential	1	1	1	4	*	3	8
Very important	4	7	3	14	2	18	16
Not important at all	26	25	48	26	41	23	17
BASE: *Unweighted*	*1212*	*1564*	*1574*	*1397*	*1638*	*1027*	*2606*

Note: the answer categories 'fairly important', 'not very important' and can't choose' have been omitted from this table

* This item was not asked in Hungary

4.3 NECESSITY OF INEQUALITY FOR GENERAL PROSPERITY (1987: B204e,f)
by country

	Britain	USA	Australia	West Germany	Netherlands	Italy	Hungary
	%	%	%	%	%	%	%
LARGE DIFFERENCES IN INCOME ARE NECESSARY FOR [COUNTRY'S] PROSPERITY							
Strongly agree	4	5	4	4	2	3	6
Agree	22	26	23	20	14	15	19
Neither agree nor disagree	24	28	31	23	20	16	17
Disagree	38	31	32	29	43	37	38
Strongly disagree	9	5	6	14	16	23	13
Can't choose	3	4	4	10	5	6	8
ALLOWING BUSINESS TO MAKE GOOD PROFITS IS THE BEST WAY TO IMPROVE EVERYONE'S STANDARD OF LIVING							
Strongly agree	10	10	10	7	4	13	16
Agree	43	37	44	33	27	45	38
Neither agree nor disagree	19	23	24	21	23	19	20
Disagree	21	23	17	20	28	14	15
Strongly disagree	3	4	3	8	8	7	4
Can't choose	3	3	3	11	10	4	8
BASE: *Unweighted*	*1212*	*1564*	*1574*	*1397*	*1638*	*1027*	*2606*

4.4 ASSESSMENT OF CONFLICT BETWEEN SOCIAL GROUPS (1987: B210a-c)
by country

IN YOUR OPINION, IN [COUNTRY] HOW MUCH CONFLICT
IS THERE BETWEEN ... ?

	Britain	USA	Australia	West Germany	Netherlands	Italy	Hungary
	%	%	%	%	%	%	%
POOR PEOPLE AND RICH PEOPLE							
Very strong conflicts	13	15	8	8	29	24	18
Strong conflicts	38	44	35	28	49	35	36
Not very strong conflicts	40	33	47	44	20	30	33
There are no conflicts	5	3	6	11	1	9	10
Can't choose	4	5	5	8	2	2	4
THE WORKING CLASS AND THE MIDDLE CLASS							
Very strong conflicts	4	3	1	1	1	12	6
Strong conflicts	16	18	17	12	21	33	31
Not very strong conflicts	64	63	63	52	71	37	44
There are no conflicts	13	12	15	27	4	12	14
Can't choose	3	5	4	8	3	5	4
THE UNEMPLOYED AND PEOPLE WITH JOBS *							
Very strong conflicts	9	9	9	6	8	23	n/a
Strong conflicts	30	37	37	31	41	35	
Not very strong conflicts	45	42	42	41	45	25	
There are no conflicts	13	8	8	15	4	15	
Can't choose	4	4	5	8	3	3	
BASE: Unweighted:	1212	1564	1574	1397	1638	1027	2606

* This item was not asked in Hungary

4.4 (continued) ASSESSMENT OF CONFLICT BETWEEN SOCIAL GROUPS (1987: B210d,e) by country

	Britain %	USA %	Australia %	West Germany %	Netherlands %	Italy %	Hungary %
MANAGEMENT AND WORKERS							
Very strong conflicts	10	9	7	10	17	17	9
Strong conflicts	45	44	43	41	51	35	32
Not very strong conflicts	38	39	42	33	27	38	44
There are no conflicts	4	3	3	8	1	8	10
Can't choose	4	5	5	7	5	3	5
FARMERS AND CITY PEOPLE							
Very strong conflicts	4	8	8	1	5	7	5
Strong conflicts	22	28	35	9	27	17	20
Not very strong conflicts	46	47	43	40	56	34	44
There are no conflicts	22	12	10	41	8	39	27
Can't choose	6	5	4	9	5	3	4
BASE: *Unweighted*	*1212*	*1564*	*1574*	*1397*	*1638*	*1027*	*2606*

4.5 SOCIO-ECONOMIC STATUS AND ATTITUDES TO INEQUALITY – GAMMAS* (1987: see notes below) by country

	Britain	USA	Australia	West Germany	Netherlands	Italy	Hungary
	γ	γ	γ	γ	γ	γ	γ
INCOME DIFFERENCES TOO LARGE (B207a)							
Family income	.207	.118	.198	.200	.417	.236	(.035)
Occupation	.240	.078	.155	.152	.240	.137	+
Education	.152	.152	.196	.199	.256	.229	(-.017)
INEQUALITY RESULTS FROM CLASS INTERESTS (scale)							
Family income	.234	.224	.186	.165	.265	.120	.180
Occupation	.254	.174	.152	.143	.141	(.078)	+
Education	.282	.235	.233	.142	.252	(.016)	.346
DEGREE OF CLASS CONFLICT (scale)							
Family income	(.032)	.094	.121	(.116)	.247	.242	+
Occupation	.054	.122	.107	.081	.097	(.053)	+
Education	(-.042)	.183	(.084)	(-.026)	(-.107)	.150	+
Base: *Unweighted*	*1212*	*1664*	*1574*	*1397*	*1638*	*1027*	*2606*

* Gamma (γ) is a measure of association which can range from nil (indicating no relationship) to +1.00 (indicating a perfect relationship). For further details, see note 7 at the end of Chapter 4. Bracketed figures are not statistically significant at the .05 per cent level.

+ Not calculated (missing data)

Notes.   SOCIAL WELFARE POLICIES: scale derives from four items (B207d; B207f; B207g).
FAMILY INCOME: Gross household income, divided into thirds.
OCCUPATION: respondent's occupation divided into eight categories: administration; professional and technical; clerical; skilled manual; sales; service; semi-skilled manual; unskilled manual.
EDUCATION: years of schooling dichotomised.
INEQUALITY RESULTS FROM CLASS INTERESTS: scale derived from two items (B204c, g).
DEGREE OF CLASS CONFLICT: scale derived from four items (B210a, b, c, d).

4.5 (continued) SOCIO-ECONOMIC STATUS AND ATTITUDES TO INEQUALITY – GAMMAS* (1987: see notes below) by country

		Britain	USA	Australia	West Germany	Netherlands	Italy	Hungary
		γ	γ	γ	γ	γ	γ	γ
SOCIAL WELFARE POLICIES (Scale)								
	Family income	.264	.312	.255	.191	.274	.283	+
	Occupation	.276	.199	(.123)	.122	.118	.076	+
	Education	.248	.272	.146	(.110)	(.060)	.267	+
REDUCE INCOME DIFFERENCES (B207b)								
	Family income	.244	.282	.214	.264	.425	.261	.091
	Occupation	.252	.171	.179	.198	.237	(.076)	+
	Education	.270	.265	.173	.174	.279	.202	.198
HELP FOR CHILDREN FROM POOR FAMILIES TO GO TO UNIVERSITY (B207c)								
	Family income	.230	.270	.230	(.124)	.323	.195	.117
	Occupation	.211	.137	(.137)	.111	.209	(.105)	+
	Education	.161	.131	.166	(.032)	.200	(.085)	.285
PROGRESSIVE TAXATION (B209)								
	Family income	.148	(.110)	(.045)	.187	(.117)	.184	.093
	Occupation	.196	(.032)	(.009)	.133	(.001)	(.012)	+
	Education	.149	(.113)	(.033)	.103	(-.035)	(.087)	(.024)
BASE:	*Unweighted*	*1212*	*1564*	*1574*	*1397*	*1638*	*1027*	*2606*

* Gamma (γ) is a measure of association which can range from nil (indicating no relationship) to +1.00 (indicating a perfect relationship). For further details, see note 7 at the end of Chapter 4. Bracketed figures are not statistically significant at the .05 per cent level.

+ Not calculated (missing data)

5 Kinship and friendship

*Janet Finch**

Relationships with family and friends may be the most rewarding features of human experience, but they are also sometimes among the most difficult. If we had to predict what people living in Italy, Hungary or Australia might have most in common, safe bets probably would be wanting to do the best for their children; striving to keep their immediate family happy and comfortable; forming and keeping close relationships with relatives and friends. In other words, people living in all sorts of different circumstances and cultures can identify with family life and strife. The worldwide popularity of television soaps, whether set in wealthy Texas or suburban Melbourne, attests to that. In this sense, family life 'travels well'.

So it is not surprising that, on first sight, the ISSP (International Social Survey Programme) data on social networks from seven different countries (Australia, Austria, Britain, Hungary, Italy, USA, West Germany) reveal many more similarities than differences. But under scrutiny variations do begin to emerge. In this chapter, we concentrate on comparisons *between* countries, although where it seems important we shall comment on *within*-country differences. We have chosen three main themes, mainly because these have long been identified in the literature as key dimensions of kin and friend relationships:

- contact and support (the two features of close relationships)
- gender divisions in family relationships
- families and friends (the twin foundations of personal networks)

In concentrating on these areas, we have in mind the question: do these

*Professor of Social Relations, Lancaster University

features of close relationships, which have seemed so important in the British context, take on the same significance when we look at data from other countries? This kind of approach allows us to go a little beyond simple description, and to generate questions for further investigation. After examining the data under these three – necessarily overlapping – headings, we ask whether there *are* any clear 'national differences', and whether any of the seven countries appears to be truly distinctive in its attitudes to personal relationships. But any conclusions we draw from this discussion must necessarily be tentative. We can do little more than speculate intelligently about *why* any differences occur, since this chapter, like the others, takes just a preliminary look at some of the more interesting results.

Contact and support

People have 'networks' of personal relationships in which some individuals are more 'special' than others. They may make fine differentiations between relationships with colleagues in the workplace and with the electrician or the plumber and with teachers at the children's school. In the latter cases, though we may meet people face-to-face, the contact is often fairly short-term, tends to be for a particular purpose, and ceases when that purpose is achieved. But relationships with relatives and friends are special because they are not concerned simply with a particular task or event. They involve mutual obligations over a much longer term (Firth, Hubert and Forge, 1969; Allan, 1979; Finch, 1989). They are about people liking and caring for each other. They give people a sense of identity and belonging.

The key features of these relationships are contact and support. Family and friends feel an obligation to keep in regular (although not necessarily frequent) contact with each other, and also feel some responsibility to offer help if it is needed. In one of the most important British studies of kinship, the authors suggest that the very knowledge that kin do exist – even if they do not see them very often – gives a certain reassurance of one's place in the world, and a sense that one is not completely isolated. People talk about their kin as 'an extension or support of themselves in an outer world'; as people upon whom they *could* rely in times of need, whether or not the need has in fact arisen (Firth, Hubert and Forge, 1969).

How important are these two elements – contact and support – to people in the seven countries studied? How often do they see their family and friends, or contact them by telephone or letter? Do they feel confident about relying on relatives or on friends in times of need? Precisely who would they turn to as their main source of help with various problems? We can answer these questions only partially: data about *contacts* with relatives help us to understand the size and shape of people's actual networks in each of the countries. But the questions asked about *support* were hypothetical: they can tell us only about people's *expectations* of whom they could turn to for help in different circumstances. But expectations *are* important: they can give us a sense of the breadth and variety of people's social networks, and tell us a lot about the extent to which individuals have multiple or limited sources of social support.[1] We look first at the kinds of networks that people in the various countries have.

Keeping in touch

Living with relatives

The most frequent contacts of all are, of course, with relatives – mainly parents, siblings and children – living in the same household, though some people share households with friends rather than relatives. In Britain an increasing proportion of young adults spend a period living in this latter type of household (Harris, 1983; Jones, 1987), but the great majority still lives either with people to whom they are related (through blood or marriage), or alone. Such households are typically quite small, with no more than two adults, and with or without dependent children. Only 12 per cent of the British population currently lives in a household with more than two adults (CSO, 1988). That the average household used to have a larger number of adults, providing a roof for (say) grandparents, unmarried brothers and maiden aunts as well, is now disputed by historians. Larger households of this kind were, however, certainly common in other European countries (Laslett and Wall, 1972; Macfarlane, 1978).

Our data show that there is still some variation between countries in the extent to which people live with adult relatives, other than their spouses or partners. It is much more the pattern in Austria, Hungary and (especially) Italy than elsewhere; and less usual in the USA and Australia. Britain and West Germany fall between these two groups. The table below gives details.[2]

Living with:	Britain	USA	Australia	West Germany	Austria	Hungary	Italy
Adult son	32%	21%	30%	40%	39%	37%	60%
Adult daughter	29%	14%	25%	26%	25%	30%	58%
Father	22%	10%	13%	28%	39%	26%	45%
Mother	21%	12%	12%	25%	36%	28%	42%
Adult brother	7%	3%	4%	7%	10%	4%	15%
Adult sister	4%	2%	3%	5%	9%	4%	14%

Note. 'Adult' was defined as aged 18 or over.

In all countries, sharing a home with parents or adult children is much more common than sharing with adult siblings. But it is the Italians who stand out. They are much more likely than any other nationality to live with *every* type of relative asked about. For instance, two in five adult Italians live in the same household as their mother, compared with about one in five Australians and Americans; three in five share their home with an adult son, compared with only one in five Americans. Hungary, Austria and West Germany are rather closer to Italy than to the English-speaking countries, especially when it comes to sharing a home with parents. Since the age profiles of respondents in the seven countries are similar, we cannot look there for an explanation of these large differences.

Analysis of the data by some of the subgroups highlights some of the differences. For instance, while only around five per cent of older (aged 45 or older) Britons share their homes with their mothers, the equivalent figure is 16 per cent in Italy and 19 per cent in Hungary. And while in the English-speaking countries it is rare for married couples to live with their parents, around one in ten married Austrians, Hungarians and Italians do so.

But it is the proportion of those who have never married who share a home with parents and adult siblings that is particularly striking. At one extreme, well over 90 per cent of the never-married Italians are living with their mother or father (or both); and at the other, less than 40 per cent of the never-married Australians and Americans likewise live with a parent. The other countries fall towards the middle, but are mostly rather closer to the Italian pattern.

	Britain	USA	Australia	West Germany	Austria	Hungary	Italy
Never-marrieds living with:							
Mother	78%	37%	38%	61%	76%	90%	94%
Father	73%	27%	36%	59%	69%	78%	92%
Adult sister	26%	9%	12%	25%	30%	24%	57%
Adult brother	42%	14%	17%	32%	38%	24%	63%

Our data suggest that leaving the parental home, other than to get married, is the norm only in Australia and the USA. In Italy and Hungary especially, it appears to be very unusual for young unmarried people to live independently of their parents.

Why are there these wide variations? Different expectations about marriage and family life could certainly be part of the reason, as could differing moral views about young people cohabiting before marriage. A survey carried out in 1981 in ten European countries showed cross-national differences, some of them quite marked, in attitudes towards sexual morality (Harding and Phillips, 1986). Those countries in which a high proportion of the population is Roman Catholic are more likely to hold strict views about sexual morality, with Italians consistently more censorious than citizens of other countries on a number of items.

Another likely explanation is different educational opportunities. We know that in Britain, for example, a higher proportion of middle-class than of working-class young people leave their parents' home before marriage – mainly because they are more likely to move away to go to college or university (Jones, 1987). Mass higher education in the USA may well be one of the reasons why such a high proportion of young Americans live away from the parental home.

Another possible explanation is clearly the availability of housing. The British housing market, for instance, has only recently begun to adapt to the needs of single-person households, and the extent to which it is practical for young people in each of the countries to set up their own households may well account for some of these differences. The high proportion of Hungarians living with their parents may well be explained by the lack of alternatives in the state-managed housing market there, especially in the cities (Pickvance, 1988). Later in this chapter, we discuss the consequences of such close family ties, in terms of the kinds of support that close relatives expect of each other.

Keeping in contact

We asked respondents about different ways in which they kept in touch with their relatives (other than those they lived with): by visiting them, talking on the telephone or writing letters. Respondents who had more than one child or sibling or 'other relative' were asked about the child, sibling and so on with whom they had *most contact*. So our survey does not provide a complete picture of patterns of contacts across the whole family network; but it does tell us something about the nature of the relationship between kin who are closest to each other.

These data must, of course, be interpreted in the light of information about where relatives live. Clearly those who live fairly close to each other are likely to meet more often than those who live hundreds of miles apart. So we asked how long it would take to get to each relative and found, predictably, large differences between the seven countries. The table below shows responses when we asked about mothers (the percentages are, as in the earlier tables, of course based on those whose mothers did not live in the same household as the respondent):

	Britain %	USA %	Australia %	West Germany %	Austria %	Hungary %	Italy %
% whose mothers live:							
Less than 15 minutes away	32	27	24	38	37	43	57
15 minutes – 1 hour away	40	31	33	30	35	35	26
1 – 5 hours away	19	19	20	22	23	19	8
More than 5 hours away	9	23	23	9	4	4	8

Italians are much more likely than respondents from other countries to live less than 15 minutes travelling distance away from their mother: well over half have mothers living this close, compared with only about a quarter of Australians and Americans, and just under a third of Britons. Conversely, Americans and Australians are much the most likely to report that their mother lives a very long way away: almost a quarter live more than five hours travelling distance – about the same number as those whose mothers live close by.* Clearly, each country's size and population density goes

---

*These differences in respect of where the respondent's mother lives are reflected in the answers given about adult children, adult siblings and other relatives.

some way to explaining these variations. Similarly, in some countries there are greater opportunities than in others for moving away from one's 'home area', through for example the greater availability of housing and jobs. But this cannot be the whole story, since in these respects Britain, West Germany and Italy are not that different. The data suggest therefore that the Italians are in some ways very distinctive in their attitudes towards the family: they seem much more inclined than people in other European nations to 'stick together'.

But does living close to relatives mean that one visits them more often than if they lived some distance away? By and large it does. People whose relatives live less than 15 minutes away are much more likely to see them every day, and frequency of contact tends to tail off as the distance which needs to be travelled increases. Essentially this holds true for all seven countries, and for all relatives asked about. This much is entirely predictable.

What is more interesting are the variations between nations in *frequency* of contact. Again we focus upon meetings with respondents' mothers, since the pattern is similar for siblings, children and other relatives. As the table below shows, it is the Italians and Hungarians who appear to be the most enthusiastic about keeping up family ties; the Australians emerge as the least concerned.

	Britain	USA	Australia	West Germany	Austria	Hungary	Italy
% living . . .							
. . . close to mother who see her daily	11%	16%	7%	20%	17%	32%	32%
. . . further away from mother who see her infrequently	34%	36%	42%	17%	17%	13%	n/c

Notes. 'close to' = one hour or less away; 'infrequently' = less often than several times a year'; n/c = not calculated because the percentage base is small.

On this evidence, the British are much closer to the other two English-speaking nations than to their European neighbours.

But there are ways of keeping in touch other than meeting; we asked about telephone calls and letters too. After all it could be that Britons, Americans and Australians compensate for having less face-to-face contact through more frequent links by other means. The table below shows the data, again for just the respondent's mother, and groups them in two different ways. The first two rows show the proportion of people who are in *daily* contact, the bottom two rows show those who are not in daily contact but who have contact with their mothers *at least once a week*.

	Britain	USA	Australia	West Germany	Austria	Hungary	Italy
Daily contacts with mother							
sees/visits	9%	9%	4%	14%	13%	25%	27%
'phones (writes)	7%	15%	7%	18%	21%	6%	29%
Contacts several times a week/at least once a week							
sees/visits	50%	37%	40%	42%	48%	46%	46%
'phones (writes)	58%	52%	56%	58%	56%	14%	44%

Note. Percentage bases exclude those respondents who live with their mother.

A number of points emerge from the patterns in this table. First, only a minority of respondents in all countries see their mothers every day; and less than about one in four (often substantially less) are in daily contact with *any* relative. As we have seen, Italians are particularly likely to see their mother daily, and a very similar proportion of Hungarians also see or visit her daily.

Second, the pattern of daily contacts by telephone (presumably they *are* by telephone rather than by letter) does *not* appear straightforwardly to act as a 'compensation' for lack of face-to-face contact. Most strikingly, Italians report the highest level of daily telephone contacts *as well as* the highest level of face-to-face contacts. Conversely, the Australians do *not* report high levels of daily telephone contact, which we would expect if only the compensation factor was at work. In the USA, the other country where people tend to live far from their relatives, daily use of the telephone is more common than in Australia, but rather less common than in, say, Austria and West Germany. And third, Hungarian respondents clearly make comparatively little use of the telephone for daily (or indeed less frequent) contact, by comparison with respondents in all other countries. This must reflect lack of access.

The figures for daily contacts should be looked at alongside those for contacts which are only slightly less frequent. If we look at the figures (on the table above) for contacts with the respondent's mother *at least once a week,* the pattern evens out quite considerably. Indeed the most striking feature of these figures is their similarity rather than their difference. The seven countries are disparate in many ways, yet in all of them around 40 to 50 per cent of people who have a mother still living visit (or have a visit from) her at least once a week.*

Frequent contact between family members, characteristic of the Italians and (to an extent) the Hungarians, means that relationships with relatives outside their households become woven into *daily* life. This itself is likely to have consequences for the kind of assistance which they can give each

---

*The discussion has focused on relationships with the respondents' mothers, but the patterns are similar for other relatives. Fewer people have very regular contact with other relatives, but the variations between countries are more or less the same.

other in times of stress or need. We turn to this topic a little later in the chapter.

Just good friends

We also asked about friendship, including a question about how frequently respondents were in contact with their 'best friend'. The answers are harder to interpret than those on kinship because friendship is, of course, more difficult to define. For example, some people may have identified their 'best friend' as the person they see most frequently, whilst others may have chosen the person with whom they have been friendly for longest. However, the data reveal the proportion of people who have at least one friend with whom they are in daily contact, and whether or not the 'best friend' tends to be of the same sex. The table below gives details.

	Britain	USA	Australia	West Germany	Austria	Hungary	Italy
One or more close friends	86%	95%	93%	77%	77%	64%	85%
% with 'best friend' seeing him/her every day	13%	19%	6%	9%	18%	38%	29%
Man and best friend is another man	85%	88%	82%	83%	79%	100%	93%
Woman and best friend is another woman	93%	90%	90%	91%	87%	87%	87%

Almost all Americans and Australians claim to have at least one close friend, as do high proportions from all other countries (though least so in Hungary where the figure is around two-thirds of respondents). But the Hungarians are the most likely to have daily contact with a 'best friend' (and are also more likely to nominate a work colleague as a best friend, which may well account for such regular contact). Frequency figures for the other countries vary quite widely, with Italy being the next highest and Australia the lowest.

Best friends are overwhelmingly likely to be of the same sex. Around nine out of ten women in every country said that their closest friend was another woman. Men's answers varied a little more. For example, about one in five Austrian men claimed that their closest friend was of the opposite sex. But virtually no Hungarian men said that their best friend was a woman.

Putting together the data on kinship contacts and on patterns of friendship, we can see that Italians stand out as most likely to have contacts with both relatives *and* friends as an integral part of their *daily* lives. The British, whilst not the lowest on these measures, are much less likely than the Italians to have the kind of lifestyle in which very frequent contacts with close friends or relatives feature strongly. Naturally this does not imply that these sorts of relationships are *less important* to the British than, for example, to the Italians. Keeping in touch regularly is not the only way that the importance of friendship and kinship can be assessed (Allan, 1979). Another is the amount of help that relatives and friends give each other. It is to the responses to questions on mutual aid that we now turn.

Helping each other

The questions we asked were of the form 'What would you do if ...' you needed to borrow money, you needed some advice and so on. Respondents were asked who they would turn to first and second for help. Various alternatives were offered, including mother, father and other relatives, friends, and other sources of help appropriate to the 'problem'. We asked about:

- household or garden jobs which you cannot manage alone;
- help around the home while you are in bed with flu;
- needing to borrow a large sum of money;
- being upset because of a problem with your spouse or partner;
- feeling a bit depressed and wanting someone to talk to;
- needing advice about an important change in your life.

The existing literature does tend to see precisely these types of assistance as integral to kin relationships – indeed, in many ways, being able to call upon relatives for help is seen as one of the defining characteristics of family life (Finch, 1987). At the same time, we have to be careful about how we interpret data of the type reported here, because they refer to *hypothetical* situations. Respondents were not asked whether they had needed to call upon relatives, friends or other agencies for help with any of these problems. So these data can tell us nothing about the actual assistance which kin or friends give day to day. Nonetheless, what the data do provide is some measure of people's feelings about whether it would be *appropriate* to call upon friends and relatives in these circumstances, and possibly of people's feelings about whether they have a *right* to make such demands.

There are striking similarities between the answers given in all countries that are worth noting before we go on to discuss the differences between them. Where the spouse (or partner) seems to be an appropriate person to turn to for help, in most countries it is the spouse (or partner) who is named. Examples are help with household or gardening jobs, domestic help in times of illness and when feeling depressed. Only when advice was needed for problems *with* a spouse were other people named – in most countries the most usual choice was a 'close friend'. The only occasion where many people would go outside their network of relatives and friends was to borrow money. In this case (hardly surprisingly) 'bank or financial institution' was the first source of help most commonly named. This pattern of 'most common choices' – although they are not always the choices of a majority – indicates that there are quite well-defined ideas about the appropriate source of help, and that these are stable across the seven countries. The feeling is widespread that it is acceptable to call upon relatives for practical help, but not for money or for personal advice (where, of course, there may be vested interests at stake). Money especially is something which should, if at all possible, be kept out of close relationships between relatives and friends.

Although these are the dominant messages, there *are* variations between countries. First, as the table below shows, there are quite large national differences in the proportions who would call first upon their spouse or partner for practical help.

	Britain	USA	Australia	West Germany	Austria	Hungary	Italy
% naming spouse/partner as first source of help							
with domestic/ gardening jobs	63%	50%	63%	54%	51%	43%	42%
when ill with flu	65%	52%	64%	59%	53%	53%	41%
when feeling depressed	53%	40%	51%	54%	48%	44%	33%

Australians and Britons are the most likely, and Italians the least likely, to rely upon their spouse or partner for practical help with household or gardening chores, or when they are ill. However, for help with a bout of depression – again an item on which 'spouse' tended to be the most common answer across all countries – Britons and Australians are no more likely than anyone else to say that they would turn to their spouse or partner. Italians are again the least likely to name their spouse.

We expected to find gender differences in responses to these questions, and we did. But these do not explain the differences between countries. Indeed the variation between men's and women's answers across all countries is remarkably consistent. Men are much more likely than women to say that they would turn first to their spouse for help when they are ill or when feeling depressed. As to help with household or gardening jobs, however, there is little difference in the proportion of women and men who name their spouse as the first source of support; presumably this is because women and men are likely to think of different types of practical jobs as their own responsibility.

Patterns of answers like these suggest that marriage (or a marriage-like relationship) means something rather different in different countries. In Australia and Britain for instance (in sharp contrast with Italy), married couples seem to have a particularly 'self-contained' view of the household; they rely on each other conspicuously more than they do on even their closest contacts outside the family unit. They make a distinction, however, between practical help and the more personal types of support needed, for example, by someone who is feeling depressed. Here Australians and Britons are no more likely than people of other nationalities to feel that they can rely on their spouses: few of our respondents expect practical support and personal closeness to be intimately intertwined. So a husband, wife or cohabitee may be fine for making a meal when you are ill, or helping to decorate the bathroom, but he or she is not necessarily the person to help if you are feeling low. This is borne out perhaps by a recent British study of couples in early married life, which shows that people who life, which shows that people who have high expectations that marriage will entail a close personal relationship are frequently disappointed by the reality (Mansfield and Collard, 1988).

Who else, apart from spouses, do people think it would be appropriate to turn to with their problems? The pattern varies somewhat from country to country, but mostly help seems to be sought within the close set of relationships involving parents and children. This is hardly surprising, since it has long been argued that the strongest forms of family obligation are to be found between parents and children (Morgan, 1975).

Although there is a general propensity across all countries to turn to parents or children, there are some variations in the *proportions* of people of different nationalities who would look to them first (and even second) for help. Thus Italians tend to be especially likely to name parents or children as their main source of support, while Australians and Americans are markedly less likely to do so. Britons too tend to be on the low side. No doubt the fact that many Italians tend to live close to their children, or in the same household, goes a long way towards explaining the pattern of answers.

When it comes to needing to borrow money, people in six of the seven countries would turn first to the bank, but a sizeable minority in every country (especially in Italy) sees parents as a suitable source of financial assistance. The table below shows the proportions of people who choose the bank, parents and children. In all countries except Italy, the bank is the most common first choice, with around 40 per cent choosing this option.

	Britain	USA	Australia	West Germany	Austria	Hungary	Italy
First source of help for borrowing money							
Bank	38%	39%	42%	45%	37%	42%	24%
Parents	17%	20%	16%	18%	18%	19%	29%
Children	6%	6%	5%	5%	6%	11%	8%

In the Italian sample, only a quarter name the bank and 29 per cent name parents (with preference split evenly between mother and father). In the past the Italian pattern may have been common elsewhere, until market sources of credit became more widespread around the middle of this century. It is also worth noting that many more people say that they would turn to their parents than would turn to their grown-up children. Although these answers obviously reflect the age profiles of the various samples, they tend to confirm a pattern noted in some of the literature on kinship – that it is seen as much more appropriate for parents to give money to their adult children, than the other way round (Hill, 1970; Cheal, 1983). This normative preference for money to flow *down* the generations seems to hold across all seven countries.

The proportions choosing relatives other than parents or children, or choosing friends, as their first source of support for most of the nominated problems tend to be small, so any variations there may be between countries are also too small to detect. The one circumstance, however, in which friends do figure prominently is when a problem arises with one's spouse or partner. The table below shows a selection of the responses.

	Britain	USA	Australia	West Germany	Austria	Hungary	Italy
First source of help over problem with spouse/ partner							
Friend	21%	30%	28%	28%	21%	13%	28%
Parents	18%	14%	12%	14%	20%	20%	14%
Clergy/priest	2%	13%	6%	2%	3%	*	2%
No-one	8%	5%	10%	20%	19%	19%	14%

Note. * = less than 0.5 per cent.

We see that friends feature prominently in all countries, and are the most popular choice except in Hungary. But when we compare the proportions choosing friends with the proportions giving other answers, there are marked variations. In Australia, West Germany, Italy and the USA, about twice as many respondents would rely on a friend for this kind of support as would turn to their parents. In Austria and Britain, however, the proportions saying that they would turn to friends and to parents are much closer, and in Hungary (where fewer people have 'best friends') many more people name their parents. It seems, then, that there are more people in these three countries who see it as appropriate to confine marital problems to the family. But they are still a minority: indeed, there is other evidence from Britain to suggest a strong resistance within *some* sectors of the population against using parents as confidants for marital problems (Brannen and Collard, 1982).

Also worth noting are the proportions in each country saying that they would turn to 'no-one' when there are marital problems. These respondents (admittedly only a small minority) presumably feel that such problems are a wholly private matter, and it appears that rather more people in Hungary, Italy and West Germany see them in this way than do Americans and Britons. Few people in any country say that they would turn first to their church (or equivalent). But here Americans stand out from the rest, with a much higher proportion (although still only 13 per cent) seeing their 'church, clergy or priest' as the most appropriate first source of help. We have other data to suggest that the USA is a 'more religious' country than almost all (if not all) the others under examination, but this is unlikely to be the whole explanation. It may well be that religious organisations in the USA have well-developed marital counselling services, and so are seen as able to provide 'specialist' help.

Kin and gender

Feminists writing about family life have suggested that women and men see the family in quite different ways. They argue that women's social relationships are much more firmly rooted in the family than are men's, and that women play a much more important role in helping their relatives

(Dalley, 1988; Finch, 1989). The data from this survey show how people across all countries are likely to look to *female* relatives for help during illness, bouts of depression and so on. Do other data from this survey lend more general support to the idea that kin relationships are closer for women than for men?

From the table below, we can see that there is indeed a general tendency for people to keep in closer contact with female relatives than with male relatives. For instance, across all seven countries, more people see a daughter at least once a week than see a son; and in six out of the seven countries, frequent contact is more common with sisters than with brothers.

	Britain	USA	Australia	West Germany	Austria	Hungary	Italy
% seeing each at least once a week							
Adult daughter	65%	53%	55%	70%	70%	67%	84%
Adult son	51%	48%	51%	61%	69%	66%	77%
Adult sister	32%	30%	24%	30%	40%	45%	51%
Adult brother	20%	26%	17%	28%	32%	47%	48%

Notes. Relatives living in the same household as the respondent are omitted from this table. 'At least once a week' includes those answering 'daily', 'several times a week' and 'at least once a week'.

Clearly, however, we need to look at the answers of women and men separately. Are they equally likely to keep in touch with female relatives, or is there a perceptible difference between relationships involving only female relatives and those where at least one party is a man? The next table shows weekly visits between sisters and between brothers and sisters. We see that, except among Hungarians, sisters are more likely to be in regular contact with each other than are sisters and brothers.

	Britain	USA	Australia	West Germany	Austria	Hungary	Italy
Visits sister at least once a week							
Sister	40%	35%	30%	34%	42%	45%	56%
Brother	23%	24%	17%	26%	38%	44%	46%

Notes. Siblings living in the same household as the respondent are omitted from this table. 'At least once a week' includes those answering 'daily', 'several times a week' and 'at least once a week'.

This pattern is particularly noticeable in Australia, Britain and the USA. In Britain, almost twice as many sisters as brothers are in weekly contact with a sister. Contacts between parents and children show similar gender variations across all countries, although they tend to be smaller. In general, the seven countries are ranged along a continuum. At one end is Hungary, in which gender does not seem to play an important role in the pattern of contacts between kin. At the other is Britain, where it seems that maintaining contacts with relatives is the 'women's business' rather than the man's. The other countries fall in between.

One possible explanation for these differences lies in the cultural rules associated with kinship in any society. It could be argued that, in Britain for instance, women are simply *expected* to be more involved with their relatives than are men, and that similar expectations are not held to the same degree elsewhere.

Certainly, some of the existing research into kinship in Britain has suggested a strong gender orientation. Firth, Hubert and Forge (1969), in their study of middle-class women, dubbed them 'kin-keepers'; and Young and Willmott (1957) described relationships between working-class mothers, daughters and sisters as 'the women's trade union'. Latterly, however, writers in this tradition have suggested that family life is becoming more 'symmetrical' and that gender divisions are consequently less prominent (Young and Willmott, 1973). Our evidence suggests that, in Britain particularly, it is still far from the case that men and women enjoy equal roles.

Another possible explanation is that women *need* to be in close contact with their relatives, especially in those countries where family members have to rely on each other for mutual aid. Feminist writers have argued that the lack of facilities in Britain – for example, for the care of children of working mothers, and of infirm elderly people – makes it necessary for women to rely on female relatives for practical support (New and David, 1985; Finch, 1989). Our data can neither prove nor disprove this hypothesis because we did not ask questions about these kinds of help.

Relatives and friends

Are relationships with close friends different in kind from relationships with relatives? Kinship and friendship are usually seen as the twin foundations for close personal relationships and for sociability; but whether friendship is as important as kinship in providing practical assistance is less clear (Allan, 1979). We have seen that, across all seven countries, more people say that they see their 'best friend' often (at least once a week) than have weekly contact with *any* relative outside their own household. So, at least at the level of sociability, it appears that friends are if anything more important than relatives.

There are, however, considerable cross-national variations. We have already seen that Hungarians and Italians are much more likely to have *daily* contact with a best friend than are people of other nationalities. We can examine the comparative importance of friends and relatives by looking at the figures for *weekly* contact with 'best friend' and with siblings*.

---

*The sibling comparison has been chosen because this kin relationship is between people of the same generation, and thus most likely to be comparable with friendship.

	Britain	USA	Australia	West Germany	Austria	Hungary	Italy
% seeing at least once a week							
Best friend	65%	65%	56%	65%	73%	73%	77%
Sister	32%	30%	24%	30%	40%	45%	51%
Brother	20%	26%	17%	28%	32%	47%	48%

Notes. Those living in the same household as the respondent are omitted from this table. 'At least once a week' includes those answering 'daily', 'several times a week' and 'at least once a week'.

In all countries, people are much more likely to see their best friend once a week than to see their sister or brother so frequently: in five out of seven countries, they are at least twice as likely to see their best friend once a week as to see their sister. But it must be remembered that siblings are clearly less likely to live nearby than are best friends, since 'best friends' may well be defined partly by frequency of contact (and many would be work colleagues).

Nonetheless, a fairly consistent pattern emerges across all the countries of the significance of friendship and kinship in people's lives. Friends are the people with whom you have most regular contact as part of your routine daily life, and who you turn to for help with personal problems. Relatives are the people who you would feel able to turn to for practical support and (to some extent) financial assistance, even though you may see them less frequently. But you would not necessarily want to go and pour out your troubles to them.

Conclusions

Of all the countries under study, Italy emerges with a particularly distinctive pattern of personal relationships and social networks (with Hungary sharing certain aspects). To Italians, relationships with both relatives and friends form a much more integral part of daily life than elsewhere. They are more likely to share a home with their relatives and also to have relatives living nearby. They are more likely to visit or telephone relatives daily, and also to be in daily contact with a 'best friend'. Relationships between parents and children seem particularly important: children are less likely than in any other country to move out of the parental home before marriage and, in adult life, children are more likely to think of turning to their parents for practical assistance, or to borrow money.

Relationships within the kin groups clearly have greater significance in daily life in Italy than elsewhere. In contrast, the marriage relationship seems to be correspondingly less important, Italians being less likely than others to look to their spouse for various types of assistance. However, while relatives may be important in Italian life socially and practically, Italians are in fact *less* likely than people in other countries to look to relatives for personal support and advice.

Britons, in contrast, seem to be rather more 'self-contained' in their approach to personal relationships. To this extent, they are closer to the majority of the other nationalities under study. But we have observed two distinctive features that tend to set Britain apart from the other nations in the way they think about the family – although, of course, this survey can tell us nothing about what happens in a *real* crisis. First, there appears to be particular emphasis upon the more 'private' relationships within the household, especially the marriage relationship (a feature which also tends to characterise Australians). British husbands and wives seem more inclined than their married counterparts elsewhere to turn to each other when they need practical help, and rather more likely to keep personal problems within the family or to themselves. Second, gender distinctions – especially the notion that family life is essentially 'women's business' – are more apparent in Britain than elsewhere. By comparison with Italy at least, the extended family seems less important, and the marriage relationship more important, in the way British people think about the family.

Notes

1.   It was decided to ask hypothetical questions about support networks because these could be asked of *everyone* regardless of their existing networks. To have asked about actual circumstances in which help was needed and given would have meant devising complex filter instructions, always inadvisable on a self-completion questionnaire when there is no interviewer present to guide the respondent through it.
2.   Respondents who had more than one adult sister, brother, daughter or son were asked to answer about the one they 'had most contact with'. So those who lived in the same household as an adult sibling, son or daughter would be very likely to have answered this series of questions in respect of that person, rather than another sibling or grown-up son or daughter who lived elsewhere. Consequently, the data presented in this section of the chapter probably give a fairly accurate picture of co-residence across the different countries.

References

ALLAN, G., *The Sociology of Kinship and Friendship,* George Allen and Unwin, London (1979).
BRANNEN, J. and COLLARD, J., *Marriages in Trouble: The Process of Seeking Help,* Tavistock, London (1982).
C S O (Central Statistical Office), *Social Trends 18,* HMSO, London (1988).
CHEAL, D., 'Intergenerational family transfers', *Journal of Marriage and the Family,* vol. 45 (1983), pp.805–13.
DALLEY, G., *Ideologies of Caring,* Macmillan, London (1988).
FINCH, J., 'Family ties', *New Society,* (March 20th, 1987), pp.16–20.
FINCH, J., *Family Obligations and Social Change,* Polity Press, Cambridge (1989).
FIRTH, R., HUBERT, J., and FORGE, A., *Families and their Relatives,* Routledge and Kegan Paul, London (1969).
HARRIS, C.C., *The Family and Industrial Society,* Allen and Unwin, London (1983).
HARDING, S., and PHILLIPS, D., with FOGARTY, M., *Contrasting Values in Western Europe,* Macmillan, London (1986).

HILL, R., *Family Development in Three Generations,* Schenkman, Cambridge, Mass., (1970).

JONES, G., 'Leaving the parental home: an analysis of early housing careers', *Journal of Social Policy,* vol.16, no.1 (1987), pp.49–74.

LASLETT, P., and WALL, R., (eds), *Household and Family in Past Time,* Cambridge University Press, Cambridge (1972).

MACFARLANE, A., *The Origins of English Individualism,* Basil Blackwell, Oxford, (1978).

MANSFIELD, P. and COLLARD, J., *The Beginning of the Rest of Your Life: A Portrait of Newly-Wed Marriage,* Macmillan, London (1988).

MORGAN, D.H.J., *Social Theory and the Family,* Routledge and Kegan Paul, London (1975).

NEW, C., and DAVID, M., *For the Children's Sake,* Penguin, Harmondsworth (1985).

PICKVANCE, C.G., 'Employers, labour markets and redistribution under state socialism: an interpretation of housing policy in Hungary 1960–83', *Sociology,* vol.22, no.2 (1988), pp.193–214.

YOUNG, M. and WILLMOTT, P., *Family and Kinship in East London,* Routledge and Kegan Paul, London (1957).

YOUNG, M. and WILLMOTT, P., *The Symmetrical Family,* Routledge and Kegan Paul, London (1973).

6 Understanding of science in Britain and the USA

*Geoffrey Evans and John Durant**

The natural sciences occupy a place of central importance in all advanced industrial societies. As systems of abstract knowledge, they constitute these societies' most distinctive and authoritative intellectual achievements. When applied in myriad ways to technology, they are the principal source of innovation in industrial, economic and social development. Wherever we turn – to agriculture, to manufacturing and service industries, or to social services such as health care – we find that new scientific discoveries and science-based technologies are at the very heart of our changing way of life.

It is this pivotal place of science that lends significance to the issue of the public understanding of science. To ask questions about public interest in, knowledge of and attitudes towards science and technology is at the same time to inquire about the extent to which people are suitably equipped for life in an advanced industrial society. Increasingly, such questions are being asked by governments striving for improved economic performance, by industrialists seeking a suitably qualified work-force, and by scientists looking for higher levels of public support for their work. For a fuller discussion, see Thomas and Durant (1987).

Over the past two years, we have conducted a survey (along with our colleagues Geoffrey Thomas at Oxford, and Patricia Prescott-Clarke at

*Geoffrey Evans is a British Academy Research Fellow at Nuffield College, Oxford and lectures in the Department of Social Psychology at the London School of Economics; John Durant is Assistant Director (Head of Research and Information Services) at the Science Museum, and Visiting Professor of the Public Understanding of Science at Imperial College, London.

SCPR) of the British public's interest in, understanding of and attitudes towards science. Coincidentally a similar project was being planned in the USA, and we took the opportunity to include an international comparative dimension. So far as we are aware, this is the first time two independent surveys on the public understanding of science have been designed expressly with a view to international comparison.[1] Brief technical details of the two surveys, carried out among approximately 2000 adults in each country, are given in Appendix I of this book.

The potential value of international comparative analysis of the public understanding of science should be clear. In its scientific and technological prowess, Britain prides itself on being fairly high up in the league of nations; but few would dispute the fact that the USA is at the top. A comparative study such as this may be expected to throw some light on the relative scientific and technological sophistication of the two countries, and hence (to the degree that such sophistication is related to industrial performance) help to illuminate larger economic issues.

In this chapter, we summarise the principal findings of our initial analyses. We look first at self-reported interest in, and self-reported informedness about science, technology and medicine. Then we look at actual levels of general scientific knowledge and specific knowledge about health risks. Next, we consider public acceptance of science in ideologically sensitive areas such as cosmology and evolutionary theory. Finally, we consider public attitudes towards science and science-based public policy issues, including the question of government expenditure on science.

These are diverse aspects of the public understanding of science. Nevertheless, our results combine to provide a clear and broadly consistent pattern of similarities and differences between the ways in which the British and the American publics relate to the world of science.

Public perceptions of science

Public interest

Interest in science is an obvious starting point for our investigation, since people who express particular interest in science may well be more knowledgeable than most. Respondents were asked how interested they were in a variety of issue areas in the news:

	Very interested		**Not at all interested**	
	Britain	**USA**	**Britain**	**USA**
New medical discoveries	49%	71%	10%	3%
New inventions and technologies	39%	46%	16%	9%
New scientific discoveries	38%	40%	18%	10%
Sports in the news	28%	–	29%	–
New films	17%	–	45%	–
Politics	16%	–	29%	–

Note. Blanks in the table indicate that a strictly comparable question was not asked in the American survey.

Two main points emerge from these findings. First, in both Britain and the USA, reported levels of public interest in science are quite high. In both countries a large proportion of respondents claimed to be very interested in science and technology and – even more so – in medicine. Comparatively few said that they had no interest. Moreover, in the British study, the self-reported interest levels in science are substantially higher than those in the three other topics offered.

Second, self-reported interest in science, and especially in new medical discoveries, is consistently higher in the USA than in Britain. Indeed, almost twice the proportion of British to American respondents claimed to have no interest at all in new scientific discoveries, and about three times the proportion claimed a complete lack of interest in new medical discoveries.

Informedness

Are higher levels of interest in science matched by higher levels of knowledge? For each of the six issue areas on which they had reported their interest, respondents were also invited to say how informed they were:

	Very well informed		Not at all informed	
	Britain	USA	Britain	USA
New medical discoveries	10%	24%	35%	17%
New inventions and technologies	9%	14%	38%	28%
New scientific discoveries	9%	12%	43%	35%
Sports in the news	28%	–	30%	–
New films	12%	–	52%	–
Politics	17%	–	28%	–

Note. Blanks in the table indicate that a strictly comparable question was not asked in the American survey.

Once again, two main points emerge from these findings. First, self-reported informedness matches self-reported interest reasonably well (at least in Britain) in the areas of sports in the news, new films and politics. But in the areas of science, technology and medicine, self-reported informedness is substantially lower than self-reported interest in both countries. In other words, there is a self-reported 'knowledge gap' in both Britain and the USA.

Second, there are consistent differences between the British and the American figures, particularly in relation to perceived knowledge about new medical discoveries. More than twice the proportion of American to British respondents said they were very well informed about new medical discoveries, and more than twice the proportion of British respondents claimed no knowledge at all. Clearly, American people see themselves as being not only more interested but also more informed about science, technology and medicine than their British counterparts.

How accurate are self-reports?

We must, of course, be cautious about accepting these self-reported views –
whether of interest or informedness – at their face value. Assertions of
interest are easily made, and they may say as much about what people
think they *ought* to be interested in as what they actually *are* interested in.
Similarly, assertions of informedness require prior judgements on the part
of respondents about what it is to be well or poorly informed about a
particular subject. Where social norms about the *importance* of science may
be expected to inflate self-reported interest levels, social norms about the
difficulty of science may be expected to deflate self-reported informedness
levels.

For these reasons, we might expect some sort of gap between the levels of
self-reported interest and informedness. Nevertheless, these self-descriptions
are likely to have some relationship to respondents' overall attitudes to
science. Several pieces of evidence support this view. First, we would expect
those who are more interested in a subject to be more informed about it;
and in both Britain and the USA this is indeed the case.[2]

Second, we would expect the more educated to be both more interested
and better informed. After all, they will have had more exposure to science
(and hence more opportunity to acquire interest in or information about
it). Once again, this expectation is borne out in both the British and the
American surveys. Among British respondents with degrees, 57 per cent
reported that they were "very interested" and only 7 per cent reported that
they were "not at all interested" in new scientific discoveries, while the
comparable figures for those with no educational qualifications were 30 per
cent ("very interested") and 28 per cent ("not at all interested").

Third, we would expect those who say they are more interested to have
more contact with or exposure to science. For instance, we asked
respondents in both countries whether they ever read science magazines.
While 13 per cent of British respondents reported that they read science
magazines, the comparable figure for the USA was 30 per cent. The
direction of this difference is in line with the results on self-reported
interest; but the magnitude of the difference suggests that other factors may
also be involved. (It may be, for example, that magazine readership
generally is higher in the USA than it is in Britain.)

Fourth, and perhaps most important, we were able to test whether or not
people are informed about a subject by asking basic questions designed to
reveal objective levels of knowledge. We refer to this evidence later, but it
suffices to say now that respondents' self-reported informedness matches
our independent assessments of informedness rather well.

Perceived relevance of science

One possible explanation for American–British differences is that
Americans may generally perceive science as more germane to their daily
lives. People who perceive something as relevant are likely to be more
interested in it, and better informed about it, than those who do not. To

examine this possibility, respondents were asked about the importance of knowing about science "in my daily life". The results were as follows:

	Britain %	USA %
Important	63	88
Not important	37	12

Note. The figures given represent the percentages of respondents who expressed a view one way or the other.

The difference between the two samples is substantial. The proportion of Britons saying that knowledge of science is *not* important in daily life is over three times as large as the corresponding proportion of Americans.

Why should more American than British people regard science as of direct personal relevance? Several possibilities suggest themselves. First, it could be that more Americans than Britons actually find themselves using science – or at least technology – in their daily lives. This may be a factor, but it is unlikely to be a particularly large one. Second, it could be that the linking of progress to scientific and technological advance is an especially strong aspect of American culture. Again, this is possible, but direct evidence is lacking. Third, it may be that attitudes towards the relevance of science are associated with educational attainment, and that the observed differences result from the higher proportion of Americans than Britons who go on to higher education. For this there is indeed evidence. In both countries, the more qualified the person, the greater is the tendency to see science as relevant. However, even among the least well-educated there is a stronger tendency for American respondents to believe that knowing about science is important. Among British respondents with no educational qualifications (40 per cent of the sample) well over half thought that science was *irrelevant* to their daily lives. Only just over a quarter of the one in ten Americans with no educational qualifications felt the same.

So, although education influences attitudes, Americans are generally more likely than the British to regard science as relevant, whatever their level of education. There does indeed seem to be a more positive evaluation of science and technology in American, as opposed to British, culture.

Understanding of science

Scientific knowledge

Since self-reporting may be unreliable, and since we needed a good measure of public knowledge, we constructed a series of questions designed to provide an *independent* estimate of the level of public understanding of science. Traditionally, this has been considered a rather difficult thing to do, since it involves setting a sort of examination paper for respondents who have no particular incentive to submit themselves to it – except, perhaps, mild curiosity about, or occasionally pride in, their own knowledge. In the event, perhaps because of the popularity of quiz shows on television, we found no real difficulty in getting answers to more than twenty elementary factual questions covering a wide range of sciences – mathematics, physics, geology, chemistry and biology.[3] From this larger set, a 'knowledge quiz' of fifteen items was also included in the American survey. The answers on this subset of comparable items are reported and discussed in the following pages.

The first and probably the most important thing to say about the 'quiz' items is that they are deliberately very elementary. Many candidate items were rejected simply on the basis of qualitative and pilot work which revealed that too few respondents would get them right, making them of little use for scaling purposes. Two items, "hot air rises" and "the centre of the earth is very hot", were included as 'morale boosters' in the expectation that almost everyone would get them right, but all but one of the other items produced significant numbers of respondents who did not know the answers.

	% giving correct answer		Correct answer
	Britain	USA	
Hot air rises	97%	97%	True
Sunlight can cause skin cancer	94%	97%	True
The centre of the earth is very hot	86%	80%	True
Which travels faster – light or sound?	75%	76%	Light
Is all radioactivity man-made or does some occur naturally?	74%	65%	Some naturally
The continents are moving slowly about on the surface of the earth	72%	80%	True
Radioactive milk can be made safe by boiling it	65%	64%	False
Does the earth go round the sun, or does the sun go round the earth?	63%	73%	Earth around sun
The oxygen we breathe comes from plants	60%	81%	True
The earliest humans lived at the same time as the dinosaurs	46%	37%	False
Lasers work by focusing sound waves	42%	36%	False
How long does it take for the earth to go round the sun?	34%	45%	1 year
Electrons are smaller than atoms	31%	43%	True
Antibiotics kill viruses as well as bacteria	29%	26%	False

Notes. In this table, the 14 items are listed, not in the order in which they were presented to respondents, but according to the proportion of Britons giving correct answers. The responses to the fifteenth item are given later in this section.

It can be seen that in purely statistical terms the 'knowledge quiz' performed rather well. Results in both surveys are approximately normally distributed, with mean scores (out of a possible 15) of 9.26 for British respondents and 10.02 for American respondents. This small but significant difference is most apparent at the extremes of the scale. Thirty-four British and a mere three American respondents scored two points or less, whereas 11 British respondents and no less than 91 Americans obtained a maximum score of 15. It is difficult to be confident about the causes of these large differences at the extremes. Perhaps fewer American than British people slip entirely through the net of the educational system; and perhaps more American than British people receive the kind of secondary and tertiary scientific education that is required to do very well on this kind of test. Whatever the reason, however, it is clear that this independent assessment confirms the aggregate self-reported knowledge figures discussed earlier: American respondents are indeed slightly better informed than their British counterparts about science, technology and medicine. (See figure below.)

Results from the Knowledge Quiz

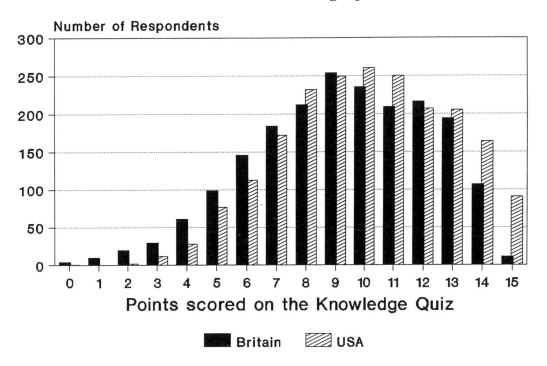

Some of the individual results of the knowledge quiz are worth further comment. Arguably, it is encouraging that a large majority of respondents got right not only the 'morale booster' questions – that hot air rises and the centre of the earth is hot – but also several others: that sunlight can cause cancer, that light travels faster than sound, that not all radioactivity is man-made and that the continents are moving. However, a number of other results are nothing like so pleasing. For example, under a half of Americans and under a third of British respondents knew that electrons are smaller than atoms. This reveals a widespread unfamiliarity with the physical model of the atom as having a central nucleus with a definite number of orbiting electrons. This model, established in the early decades of this century, has given us not only our current understanding of what the world is made of but also nuclear weapons and nuclear power generation.

Similarly, although a majority of respondents in both countries knew that the earth goes round the sun, only just over one third of British and just under one half of American respondents knew that its orbit lasted one year. Interestingly, the question about the relative antiquity of humans and dinosaurs produced almost exactly the opposite result; just over one third of American and just under one half of British respondents answered correctly. (We shall say more about this item below.)

The lowest scores of all were obtained on the item about antibiotics. Here, only a quarter of American and under a third of British respondents knew that antibiotics are ineffective against viruses. Significantly, only 17 per cent of British and 11 per cent of American respondents answered "don't know" on this item (as compared, for example, with 45 per cent and 37 per cent, respectively, for the item on electrons and atoms). This suggests that a positive misconception, as opposed to mere lack of knowledge, is involved here.

Perhaps the most surprising answers are to the fifteenth quiz item, not yet discussed. Probabilistic reasoning is a crucial element in much of modern science and technology, and concern has been expressed about the general public's ability to interpret it at all accurately or appropriately (see Royal Society, 1985). In fact, as the table below shows, almost a two to one majority of both the British and the American publics clearly do understand the basics of probabilistic reasoning. We put the following example to respondents and asked them to interpret it by choosing one of four possible meanings:

Doctors tell a couple that their genetic make-up means that they've got a one in four chance of having a child with an inherited illness.

	% answering correctly		Correct answer
Does this mean that . . .	Britain	USA	
. . . if they have only three children, none will have the illness?	84%	91%	No
. . . if their first child has the illness, the next three will not?	80%	89%	No
. . . each of the couple's children has the same risk of suffering from the illness?	82%	74%	Yes
. . . if their first three children are healthy, the fourth will have the illness?	80%	86%	No
Percentage answering all four correctly	66%	62%	

It should be stressed that the criteria for success on this item are rather tough: not only must respondents identify the third option as correct, but also they must identify all other options as incorrect. Naturally, a single multiple-choice question cannot possibly do justice to this subject. Nevertheless, the results do suggest that most people in Britain and the USA (and slightly more in the former than the latter) do understand the basic concept of chance, in spite of their relative ignorance about some elementary features of the natural world.

Knowledge of risks to health

Medicine is arguably the most direct way in which modern science affects the well-being of the general public. Still with a view to assessing knowledge, we decided therefore to focus on a major area of current concern, heart disease. We invited respondents to pick from a list of potential risk factors those that contribute to heart disease. The results were as follows:

	% saying each factor contributes to heart disease		
	Britain	**USA**	
Stress	95%	96%	
Not taking much exercise	91%	91%	Broadly
Eating a lot of animal fat	88%	94%	correct
Smoking	83%	95%	
Eating food with a lot of additives	57%	66%	
Lack of vitamins	44%	49%	Broadly
Eating very little fresh fruit	42%	50%	incorrect
Eating very little fibre	39%	50%	
Percentage identifying all eight correctly	9%	8%	

Note. In this table too, the items are listed according to the proportion of British respondents giving correct answers.

Clearly, most British and American respondents knew that smoking, eating a lot of animal fat, lack of exercise and stress are all genuine risk factors. At the same time, however, substantial numbers in both countries also believed that the other suggested factors are contributory causes of heart disease.

At first sight, these results appear to confirm the American respondents' view of themselves as being better informed about medical matters than their British counterparts. For example, 12 per cent more Americans than Britons acknowledged the well-established link between smoking and heart disease. However, the notion that this difference reflects superior medical knowledge on the part of the American respondents is undermined when we turn to the answers to the four non-genuine risk factors in the list. Substantially more American than British respondents incorrectly identified each of these. Indeed, the average difference in scores on the non-genuine risk factors (eight per cent) is about twice that on the genuine ones. This relative failure of Americans to discriminate between genuine and non-genuine risk factors is reflected in the fact that the proportion of respondents categorising all eight risk factors correctly is virtually the same in Britain (nine per cent) as it is in the USA (eight per cent). The main difference between the distributions turns out to be that Americans are more inclined than the British to see *all* the risks as contributory factors.

There may of course be another way of interpreting these figures – as showing a recognition on both sides of the Atlantic that all the factors presented are simply not conducive to good health in general (which is indeed the case). But this was not the question we asked respondents to consider.

Acceptance of scientific theories

It is one thing to know what science says about the world, and quite another to accept it. In certain cases, sections of the public are sceptical about the findings of science for what are essentially ideological reasons. In the USA, in particular, religious fundamentalists have opposed scientific theories of human origins for the greater part of the twentieth century. In the 1920s, fundamentalist campaigns led to several States passing anti-evolution legislation; and in the 1980s, there has been another spate of legal battles over so-called 'equal time' bills, according to which public schools and colleges are required to be even-handed in their teaching of evolutionary theory and the biblical account of creation. Interestingly, Christian fundamentalism is, so far, distinctive of the USA; its nearest equivalents in Britain, for example, are far less culturally significant (see Durant, 1985).

We included two items related to the question of the acceptance of the scientific world-picture, one on the 'Big Bang' – the colloquial name given to the explosive event with which most cosmologists believe the universe began – and another on human evolution. As the centre-piece of modern cosmology, the notion of the Big Bang is a scientific answer to the question of how the universe came into being; and for this reason, at least, we may expect it to impinge on religious sensibilities. Similarly, the question of human origins has always been the most controversial aspect of evolutionary theory – for example, in 1925 it was the central issue in the infamous 'monkey trial' in Dayton, Tennessee.

The responses to these two questions provide an interesting contrast with those on interest and knowledge:

	True		False		Don't know	
	Britain	USA	Britain	USA	Britain	USA
The universe began with a huge explosion	64%	55%	23%	16%	13%	29%
Human beings as we know them today developed from earlier species of animals	79%	47%	15%	41%	6%	12%

On both issues, it will be seen that there are higher levels of public acceptance of the scientific view of the world in Britain than in the USA. For the Big Bang, the difference is fairly modest; but on the question of human origins, it is very large indeed: while almost four-fifths of British respondents accept the Darwinian theory of human origins (and only 15 per cent reject it), Americans are almost evenly divided. Put another way, almost three times as many American as British respondents reject the idea of human evolution (41 per cent to 15 per cent).

Given what has already been said, it would seem plausible that the strength of Christian fundamentalism in the USA is the main cause of these differences. In addition, however, we must consider the possibility that ignorance of the relevant scientific theories may be involved. To assess the relative importance of these two factors – religion and ignorance – we have looked at the answers to the Big Bang and human evolution items in relation to responses on two other relevant questions. One was on the relative antiquity of humans and dinosaurs, and the other was an agree/disagree item: "we depend too much on science and not enough on faith". The latter is our only direct comparative measure of respondents' views on the relationship between science and religious belief. (The British survey included measures of religious affiliation, religious observance and religious belief, but the American study did not.)

The results (expressed as Pearson rank order correlations*) reveal a striking pattern of associations:

	Big Bang		Humans and dinosaurs		Science and faith	
	Britain	USA	Britain	USA	Britain	USA
Human evolution	.34	.45	.12	.01	−.19	−.31
Big Bang			.14	.07	−.12	−.20
Humans and dinosaurs					−.08	−.11

In Britain and the USA, acceptance of human evolution is moderately closely associated with acceptance of the Big Bang. In both countries it is also associated with *rejection* of the proposition that we depend too much on science and not enough on faith. In both cases, the strength of association between 'belief' in science *versus* faith and the other items is in the following order:

> human evolution
> Big Bang
> humans and dinosaurs

This order may be taken to represent a sequence of religious sensitivity. In other words, it appears that rejection of human evolution depends more on religious belief than does rejection of the Big Bang; and rejection of the Big Bang depends more on religious belief than does ignorance of the relative antiquity of dinosaurs and humans.

In these respects the British and American results have much in common. However, there is one important difference between the two. In the British results, acceptance of the Big Bang and human evolution are as closely correlated with *knowledge* of the relative ages of humans and dinosaurs as they are with *attitudes* to the relative importance of science

---

*These correlations can range from 1.00 to −1.00. The closer they are to 1.00, the more strongly the two statements are positively related, so that someone who agrees with one is likely to agree with the other. The closer they are to −1.00, the more strongly the two statements are negatively related, so that someone who agrees with one disagrees with the other. A score of zero would mean there was no relationship between the two answers.

and faith. The American results stand in sharp contrast. Acceptance of the Big Bang and human evolution are *not* significantly correlated with knowledge of the relative ages of humans and dinosaurs; but they *are* rather more strongly correlated with respondents' views on science *versus* faith. In essence, for Americans, acceptance of the Big Bang, and (especially) human evolution, is rather less dependent on scientific knowledge and rather more dependent on religious belief than it is for the British.

For the British data, we undertook a regression analysis to determine the extent to which religious factors (such as affiliation, observance and belief) as opposed to other factors (such as educational level and scientific knowledge) contributed to the differences in people's answers to the Big Bang and human evolution items. Whereas for the Big Bang item, scientific knowledge emerged as the *only* significant independent influence, for the human evolution item *both* scientific knowledge *and* religious belief emerged as significant independent influences. This confirms that acceptance of evolution in Britain depends to an extent on religious belief, while acceptance of the Big Bang does not. Although strictly comparable data are not available for the American respondents, the other results we have suggest that evolution is an even more religiously sensitive issue there.

Public attitudes to science

We turn now to the wider issue of British and American public attitudes towards science. The first question to ask is whether higher levels of interest and informedness are associated with more favourable attitudes towards science and technology. We invited respondents to agree or disagree with a number of statements. The questions and answers were as follows:

	% agreeing		% disagreeing	
	Britain	USA	Britain	USA
Even if it brings no immediate benefits, scientific research which advances the frontiers of knowledge should be supported by the government	93%	86%	7%	14%
Science and technology are making our lives healthier, easier, and more comfortable	84%	89%	16%	11%
Science makes our way of life change too fast	60%	37%	40%	63%
We depend too much on science and not enough on faith	56%	51%	44%	49%
Scientists should be allowed to do research that causes pain and injury to animals like dogs and chimpanzees if it produces new information about human health problems	40%	56%	60%	44%
More jobs will be created than lost as a result of computers and factory automation	40%	46%	60%	54%

Note. The response categories for these attitude questions were slightly different in the two surveys. The British survey had a category "neither agree nor disagree", and the American survey did not. So only respondents who expressed either agreement or disagreement are included in this table.

In general, attitudes on these items in both Britain and the USA are fairly positive. Americans, however, are generally more favourably disposed than the British towards science and science-based technologies such as computers and factory automation. And substantially more Americans than Britons *disagree* that science makes our way of life change too fast.

This pattern extends even to those areas in which moral and religious sensibilities are almost certainly involved. For example, opinion in both Britain and America is sharply divided on the use of animals in medical research; but whereas in Britain the balance of opinion is against current scientific practice, in the USA it is in favour. On the question of science *versus* faith, where attitudes are also divided, this pattern still holds – surprisingly, perhaps, in view of what we have learned so far about Americans' religious sensitivities.

The one exception to the general pattern is on government support for scientific research. There is indeed overwhelming support for government expenditure on basic science in *both* Britain and the USA but the other answers would have led us to expect that the level of public support in the USA would be even higher than in Britain. In fact, the reverse is true. The obvious explanation for this apparent anomaly is that Britons and Americans have different views on the *general* question of government expenditure. (This possibility has already been raised in Chapter 3 in the context of welfare provision.) To test this idea, we asked respondents to say whether they thought the government was spending too much, too little or about the right amount on a number of different goals. The results were as follows:

| | % saying that government spends | | | |
| | ... too little | | ... too much | |
	Britain	USA	Britain	USA
Health care	86%	68%	1%	3%
Helping older people	82%	75%	1%	3%
Education	80%	78%	2%	19%
Helping people on low incomes	74%	57%	8%	13%
Reducing pollution	71%	77%	2%	3%
Scientific research	53%	35%	8%	13%
Exploring space	13%	7%	48%	41%
Developing weapons for national defence	7%	10%	55%	55%

Notes. The items are listed not in the order in which they were presented to respondents but according to the proportion of Britons saying that there was too little spending on each item. The percentages are based on the total giving an opinion (i.e. excluding the 'don't knows').

Clearly, American and British respondents *do* have different views on the question of government expenditure. Not just in the field of scientific research, but also over a whole range of social welfare programmes, Americans are less supportive of government expenditure than their British counterparts. Only in the areas of reducing pollution and of defence expenditure are American respondents more in favour of increased government expenditure – and even here the differences are not great.

These results are more or less what we might have expected. After all, for most of the post-war period, the USA has been known as the home of the free market and of the light hand of government. In recent years, of course, Britain too has been adopting this posture; but our results suggest that public attitudes towards the role of government in the two countries remain distinct. Despite having a generally more positive attitude towards science, Americans are less inclined than their British counterparts to favour increased government spending on scientific research.

Conclusion

We have found that, compared with the British, American respondents are rather more interested in science, technology and medicine, and they regard themselves as being rather better informed about all these subjects. Americans also tend to see science as more relevant to their daily lives. Furthermore, our own assessment indicates that Americans are indeed a little more knowledgeable about science, and that they possess slightly more positive attitudes towards it. Consistently, the American respondents tend to be more attentive to, and appreciative of, science than their British counterparts. Conversely, we may say that the British respondents reveal higher levels of apathy and indifference towards science. On the basis of our results, it seems fair to say that in general the American public cares more about science than does the British public.

However, we must immediately enter three important qualifications. First, although Americans may care more about science, they are not always more knowledgeable than the British (consider, for example, the findings on risk factors for heart disease). Second, Americans are less willing than the British to accept scientific conclusions in religiously sensitive areas such as evolutionary theory. Third, despite professing to care more about science, Americans are actually less supportive than the British of increases in government expenditure in this field.

Finally, what bearing do these results have upon the wider public policy issues with which we began? Certainly, we have found evidence of considerable public interest in, and support for, science in both Britain and the USA. If our results reflect stable public intellectual orientations and attitudes then it seems that large majorities of the British and the American populations accept the importance of science, both as it affects personal life and as it contributes to the industrial and economic well-being of society. Indeed, the British and American scientific communities may well take comfort from the fact that public support for government expenditure on science, while not as great as for health and other social services, is certainly considerable.

Nevertheless, such comfort should be tempered with two *caveats*. First, public ignorance of some of the findings of science is very great; and second, public doubts about certain aspects of current scientific practice (such as the use of animals in medical research) are substantial. In both cases, the British public appears less in tune with scientific knowledge and practice than the American public. British policy-makers, industrialists and scientists will surely view with concern the relatively high levels of public ignorance of and apathy towards science in their own country. Such concern is appropriate, if only because uninformed interest and passive approval are, to say the least, an insubstantial foundation upon which to build continuing public support for the scientific enterprise.

Notes

1. For a recent attempt to compare results on two independently conducted surveys on the public understanding of science, see National Science Board (1987).
2. Spearman's r = .51 (Britain) and .38 (USA).
3. On the basis of these questions, we have constructed from the British survey data a battery of items that together constitute the Oxford Scientific Knowledge Scale. For more details of this scale, and of the associations between this and other variables, see Durant, J.R. *et al* (1989).

References

DURANT, J.R., (ed.), *Darwinism and Divinity: Essays on Evolution and Religious Belief,* Basil Blackwell, London (1985).

DURANT, J.R., EVANS, G.A and THOMAS, G.P., 'The public understanding of science' *Nature,* no. 340 (6 July 1989), pp. 11-14.

NATIONAL SCIENCE BOARD *Science and Engineering Indicators – 1987,* Washington, D.C. (1987), chapter 8.

ROYAL SOCIETY, *The Public Understanding of Science,* London (1985).

THOMAS, G.P. and DURANT, J.R., 'Why should we promote the public understanding of science?', in: Shortland, M. (ed.), *Scientific Literacy Papers,* Rewley House, Oxford (1987), pp. 1-14.

Acknowledgements

The British survey is a joint Oxford University Department for External Studies (OUDES)/Social and Community Planning Research (SCPR) project, funded by the Economic and Social Research Council (ESRC) under grant numbers A09250013 and A418254007. The American survey was funded by the National Science Foundation, under NSF grant number SRS8807409 and conducted by Jon Miller and his associates at Northern Illinois University. The authors wish to acknowledge the contributions of their co-researchers, Dr. Geoffrey Thomas (OUDES) and Patricia Prescott-Clarke (SCPR), as well as the advice and assistance of Don Buzzelli, Barry Hedges, Roger Jowell and Jon Miller.

7 Pride in one's country: Britain and West Germany

Richard Topf, Peter Mohler and Anthony Heath*

This year is the fortieth anniversary of West Germany's second republic. The Federal Republic is now widely regarded by many commentators not only as one of the leading economic forces in the Western world, but also as a model of stable liberal democracy. Yet celebrations in West Germany have been muted. Of all the citizens of the European Community countries, West Germans seem to be the most hesitant to express any sense of national pride. For instance, in a recent Eurobarometer survey, over half of the British respondents said that they were very proud to be British, compared with just one fifth of West Germans who said that they were very proud to be German.[1] Even more strikingly, among all European Community countries only in West Germany do over ten per cent of all respondents deny feeling *any* sense of national pride.

In West Germany, any overt expression of national pride in the political sphere is widely considered to be unacceptable – an understandable reaction to the nationalism of the Third Reich. The very strong response by all established West German politicians to the recent, limited successes of the far-right Republican Party in local and European Parliamentary elections bears testimony to this continuing sensitivity. Still, the marked contrast in levels of national pride between West Germany and the other European Community nations poses a challenge to well-established theories of how pluralist democracies work.

---

*Richard Topf is Senior Lecturer in Politics, City of London Polytechnic and Member of Nuffield College, Oxford; Peter Mohler is Executive Director of the Centre for Survey Methodology and Analysis (ZUMA) at Mannheim, Program Director of ALLBUS, the German General Social Survey, and teacher in sociology at the University of Frankfurt; Anthony Heath is Official Fellow at Nuffield College, Oxford.

National pride in liberal democracies

Most of those who study the workings of liberal democracies regard nationalism *per se* as an ideology of doubtful virtue associated, for example, with illiberal attitudes towards minority groups, if not with the extremes of Fascism and Nazism. Nonetheless, certain forms of national pride may perform important and beneficial functions within a liberal democracy. For instance, people's attachment to collective symbols of nationhood may serve to bind them together with a sense of shared identity, and hence help overcome internal divisions within society. The attachment of the British people to their monarchy, and of the Americans and French to the symbols of their respective Revolutions, are examples of this. National pride in *shared* national symbols may lead to a greater sense of integration and cohesion, and so may reduce the likelihood of internal division and strife (see Shils and Young, 1956; Birnbaum, 1955; Blumler *et al*, 1971; Lukes, 1977). For example, in the 1950s Shils and Young wrote:

> Over the past century, British society, despite distinctions of nationality and social status, has achieved a degree of moral unity equalled by no other large national state... The combination of constitutional monarchy and political democracy has itself played a part in the creation and maintenance of [this] moral consensus (pp.76–77)

Even stronger were Bagehot's remarks in the late nineteenth century:

> The English Monarchy strengthens our government with the strength of religion... It gives now a vast strength to the entire constitution, by enlisting on its behalf the credulous obedience of enormous masses.

More particularly it is argued that pride in the political institutions which buttress democracy, especially when combined with a sense of political efficacy encouraging the citizen to participate in the democratic system, may be an important factor in sustaining long-term political stability. Thus the absence of such pride may indicate a lack of attachment to the political system and a corresponding potential for political instability (see Almond and Verba, 1963).

Background evidence

One of the seminal studies of the relationship between levels of national pride and the functioning of democratic political systems is Almond and Verba's *The Civic Culture*. Their comparative survey of five countries, conducted in 1959 (just ten years after the creation of the German Federal Republic) found that, although West Germans did exhibit political awareness and skills, they almost completely lacked pride in their political system and institutions. As the table below shows, only seven per cent of West Germans named any aspect of their political institutions as their main source of national pride, and only one in 20 in the achievements of their developing welfare state. In contrast, just under half (45 per cent) of

British respondents said their first object of national pride was some aspect of the British political system.

	1959	
	Britain	West Germany
% naming each as first source of national pride:	%	%
political-legal system	45	7
welfare state	13	5
economic achievements	3	28
arts and culture	2	4
science and technology	3	3
other institutions/systems	30	42
nothing	4	6

Insofar as West Germans revealed pride in any specific aspect of their new nation-state, it was in their 'economic miracle', ranked first by just over a quarter of respondents (compared with just three per cent in Britain).

At that time then, these and other survey findings led the authors to conclude that, compared with Britain's political system, the future of stable liberal democracy in West Germany was still in doubt – as it turned out an unduly pessimistic prognosis. Indeed, some ten years ago Almond and Verba were themselves to endorse the view that West Germany had become one of the exemplary liberal democracies, whilst in Britain the democratic virtues had declined (see Almond and Verba, 1980; Heath and Topf, 1987; Jowell and Topf, 1988; Topf, 1989).

The present study

The results reported in this chapter are based on a new comparative survey of national pride in Britain and West Germany.* We were especially anxious to find out whether or not citizens' feelings of pride in their respective countries were, with the maturing of West German political culture, now more similar to each other than they were when Almond and Verba looked at this issue 30 years ago. We also wanted to discover whether such feelings of pride as did exist were evenly distributed throughout the respective societies, or whether there were particular groups within them which had little or no admiration for the main national symbols of their societies. Finally, we wanted to test whether there is an association between a sense of national pride in a political system and active citizenship within that system.

---

*The questions were asked in West Germany on the 1988 ALLBUS General Social Survey, a joint project of ZUMA at Mannheim and of the Central Archive for Empirical Social Research (ZA) at Cologne directed by Peter Ph Mohler and Michael Braun. In Britain they were asked on the 1987 SCPR/Oxford *British General Election* survey. Further details about both are given in Appendix I. The work was part-funded by the Anglo-German Foundation.

In their 1959 study, Almond and Verba asked their respondents to name, in their own words, the things about their respective countries of which they were most proud: the researchers then coded the responses. Whilst there is undoubted value in this approach (respondents are free to express themselves as they wish), it also creates problems particularly in cross-national and cross-cultural research. In particular, analysis of the responses depends very heavily upon the actual vocabulary used by respondents, upon how the researchers interpret the meaning of those responses, and then on the categories devised to code them. Thus in the Almond and Verba survey, the crucial category of pride in the 'political-legal system' was something of a 'catch-all': it embraced both specific political institutions, such as parliaments, as well as abstract qualities such as freedom, justice and democracy.

Rather than follow Almond and Verba's approach and face similar problems, we decided to offer our respondents an explicit choice of possible objects of pride which corresponded to the intentions underlying the original categories. The question was as follows (the German text is given at the end of this chapter[2]):

> Listed below are some things people have said make them proud of Britain/*Germany*. Please write '1' in the box next to the thing that makes you feel proudest of Britain/*Germany*. Then write a '2' in the box next to the thing that makes you feel next proudest of Britain/*Germany* and '3' next to the third thing:
>
> – British/*German* scientific achievements
> – The British Parliament/*German Bundestag*
> – British/*German* sporting achievements
> – The British monarchy/*German Basic Law*
> – British/*German* theatre and the arts
> – British/*German* economic achievements
> – The British/*German* health and welfare system
>
> OR TICK
>
> – None of these make me proud of Britain/*Germany*

So, instead of just the single category of 'political-legal system', our choices included the monarchy in Britain and the Basic Law *(Grundgesetz)* in West Germany, as well as the respective legislatures, namely Parliament and the *Bundestag.*

Few question the symbolic importance of the monarchy in Britain. Kavanagh (1985) reflects the views of most commentators when he writes that:

> Today the monarchy is the most prominent symbol in British public life and still stimulates popular emotions... Supporters of the monarchy as an institution are more likely than anti-monarchists to support the political system and comply with its basic laws. (p.51)

West Germany has no institution directly comparable to the British monarchy, which is not only an abstract symbol of legitimacy but at the same time an identifiable family about which 'personal' feelings may be held. However, the Basic Law is an unquestioned symbol of the Federal Republic, comparable to the United States Constitution. The *Grundgesetz,* ratified in May 1949, was drafted largely in response to the threat posed by the Berlin blockade and while the country was still occupied by the Allied forces. It was intended as a transitional arrangement which would cease to have effect once all the German people could decide on a constitution. Unlike the earlier Weimar Constitution, the Law begins with an extensive Bill of Rights which cannot be amended by the *Bundestag* or courts.

Under the Basic Law, it is the duty of responsible citizens not only to obey legitimate decisions of public officials, but also actively to oppose illegitimate acts of governments. Later articles, which also cannot be amended, provide for the Republic's federal structure and ensure a balance of power and of financial controls between the Federal government and the State governments (see Finer, 1979, for further details). So we considered it important to establish the extent to which this symbol had become established in the West German political culture. Unlike parliaments, of course, both monarchy and the Basic Law, very different though they are from each other, stand largely outside the sphere of national party politics.

Objects of national pride

The table below shows our respondents' first choices, and the results are striking. The Basic Law in West Germany and the monarchy in Britain now attract fairly similar levels of support as sources of national pride, with only seven percentage points separating them as first choices.

| | Britain | | West Germany | |
	1st choice %	All choosing	1st choice %	All choosing
% expressing national pride in:				
monarchy	37	65%	–	–
Basic Law	–	–	30	51%
scientific achievements	22	61%	8	38%
welfare state	16	52%	11	40%
Parliament	8	33%	1	10%
sporting achievements	5	29%	7	21%
artistic achievements	3	21%	6	21%
economic achievements	2	16%	17	51%
nothing	7	n/a	20	n/a

Notes. 'All choosing' = all ranking each item first, second or third. For the second and third choices, see **Figures 7.1** and **7.2**.

This is a significant change since 1959 when (taking first choices only) pride in all aspects of the political system in West Germany was only seven per cent compared with 45 per cent in Britain. (Even more similarity is apparent when we consider all three choices made by our respondents; 65 per cent of British respondents now give the monarchy as one of their

three choices, compared with 51 per cent of German respondents who give
the Basic Law as one of theirs.)

The evidence so far is that support for the respective political orders of
the two countries has converged over the last 30 years; levels of attachment
to the foremost political symbols in both Britain and West Germany are
now similar. We must, of course, be careful when comparing our 'forced-
choice' responses with those obtained by Almond and Verba's open-ended
question; nonetheless, it does appear that in West Germany pride in the
political order has increased to something much nearer the British level.

Figure 7.1   National pride in Britain 1987

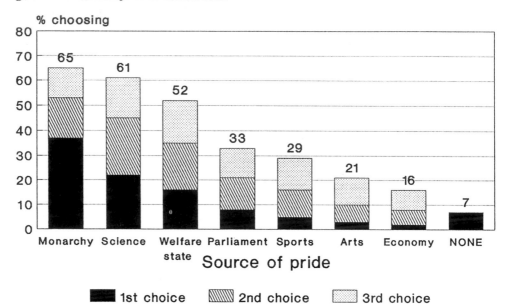

Figure 7.2   National pride in West Germany 1988

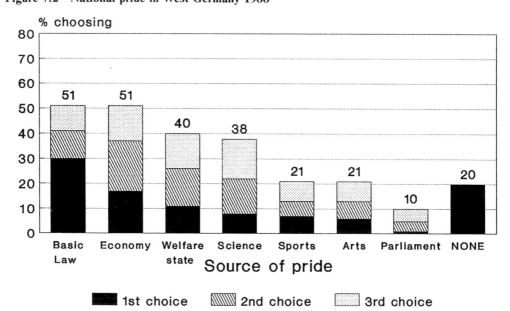

As well as the monarchy and Basic Law, we offered our respondents five further options. Three of these – the parliaments, economic achievements and welfare provision of each country – are all in some way linked to the political order. It has long been argued that Parliament is a potent symbol of democracy, especially for Britain where Bright once described England as 'the mother of Parliaments'.* As we have noted, economic achievments were the principal focus of German pride 30 years ago, while claims are now made by some that there has been an 'economic miracle' in Britain over the last decade. Finally, the welfare state is seen by many in both countries as one of the major political achievements of the postwar era.

From the preceding tables, we see that welfare achievements are indeed among the top three objects of pride in both countries, and the first choice of 16 per cent of Britons and 11 per cent of West Germans. Economic achievements now rank second in the Federal Republic (whereas in 1959 they were first), but at 17 per cent they are now well behind the Basic Law as first choice. In Britain, on the other hand, despite the rhetoric of politicians, a mere two per cent of respondents named economic achievements as the main focus of pride – almost exactly the same as in 1959.

Our data also show that in both countries few citizens name their Parliament as the first object of national pride. Only eight per cent of Britons gave it as their first choice, in a country where, as we have seen, around half the population claim to be very proud to be British. Might this be partly an indictment of the present workings of parliamentary democracy – even more so than the high levels of distrust in politicians reported in earlier volumes in this series?

However, the proportion in West Germany expressing pride in their parliament is even lower than in Britain: just one per cent of West Germans gave the *Bundestag* as their first choice. This may in part be a reflection of the scandals surrounding some national politicians in the Federal Republic at the time of our survey in mid-1988; but even so the low levels of pride expressed in the parliaments of both countries is clearly a finding which demands further investigation. Even if we consider all three choices made by our respondents, in Britain parliament remains in fourth place; and in West Germany the *Bundestag* clearly remains the least admired of the seven institutions asked about: only 10 per cent mentioned it at all, well below the proportions naming German arts, science and sport. It should also be noted that Britons rank scientific achievements second only to the monarchy as a source of pride (mentioned by 22 per cent compared to eight per cent of West Germans). It seems then that the British do feel proud of the nation's scientists (and, as Chapter 6 shows, over half feel that the government spends too little on scientific research).

One further, important finding emerges. We gave our respondents the option of saying, specifically, that they felt pride in *none* of the items we offered them. Whereas in Britain only seven per cent of respondents took this option, in West Germany 20 per cent of respondents said 'none', making it second only to the Basic Law. This puts the low ranking of the

---

*This phrase is often misquoted, most commonly as "Parliament, the mother of democracy".

Bundestag in an even more gloomy light: one in five of respondents preferred to say 'none', rather than profess pride in their *Bundestag* – or indeed in anything else.

Cultural homogeneity

Although West Germans are still conspicuously reluctant to express pride in being German, the relative ranking of the different symbols of national pride in Britain and West Germany appears far closer now than it was a generation ago. On the basis of this evidence alone, however, we cannot assume that both countries now enjoy similar levels of political cohesion. It could well be that the overall patterns mask significant differences *between* groups within the respective societies. Moreover, any such subgroup differences in feelings of national pride may have important implications for national integration and political stability. We therefore examined the data for socio-demographic variations. We focus on the first choices that our respondents made, but the distribution of total choices reveals much the same pattern.

British pride in the monarchy

The monarchy is of particular interest given its prominence as a source of national pride. However, attachment to the monarchy varies considerably between different social groups – more so than to other objects of national pride.

% in each group naming the monarchy first as source of national pride	Britain
Sex:	
men	29%
women	46%
Age:	
18–24	28%
25–44	32%
45–59	42%
60+	47%
Religion:	
Church of England	47%
Roman Catholic	30%
None	26%
Education:	
graduates	18%
with intermediate qualifications	37%
with no qualifications	42%

We can see that the monarchy appeals to a markedly higher proportion of women than of men, to the over-sixties more than to 18–24 year olds, and to those with intermediate or no educational qualifications more than to graduates.

There are also variations in attitudes towards the monarchy between people of different religions and social classes. Almost half (47 per cent) of Church of England members chose the monarchy as their first object of national pride, compared with 30 per cent of Roman Catholics, and a quarter of people without religious convictions. Analysis by respondents' social class produced a rather more complex picture, with the monarchy given as first choice by 44 per cent of routine non-manual workers, 31 per cent of the salariat, and 37 per cent of manual workers. These patterns are, of course, linked: for instance, both religion and class are strongly associated with age and education, and women are very strongly represented among routine non-manual workers.

Finally, we considered regional differences. Recently much attention has been paid in Britain to the question of the so-called North/South divide, and to ideas about the distinctiveness of the three British nations, the English, Scots, and Welsh (for example, Curtice 1988). The monarchy is, at least in recent history, largely an *English* monarchy and might be expected to raise more ambiguous feelings in Scotland and Wales. This is indeed what we found, as the table below shows. (**Table 7.1** gives full details.)

% in each region naming the monarchy first as source of national pride	Britain
Scotland	26%
Wales	28%
Greater London	32%
North/Yorkshire and Humberside	39%
Midlands	40%
East Anglia/South East	41%
South West	42%

Note. All regional analyses based on (comparatively) small subsamples are subject to larger than average sampling errors. Nonetheless, the difference between Scotland and Wales on the one hand, and the south of England on the other, is statistically significant.

West German pride in the Basic Law

In West Germany, pride in the Basic Law also revealed some of the largest differences between socio-demographic groups, but even so, they were consistently smaller than those in Britain in respect of the monarchy. The direction of the differences too was sometimes the opposite of that found in Britain. For example, the Basic Law found more favour among men than among women, and among the highly educated than among people with intermediate or low educational qualifications.

	West Germany
% in each group naming the Basic Law first as source of national pride	
Sex:	
men	33%
women	28%
Age:	
18–24	25%
25–44	31%
45–59	30%
60+	32%
Religion:	
Protestant	30%
Roman Catholic	30%
None	24%
Education:	
graduates	37%
with intermediate qualifications	31%
with low qualifications	28%

As in Britain in respect of the monarchy, however, the Basic Law was a greater source of national pride to the old than to the young, although the age differences in West Germany were much less sharp (see **Table 7.2**). The fact that some of these subgroup differences are in the reverse direction in the two countries almost certainly owes something to the nature of the two symbols. The more abstract nature of the Basic Law, for example, compared with the distinctly personal nature of the monarchy, may account for the greater support the former receives from graduates.

In West Germany regional differences have seldom surfaced as the sort of issue they represent in Britain. Nonetheless some aspects of West German political culture are occasionally explained in these terms. For instance, it has been argued recently that, should an extreme right-wing party with a nationalistic flavour become a potent force in the Republic, then Bavaria is a predictable place for it to emerge. It should be remembered that the Basic Law is a symbol of West German federalism, and the guarantee of an important degree of autonomy for the separate West German states, many of which were created for the first time by the Basic Law itself. Our data show that those living in the southern states of West Germany are noticeably less proud of the Basic Law than those living in the northern ones (again, see **Table 7.2**). However, the geographical differences are much smaller than those found in Britain in respect of the monarchy.[3]

British pride in Parliament

In both Britain and West Germany we found large differences between socio-demographic groups in the degree of pride they expressed in the monarchy and the Basic Law. There are differences too (but rather less striking ones) among subgroups in Britain in attitudes towards Parliament,* and they represent an important contrast with those found towards the monarchy. Pride in Parliament (as a first choice) was characteristic of men rather than women, of graduates rather than of people with intermediate or no educational qualifications, and of the salariat rather than of manual workers.

% in each group naming Parliament as first source of national pride	Britain
Sex:	
men	10%
women	6%
Education:	
graduates	14%
with intermediate qualifications	8%
with no qualifications	7%
Social class:	
salariat	13%
manual workers	5%

In demographic terms then, British pride in Parliament looks more like the West Germans' pride in their Basic Law than like British pride in the monarchy. Again this is unsurprising given the nature of the three institutions.

We then looked at the data in another way, comparing British respondents who placed Parliament *or* the monarchy first with West German respondents who placed the *Bundestag or* the Basic Law first. This reduces the differences between the two nations but does not eliminate them. Yet the most striking feature of this analysis is the high proportion of the young, the more highly educated and the non-religious in *both* countries who chose *neither* of these two symbols of the political order as their first source of national pride. In this respect, at least, the two countries are very similar. This raises the question of whether we are witnessing a 'life-cycle' effect or a 'generational' effect. Will younger Britons become more attached to institutions like the monarchy and Parliament as they grow older? Or will the present attitudes of this younger, more educated but less religious generation persist into middle age and beyond? If they do then we can expect British and West German patterns of national pride to converge further as the years pass.[4] For further evidence, see Commission of the European Communities (1982).

---

*So few West German respondents gave the *Bundestag* as their first choice that we did not undertake subgroup analysis.

Economic achievements and the welfare state

As we have seen, 30 years ago economic achievements were the ones of which West Germans were proudest; people of all ages concurred. Now, tellingly, we find that twice as many in the oldest age group are proud of their country's economic achievements as in the youngest (20 per cent of those aged 45 or over compared with just 10 per cent of 18–24 year olds nominate the economy as their first choice). No comparable age differences are apparent among the British sample (even when we take first, second and third choices into account). Full details are given in **Tables 7.1** and **7.2**. Here there is almost certainly a 'generational' difference among West Germans. The postwar German economic miracle clearly filled an emotional vacuum for those older Germans who had experienced the humiliation of the Third Reich. We also suspect that a 'greener' generation is growing up which is more sceptical of economic growth *per se*.

In Britain, pride in the postwar creation of the welfare state seems to be in some respects equivalent to German pride in the economy. As we have noted, 16 per cent of Britons gave the welfare state as their first choice, while 17 per cent of West Germans gave economic achievements as their first choice. And although there are not noticeable differences according to the respondent's age for *first* choice, a marked age-gradient emerges when we look at *all three* choices. While 57 per cent of the over-sixties in Britain named the welfare state as one of their three options, the equivalent figure for respondents aged under 25 years was only 35 per cent. Perhaps younger people are more inclined to be critical of current shortcomings in welfare provision than to be grateful that the welfare state exists at all.

Who lacks national pride?

If feelings of pride in a country's political symbols, social institutions and scientific and other achievements are indeed an indication of the health of a democratic state, then it follows that denial of pride in these symbols, institutions and achievements must be of concern. Moreover, when subgroups stand out as lacking pride in any of their country's symbols, institutions or achievements, they may well be, to an extent at least, disaffected or less well-integrated into the political order.

We found that, in both Britain and West Germany, age was the most powerful discriminator, with the youngest group (aged 18–24) being by far the most likely to say they were not proud of anything. In Britain 14 percentage points separated the youngest and oldest cohorts whilst in West Germany the difference was 10 percentage points. Lack of religious conviction (which is of course strongly associated with age) also counted in both countries; people without a religion were particularly likely to lack national pride (see **Tables 7.1** and **7.2**). Again we cannot tell whether we are witnessing a life-cycle or a generational effect. As is so often the case, it may well be both.

In both countries, disaffection is rather greater among the more marginal, less established groups (see also Burklin, 1985). The least well-educated, and the overlapping group of manual workers – those in both nations with the least power and resources – were more likely to say 'none'. But these differences are only small.

Attitudes to democracy

We have seen that, whilst the monarchy and the Basic Law were ranked first among objects of pride – and by a substantial margin – Parliament was ranked low in Britain and last in West Germany. Potentially this is a more ominous sign of disillusionment with the prevailing political order. As a check on the weight we should attach to this finding, we asked respondents in both countries how well or badly they thought their respective systems of democracy were working. As the table below shows, the results were almost identical in the two countries.

	Britain	West Germany
	%	%
System of democracy . . .		
. . . works well and needs no changes	15	18
. . . works well and needs some changes	66	64
. . . does not work well and needs a lot of changes	15	15
. . . does not work well and needs to be completely changed	4	2

Somewhat under a fifth of both populations believe that the system is working well and needs no changes, and almost the same proportion believes that a lot of changes are necessary. These findings seem to confirm that, in this respect at least, the political cultures of Britain and West Germany are converging.

As we have noted, comparatively few people in either country name their parliament as a particular object of national pride. Nonetheless, far more people in both countries believe that their democratic systems are working well. This suggests that the lack of esteem for parliament may be a specific reflection of the distrust and cynicism about national politicians (already noted by Jowell and Topf, 1988, as characteristic of the British), rather than of a wider rejection of the parliamentary system of government *per se*.

In both countries, hardly surprisingly, we found that people who took pride in none of the institutions or achievements we named were those most likely to be dissatisfied with the democratic system. But it was in Britain that the difference was most pronounced: 80 per cent of respondents overall thought that the democratic system worked well and needed little or no change, but this proportion almost halved (to 43 per cent) among people who felt no pride in the various symbols. In West Germany the fall was much less dramatic. Overall, 84 per cent of Germans thought their democratic system worked well, needing little or no change, as did 76 per cent of those who felt no pride in any of its symbols or institutions.

Different connotations of the phrase 'national pride' may well account for the difference between the two sets of results. As we have noted, expressions of national pride in Germany have been inextricably associated with the excesses of Nazism. The rather large and heterogeneous group who deny having any national pride probably does so for a wide variety of reasons – some renouncing it because of these negative historical connotations, others because of disaffection with the current social and political order. In Britain, on the other hand, these sorts of negative historical connotations are hardly present. We are dealing with an altogether smaller and more homogeneous group that stands out rather markedly in their disaffection with the democratic system. We shall look at this group in more detail in the future.

National pride and political participation

The thesis advanced by Almond and Verba and their contemporaries was that there is a strong association between one's pride in the political system and one's part in its democratic processes. In the longer term, they argued, the legitimacy and stability of the system itself depended upon such an association. An absence of pride in one's country's main political processes and institutions may well indicate a perceived inability to play a part in them, whether because people lack the necessary skills, or because the system itself puts obstacles in the way. Any system that fails to provide an outlet for at least a measure of citizen participation, it is argued, is vulnerable to undemocratic forms of action such as violent protest and eventually to instability.

Thirty years ago, following a long-standing liberal tradition, Almond and Verba (1963) concluded that the key to maintaining and strengthening exemplary democracies was, above all, education. They emphasised that in Britain, but not in West Germany, pride in political institutions was strongly associated with levels of educational attainment (see also Heath and Topf, 1986). They reported that in Britain three-quarters of graduates expressed pride in such institutions compared with well under half of respondents (41 per cent) with no educational qualifications. Moreover, as they put it:

> The educated classes possess the keys to political participation and involvement, while those with less education are less well-equipped. (p.381).

In *The 1987 Report,* we concluded that this remained true for Britain (Heath and Topf, 1987). But at that time we had no data on national pride, and no comparable data from another European democracy. This time we are able to examine the relationships between pride (or the absence of it) in political symbols, political participation and education. So we can now look at and draw comparisons between these relationships in both Britain and West Germany.

We focus here on only two measures of political participation: turning out to vote in national elections, which is the minimal form of participation in the democratic system, and taking part in a number of other political activities, ranging (in Britain) from helping election candidates to writing to MPs and signing petitions, and (in West Germany) from taking part in citizens' initiatives to joining protest groups. We constructed a single measure to combine these two sets of activities.

Our analysis shows complex but intriguing differences between the two countries. Britons who are politically active are *less* likely to be proud of the monarchy *and* less likely to be proud of nothing, than people who are politically passive, doing little more than voting. At least partly, this is likely to be related to the different views and levels of activism reported by Labour Party supporters (see **Table 7.1** for an analysis by party identification). Moreover, barely one in ten of politically active Britons express pride in their Parliament:

	Political participation in Britain	
	Politically inactive %	Politically very active %
% naming each first as source of national pride		
monarchy	36	28
welfare state	14	20
Parliament	5	11
economic achievements	–	2
others	29	33
none	15	6

In contrast, West Germans who are politically active are significantly *more* likely to be proud of the Basic Law than their politically inactive counterparts, but they are less than half as likely to be proud of their country's economic achievements.

	Political participation in West Germany	
	Politically inactive %	Politically very active %
% naming each first as source of national pride		
Basic Law	26	38
economic achievements	21	9
welfare state	12	11
Bundestag	1	1
others	18	21
none	22	21

If we take seriously the link between pride in a nation's political symbols and active citizenship, and regard them as parallel indicators of the health and stability of a democratic system, then it would appear that it is no longer West Germany's liberal democracy but Britain's which gives cause for concern.

Notes

1   The data in the following figure are taken from Eurobarometer 26, Dec. 1986:

National pride by EC country
1986 Eurobarometer

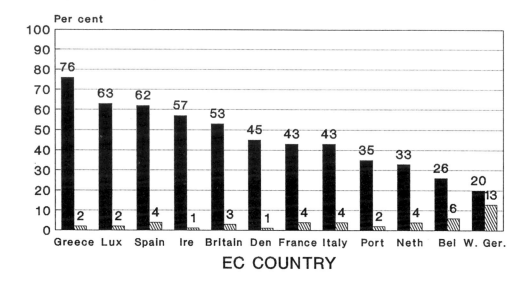

2.   The German text of the question on national pride is as follows:
    18   Auf diesen Kärtchen finden Sie eine Reihe von Dingen, auf die man als Deutscher stolz sein kann. Wählen Sie bitte diejenigen *drei* Dinge aus, auf die Sie am meisten stolz sind.

        – Das Grundgesetz
        – Der Bundestag
        – Die Leistungen der deutschen Sportler
        – Die wirtschaftlichen Erfolge
        – Die deutsche Kunst und Literatur
        – Die wissenschaftlichen Leistungen
        – Die sozialstaatlichen Leistungen

    18a   Auf was sind Sie am meisten stolz?

    18b
    18c   Und was kommt an zweiter und dritter Stelle?

3.   The relative size of the regional differences within the two countries is evident from the following map:

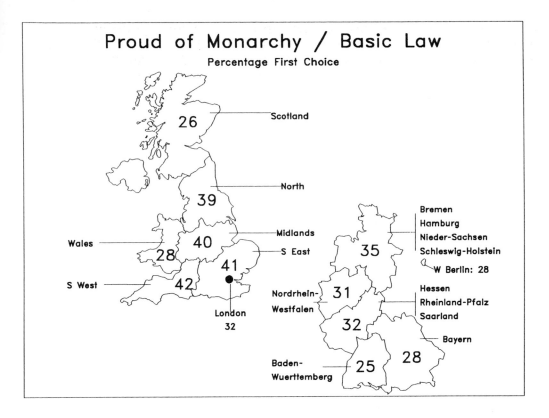

Proud of Monarchy / Basic Law
Percentage First Choice

4.   It should perhaps be noted that in a survey carried out in all the EC nations in 1987 (EC, 1988), the West Germans were found to be rather more satisfied with the way democracy worked in their country than were the British with the way it worked in theirs. Young people (aged under 25) and their elders held virtually identical views (p.36).

References

ALMOND, G.A. and VERBA, S., *The Civic Culture: Political Attitudes and Democracy in Five Nations,* Princeton University Press, Princeton (1963).

ALMOND, G.A. and VERBA, S. (eds), *The Civic Culture Revisited,* Little Brown, Boston (1980).

BIRNBAUM, N., 'Monarchs and Sociologists: A Reply to Professor Shils and Mr. Young', *Sociological Review,* no.1 (1955), pp.8–23.

BLUMLER, J.G., BROWN, J.R., EWBANK, A.J. and NOSSITER, T.J., 'Attitudes to the Monarchy: Their Structure and Development during a Ceremonial Occasion', *Political Studies,* vol.XIX (1971), pp.149–71.

BURKLIN, W., 'The German Greens: the post-industrial non-established and the party system', *International Political Science Review,* 6 (1985), pp.463–81.

COMMISSION OF THE EUROPEAN COMMUNITIES, *Young Europeans: an Explanatory Study of 15–24 Year Olds in EEC Countries,* EEC, Brussels (1982).

CURTICE, J., 'One Nation?' in Jowell, R., Witherspoon, S. and Brook, L., (eds), *British Social Attitudes: The 5th Report,* Gower, Aldershot (1988).

EC (European Community), *Young Europeans in 1987,* EC Brussels (1988).

FINER, S.E., *Five Constitutions,* Penguin Books, Harmondsworth (1979).

GIBBINS, J. (ed.), *Contemporary Political Culture: Politics in a Postmodern Age,* Sage, London (1989).

HEATH, A. and TOPF, R., 'Educational Expansion and Political Change in Britain: 1964–1983', *European Journal of Political Research,* no.14 (1986), pp.543–567.

HEATH, A. and TOPF, R., 'Political Culture' in Jowell, R., Witherspoon, S. and Brook, L. (eds), *British Social Attitudes: the 1987 Report,* Gower, Aldershot (1987).

JOWELL, R., and TOPF, R. 'Trust in the Establishment' in Jowell, R., Witherspoon, S. and Brook, L. (eds) *British Social Attitudes: the 5th Report,* Gower, Aldershot (1988).

KAVANAGH, D., *British Politics: Continuities and Change,* OUP, Oxford (1985).

LUKES, S.M., *Essays in Social Theory,* Macmillan, London (1977).

SHILS, E, and YOUNG, M., 'The Meaning of the Coronation', *The Sociological Review,* ns.1, no.2 (1956), pp.63–71.

TOPF, R., 'Political Change and Political Culture in Britain: 1959–87', in Gibbins, J. (ed.), *Contemporary Political Culture: Politics in a Postmodern Age,* Sage, London (1989).

Acknowledgements

This research was supported by a grant from the Anglo-German Foundation whose generous help we should like to acknowledge. The SCPR/Oxford *1987 General Election Survey* (on which the national pride questions were asked in Britain) was funded jointly by the Sainsbury Family Charitable Trusts, the ESRC (under Grant No E12 25 0001) and Pergamon Press which will publish the complete findings in 1990.

7.1 BRITISH PRIDE IN NATIONAL INSTITUTIONS AND ACHIEVEMENTS
by sex, age, compressed Goldthorpe class schema and education

FIRST SOURCE OF NATIONAL PRIDE	TOTAL	SEX		AGE				COMPRESSED GOLDTHORPE CLASS SCHEMA			EDUCATION		
		Men	Women	18-24	25-44	45-59	60+	Salariat	Non-manual	Manual	Degree	Intermediate	None
	%	%	%	%	%	%	%	%	%	%	%	%	%
Monarchy	37	29	46	28	32	42	47	31	44	37	18	37	42
Scientific achievements	22	26	18	16	24	22	21	28	19	21	28	23	19
Health and welfare system	16	17	14	13	19	15	13	14	15	18	19	15	16
Parliament	8	10	6	5	7	10	9	13	7	5	14	8	7
Sporting achievements	5	7	3	13	6	3	2	4	3	8	4	5	5
Theatre and the arts	3	2	4	6	3	2	1	4	3	1	10	3	1
Economic achievements	2	3	2	1	2	2	3	2	2	2	2	2	2
Nothing	7	7	8	18	8	5	4	5	6	10	6	7	8
BASE: *Unweighted*	3266	1590	1676	420	1248	746	830	815	1159	1144	280	1722	1257

7.1 (continued) BRITISH PRIDE IN NATIONAL INSTITUTIONS AND ACHIEVEMENTS by religion, region and party identification

FIRST SOURCE OF NATIONAL PRIDE	TOTAL	RELIGION				REGION							PARTY IDENTIFICATION		
		Church of England	Roman Catholic	Other	No religion	Scotland	North	Midlands	Wales	South West	South East	Greater London	Conservative	Alliance	Labour
	%	%	%	%	%	%	%	%	%	%	%	%	%	%	%
Monarchy	37	47	30	40	26	26	39	40	28	42	41	32	47	34	28
Scientific achievements	22	21	8	22	25	21	21	22	22	24	22	21	21	28	19
Health and welfare system	16	10	11	17	20	28	15	15	22	13	13	14	9	17	25
Parliament	8	8	2	8	6	4	7	8	10	7	8	12	11	8	4
Sporting achievements	5	4	7	4	6	6	6	5	3	4	5	3	3	5	7
Theatre and the arts	3	2	6	3	4	2	2	2	2	2	3	6	2	4	3
Economic achievements	2	3	17	2	2	3	2	3	1	4	3	1	5	1	1
Nothing	7	5	20	5	11	9	8	5	11	5	6	11	2	5	13
BASE: Unweighted	3266	1369	313	491	1038	299	860	565	179	300	741	322	1217	681	837

7.2 WEST GERMAN PRIDE IN NATIONAL INSTITUTIONS AND ACHIEVEMENTS
by sex, age, compressed Goldthorpe class schema and education

	TOTAL	SEX		AGE				COMPRESSED GOLDTHORPE CLASS SCHEMA			EDUCATION		
		Men	Women	18-24	25-44	45-59	60+	Salariat	Non-manual	Manual	Degree	Intermediate	Low
	%	%	%	%	%	%	%	%	%	%	%	%	%
FIRST SOURCE OF NATIONAL PRIDE													
Basic Law	30	33	28	25	31	30	32	38	28	27	37	31	28
Economic achievements	17	19	15	10	16	20	21	15	20	15	13	16	19
Health and welfare system	11	10	12	9	11	10	11	10	11	12	8	11	11
Scientific achievements	8	8	7	12	7	8	7	10	7	9	12	9	7
Sporting achievements	7	7	7	6	6	7	6	3	9	10	1	6	9
Theatre and the arts	7	7	8	9	7	4	6	8	5	4	11	9	4
Bundestag	1	1	1	1	1	2	2	1	1	3	2	1	2
Nothing	20	17	23	26	21	19	16	16	20	20	19	19	21
BASE:	*3018*	*1343*	*1675*	*437*	*1104*	*680*	*797*	*648*	*1148*	*269*	*200*	*1212*	*1605*

7.2 (continued) WEST GERMAN PRIDE IN NATIONAL INSTITUTIONS AND ACHIEVEMENTS by religion, region and party identification

FIRST SOURCE OF NATIONAL PRIDE	TOTAL	RELIGION				REGION*								PARTY IDENTIFICATION			
		Prot-estant	Roman Catholic	Other religion	No religion	Baden Württem-berg	Bayern (Bavaria)	Berlin	Hessen	Nordrhein-Westfalen	Neider-Sachsen	Rheinland-Pfalz	Schleswig-Holstein	CDU/CSU	SDP	FDP	Grünen (Greens)
	%	%	%	%	%	%	%	%	%	%	%	%	%	%	%	%	%
Basic Law	30	30	30	23	24	25	28	28	28	31	32	35	43	31	33	42	30
Economic achievements	17	19	17	13	13	23	16	11	15	17	14	13	23	24	17	17	7
Health & welfare system	11	11	11	8	7	14	14	5	9	10	9	4	11	11	11	9	10
Scientific achievements	8	7	8	8	9	9	7	6	5	8	12	8	5	5	8	11	7
Sporting achievements	7	8	7	8	6	6	6	9	8	6	11	10	2	6	8	6	3
Theatre and the arts	7	6	6	9	8	4	6	13	11	6	5	6	4	5	5	6	13
Bundestag	1	1	2	-	1	1	1	2	2	1	1	2	1	2	1	1	2
Nothing	20	19	20	23	24	20	24	26	23	20	17	22	11	16	17	8	28
BASE:	3018	1865	1375	102	231	449	547	134	242	839	337	165	134	791	841	161	206

* Bremen, Hamburg and Saarland have been omitted since the subsample bases of each of these regions is small

8 Interim report: The changing family

Stephen Harding*

A spate of recent statistics comparing family life in Britain with that in other countries has set alarm bells ringing. Divorce rates in Britain, where a third of marriages are likely to end in the courts, are the highest in the European Community, though still some way behind those in the USA. At one in fourteen, Britain is joint first in the EC for one-parent families, and third for the number of children born outside marriage (Family Policy Studies Centre, 1989). To some social commentators, such developments sound the death knell for the family. "The British social fabric will collapse inside two generations" warned Richard Whitfield, Chairman of the National Campaign for the Family (Grice, 1989). Others, less gloomily, consider that marriage and the family are passing through a period of profound change: roles are no longer 'culturally prescribed' but rather 'negotiated', with people increasingly making up their own rules for living together (Hannan, 1977; Rapaport *et al*, 1977).

We felt it would be useful to broaden the scope of this debate. Are the trends that we see in Britain really that different from those taking place elsewhere? If they are similar, are there social and cultural factors at work which might impede or accelerate the rate of change? A series of questions asked in 1988 as part of the International Social Survey Programme enables us to start looking for answers. So far we have results from four very contrasting countries: West Germany, Hungary, the Republic of Ireland and the USA. This interim report will be amplified in due course as information from other countries, including Britain, becomes available.[1] (We have some directly comparable data for Britain from earlier *British Social Attitudes* surveys and these have been included and discussed where appropriate.)

---

*Associate Director of ISR International Survey Research Ltd.

First we consider attitudes towards women in employment, and the perceived consequences for family life. Next we look at attitudes towards family size and child-rearing, and finally at attitudes towards divorce.

Women at work and at home

It is only recently that large numbers of women, particularly those with young children, have taken on paid work outside the home. (Of course in earlier times, many women worked on homesteads and farms.) The proportion of economically active women in the total working population has risen sharply in the past two decades, and now stands at about 30 per cent in the Republic of Ireland, about 40 per cent in West Germany and the USA and about 50 per cent in Hungary (Jallinoja, 1989). In Britain, the increase was particularly marked during the 1970s, but continues to grow: in 1986, two-thirds of all women of working age (and just over half of women with dependent children) were in paid employment or looking for work (CSO, 1989).

To a large extent, these changes have come about because greater numbers of women, either through choice or necessity, return to work after having had children – often to low paid, part-time jobs. However, our survey results show that the picture for mothers of young children is still very different across the four countries. All the women who were interviewed were asked, first, if they had gone out to work when any of their children were under school age and, second, if they had done so when any of their children were at school.

	USA	West Germany	Hungary	Republic of Ireland
% of women in work when child was under school age				
with full-time job	22%	44%	48%	14%
with part-time job	21%	11%	4%	12%
% of women in work when child was at school				
with full-time job	33%	40%	58%	11%
with part-time job	22%	11%	2%	16%

So it is quite common in Hungary and West Germany for mothers of even quite young children to have full-time jobs, but less usual in the USA (where part-time working is relatively more common) and rarer still in the Republic of Ireland.* Indeed few Irish women even with school-age children have taken on paid work of any sort outside the home. At the other extreme, well over half of Hungarian women have had full-time jobs while a child of theirs was still at school.

---

*We do not have British data for this question but we know from other sources that for mothers of pre-school and school-age children to have full-time or (especially) part-time jobs is common in the UK too (OPCS, 1989).

Clearly, the trend for a growing number of married women to seek paid work has ramifications for family life and, in particular, for the woman's role within the family. Our data reveal considerable ambivalence as to whether it is a good thing or not. Few people disapprove in principle of a woman going out to work: majorities (usually very substantial majorities) in each country acknowledge that there are advantages from her point of view. Respondents were asked to agree or disagree with the proposition:

Having a job is the best way for a woman to be an independent person

	Britain	USA	West Germany	Hungary	Republic of Ireland
	%	%	%	%	%
Strongly agree/agree	60	43	65	54	58
Neither agree nor disagree	25	23	16	16	12
Disagree/strongly disagree	15	31	14	28	29

Note. We can include data for Britain here since this question was asked in 1987.

West Germans and Britons are especially keen on the idea; Americans are, however, markedly more ambivalent. At present, we can only speculate as to how far people in different sub-groups within the different countries vary in their attitudes. We do know from earlier *British Social Attitudes* surveys, and from other sources, that the views of British women – especially women of working age – are less 'traditional' than those of the population as a whole (Witherspoon, 1988, p.190). It would be surprising if differences such as these were not found in all the countries under examination here.

However, when respondents were asked to take family commitments into account, their enthusiasm for women working outside the home rapidly diminishes. About two-thirds of respondents in all four countries would agree that a working mother can establish as close a relationship with her children as one who does not go out to work, but many more are concerned about the effect of the mother's job on very young children in the family. The statement put to respondents was deliberately stark:

A pre-school child is likely to suffer if his or her mother works

Even so, it was endorsed by a majority in three of the four countries. Again, it was only among Americans that opinion was more or less evenly divided:

	USA	West Germany	Hungary	Republic of Ireland
	%	%	%	%
Strongly agree/agree	43	69	70	51
Neither agree nor disagree	13	11	11	9
Disagree/strongly disagree	44	15	18	39

West Germans and Hungarians especially are opposed to mothers of young children going out to work, though we should remember that large numbers of women in those two countries do in fact have full-time jobs. (In Hungary, some mothers do take long maternity leave, available until the child is three years old; see Sas, 1981).

As for Britain, data from an earlier *British Social Attitudes* survey reveal a similarly widespread disapproval of mothers with young children working outside the home (Ashford, 1987). Among four options, 76 per cent of respondents preferred a 'traditional' work arrangement (father working full-time and mother at home) in households with children under five years old. If the children were in their early teens, however, traditional arrangements received far less support (19 per cent), and a 'compromise' arrangement (father working full-time, mother working part-time) emerged as the preferred option (favoured by three in five respondents).

A similar pattern emerges in responses to this proposition:

All in all, family life suffers when the woman has a full-time job.

	USA	West Germany	Hungary	Republic of Ireland
	%	%	%	%
Strongly agree/agree	35	57	62	53
Neither agree nor disagree	15	14	13	9
Disagree/strongly disagree	49	25	24	37

Attitudes of Americans seem the most 'progressive', in the sense of actually endorsing the longstanding trend there towards the integration of women into the labour force.* Hungarians, in contrast, appear at first glance to be the most 'traditional'; nine in every ten also accept the view that "being a housewife is just as fulfilling as working for pay", compared with 64 per cent of the Irish, 52 per cent of Americans and 46 per cent of West Germans. However, the strength of feeling among Hungarians is unlikely to have much to do with nostalgic stereotypes of the woman at home. A much more probable explanation is that, out of economic necessity, large numbers of Hungarian women – even with pre-school children – are obliged to work full-time, whereas American women, say, feel that they have much more choice as to whether they work or not. As we have already seen, Hungarians are also most likely to express concern at the consequences for family life of a woman's heavy work commitment outside the home.

The economic strains that the need to work can impose on family life may also help explain the cross-national differences in response to the following statement (here we can add in data for Britain since precisely the same question was asked on the 1987 *British Social Attitudes* survey).

---

*The available data suggest that on this issue the British are much less 'progressive' than Americans. In 1987 we asked if "a woman and her family will all be happier if she goes out to work". Only 14 per cent agreed; nearly half (46 per cent) disagreed.

A job is all right, but what most women really want is a home and children

	Britain	USA	West Germany	Hungary	Republic of Ireland
	%	%	%	%	%
Strongly agree/agree	36	33	38	76	56
Neither agree nor disagree	22	26	19	12	13
Disagree/strongly disagree	42	38	33	12	30

In *The 5th Report,* we noted "just how divided [British] respondents are about the appropriate role for women, and about how to balance women's rights with family responsibilities" (Witherspoon, 1988, p.190). The same, it appears, is true of American and West German respondents. In the Republic of Ireland, where family roles are still comparatively 'traditional', a surprisingly large minority questions the orthodox view of a woman's proper place. From responses like these, and to other similar questions, it seems that the Hungarians alone show a distinct preference for the 'traditional' pattern of work arrangements, although except during maternity leave they are the farthest from being able to achieve it. This again suggests that many Hungarian women feel compelled to go out to work just to make ends meet.

The economic reality of *having* to go out to work is also well illustrated by the responses to the next question. We asked whether

Both the husband and the wife should contribute to the household income

	USA	West Germany	Hungary	Republic of Ireland
	%	%	%	%
Strongly agree/agree	49	47	84	64
Neither agree nor disagree	30	21	8	14
Disagree/strongly disagree	19	26	7	20

Quite evidently, those living in the two more affluent countries are much less likely to regard a dual income as a necessity. The Irish, on the other hand, would appear to have less choice in the matter, and the Hungarians very little indeed. But here again we see something of a paradox. Only a small minority of respondents in any of the four nations strongly disapproved of the notion that both partners in a marriage should make a financial contribution towards running the family home. Yet, as we have seen in answers to other questions, there is (except in the USA) fairly strong resistance to the idea that a woman should actually go out and earn money when there are young children in the home – precisely the time when the need for extra income is likely to be growing.

itself. A 'modern' or secularised view of the family and personal relationships would put particular emphasis on *individual* choice – including the choice not to have children. On this model, parents who do choose to have children place emphasis on the personal pleasure they take in the relationship with them. Simons and Heald (1987) contrast this with an alternative view, described by them as 'fundamentalist', which suggests that a country's social norms in respect of family life and the importance of childrearing derive from religiously-inspired prescriptions (see also Simons, 1989). According to this model, reproductive behaviour is

> governed by truths which transcend purposes and circumstances of individuals... The rule governing minimum family size is whatever is implicit in the family sizes of recent generations. (p.3)

To test their 'fundamentalist' hypothesis, Simons and Heald used data from an international survey mounted in 1981 by the European Values Systems Study Group (EVSSG) (Harding and Phillips, 1986). Respondents in twelve Western European countries were asked whether they agreed or disagreed that "It is parents' duty to do their best for their children, even at the expense of their own well being". Responses were highly correlated with the fertility rate in each country, leading Simons and Heald to conclude that a low fertility rate is "due to an absence of the fundamentalism expressed in familist sentiments" – that is to greater 'individualism' – in those countries. With this in mind, they predicted that:

> the change in values that would herald a persistent fertility decline would probably be detectable in values data long before it could be reliably inferred from fertility statistics. (p.7)

Responses to a question on parenthood asked in the 1988 ISSP survey enable us to test the 'fundamentalist' hypothesis further. Whereas the EVSSG question asked about parental duty, the ISSP item expresses the opposite sentiment. Respondents were asked whether they agreed or disagreed that "having children interferes too much with the freedom of parents". Responses are revealing.

	USA	West Germany	Hungary	Republic of Ireland
	%	%	%	%
Strongly agree/agree	11	32	28	8
Neither agree nor disagree	13	19	18	7
Disagree/strongly disagree	74	44	52	84

That one third of West Germans regard children as interfering too much with adult lives is striking testimony to the evident decline in familist sentiment, reflected in concrete form in the rapidly diminishing young population of West Germany. Figures from Hungary suggest that a similarly individualistic or pragmatic orientation is common there too.

Attitudes of American respondents may at first glance make us pause: after all, more Americans than West Germans, Hungarians or Irish said that it was desirable to have no children at all. But we should remember the traditionalism that characterises mainstream American values, especially in the spheres of family and religion (Rokeach, 1974; Greeley, 1972). Clearly not all social groups share these values to the same extent – young professionals, for instance, do not – but there is little evidence in the USA of the widespread rejection of religiously-based prescriptions about family life – a rejection which is characteristic of more secularised European nations such as West Germany and Hungary.

That an overwhelming majority of the Irish reject the proposition comes as no surprise. After all, the Republic is still very much a nation of practising Catholics, and the Roman Catholic Church is 'fundamentalist' in its teachings on marriage and the family, periodically reaffirming its stance by opposing efforts to liberalise laws on contraception, abortion and divorce.

Attitudes towards children and childrearing involve making choices among available alternatives. In making decisions about family size, in common with many other decisions, people have to weigh benefits against costs. Individual governments are able – through fiscal and other policies – to provide help with the responsibilities and financial burdens of family building and childrearing, and so increase the attractiveness of that sort of lifestyle – particularly for women. If they fail (through commission or omission) then the costs – in direct financial terms, and indirectly in terms of perceived loss of freedom – make it increasingly likely that predictions like those of Jacques Chirac will turn out to be true.

Divorce

The divorce rate in European Community countries increased four-fold between 1960 and 1985 (Eurostat, 1987) and shows every sign of rising still further. The one exception to the trend is the Republic of Ireland where divorce remains illegal (in other 'traditionally Catholic' countries, like Italy and Spain, public demand recently led to its legalisation).[2] Divorce rates are also high in Hungary, where some 40 per cent of marriages end in the courts (Clare, 1986). However, even these figures pale into insignificance beside those for the USA where it is now estimated that two-thirds of new marriages will end in divorce (Norton and Moorman, 1987). Twenty-six per cent of American respondents to our survey said that they had been divorced (the equivalent figure for West Germany and Hungary being eight per cent and for the Republic of Ireland only one per cent).

The question of interest to us, however, is what people feel about the *availability* of divorce. We asked first:

> *In general, would you say that the law now makes it easy or difficult for people who want to get divorced?*

Legislation in the four countries varies considerably and this is reflected in responses.

	USA	West Germany	Hungary	Republic of Ireland
	%	%	%	%
Very/fairly easy	73	29	51	7
Neither easy nor difficult	14	22	25	1
Fairly/very difficult	9	24	19	49
Impossible*	n/a	1	1	41
Can't choose	3	25	4	2

Note. * This answer category was not printed on the questionnaire, but was volunteered by some respondents.

A large majority of Americans considered divorce to be easily obtainable, as did a majority of Hungarians. In both countries, court proceedings are well organised, and divorce is relatively quickly obtained. In West Germany, divorce proceedings are protracted and expensive, and are particularly difficult in its predominantly Catholic states. In the Republic of Ireland divorce remains illegal, so presumably respondents not answering 'impossible' are referring to divorces obtained abroad.

In two follow-up questions, we asked respondents to state how easy or difficult it *should* be to get a divorce. The first question concerned couples without young children.

In general, how easy or difficult do you think the law should make it for couples without young children to get a divorce?

	USA	West Germany	Hungary	Republic of Ireland
	%	%	%	%
Very/fairly easy	38	31	61	41
Neither easy nor difficult	30	36	28	7
Fairly/very difficult	26	15	9	42
Impossible	n/a	1	1	7
Can't choose	6	17	2	3

What clearly emerges is that, unlike the Hungarians and the Irish who think that divorce ought to be easier to obtain than they claimed it actually was, many Americans believe that the quick and easy divorce proceedings there have gone too far. Only nine per cent felt that divorce *was* difficult to obtain, whereas over a quarter felt that it *ought* to be difficult, even for couples without young children.

Three in five Hungarians favour easy divorce, the highest figure by far. West Germans appear to favour a slight liberalisation of divorce law, but a relatively high percentage stated that they couldn't choose between the alternatives offered. But it is respondents from the Republic of Ireland who clearly seek the most sweeping change in policy: only a very small minority (seven per cent) said that it should be impossible to get a divorce, which is the current position. Indeed, around 40 per cent believe that divorce for couples without young children should be easy. Although a similar percentage believe that it should be difficult, our figures reveal a considerable gulf between public attitudes on the one hand, and public policy and the stance of the Roman Catholic Church on the other.

Attitudes were markedly different when we asked about couples with young children. Less than a fifth of respondents in any of the four countries consider that in these circumstances, divorce should be easy:

And what about couples with young children? How easy should the law make it for them to get a divorce?

	USA %	West Germany %	Hungary %	Republic of Ireland %
Very/fairly easy	14	13	14	17
Neither easy nor difficult	31	33	27	8
Fairly/very difficult	50	37	49	60
Impossible	n/a	3	6	12
Can't choose	6	15	3	3

It appears that respondents in all four countries would like to see the law discriminate between couples with and without young children, the Hungarians and Irish being especially keen that a distinction be made in order to keep couples with young families together. But barely more than one in ten respondents in the Republic of Ireland favour retaining a law that makes divorce even in these circumstances impossible to obtain. By contrast, Americans and Hungarians perceive the divorce laws as having become much too liberal, at least where young children are concerned.

We have no directly comparable figures for Britain yet, but would be surprised if the attitudes of the British differ much from those expressed by citizens of other European countries. In 1987, almost four times as many *British Social Attitudes* respondents thought that divorce should be more difficult to obtain as thought it should be easier; half opted for the *status quo*. These figures, unsurprisingly, conceal sharp subgroup differences (see Ashford, 1987) which are no doubt paralleled in the other ISSP countries, and we hope to discuss these in a future volume in this series of reports.

Conclusions

Alongside ever-increasing divorce rates in most Western countries, marriage (and remarriage) is more popular than ever. In Britain for instance, in 1911 just over half of women aged between 19 and 40 were married. By 1961, the figure was 80 per cent, and today it is estimated that less than eight per cent of women will remain unmarried during their lifetime (Clare, 1986). However, the nature of the marriage relationship has undergone changes: divorce and remarriage are far more common, acknowledging in effect that the institution remains intact even though the specific partnerships involved may not. The desire to have large families is waning rapidly, and the decision to have children at all appears to be increasingly dependent on the calculation (implicit or explicit) or the potential advantages and disadvantages. For an apparently increasing number of people, the sacrifices are outweighing the rewards. It has been argued that such trends form part of a broader movement away from culturally prescribed to negotiated roles, a change taking place not just in Britain but in developed nations everywhere. The extent to which such an evolution has occurred in any country clearly depends on cultural, economic and social factors prevailing there. For instance, paid work for Hungarian women is only partly a matter for personal choice; similarly, religious beliefs and restrictive laws continue to have a restraining effect on the nature of relationships among the Irish. Nonetheless, these trends towards 'negotiated' arrangements seem inexorable. But inevitably new constraints will take the place of old ones. Couples and families are bound to come under increasing strain as they seek to reconcile traditional prescriptions with individual preferences.

Notes

1. This chapter was written before data for the four countries discussed had been archived at Cologne. Only marginals were available at the time. We are grateful to Tom W.Smith for compiling them and making them available to us so that we could incorporate them into this Report. Technical details of the four ISSP surveys on which this chapter is based will be found in Appendix I.
2. The divorce rates per 1,000 existing marriages in EC countries in 1981 and 1986 are as follows:

	1981	1986
United Kingdom	11.9	12.9
Denmark	12.1	12.8
Netherlands	8.3	8.7
France	6.8	8.5
West Germany	7.2	8.3
Luxembourg	5.9	7.5*
Belgium	6.1	7.3
Greece	2.5	3.0*
Italy	0.9	1.0
Republic of Ireland	0.0	0.0

Rates for Portugal and Spain are not available. * = 1985 figures.
Source: *Social Trends 19*, HMSO, London (1989), Table 2.20.

References

ASHFORD, S., 'Family Matters', in Jowell, R., Witherspoon, S. and Brook, L. (eds), *British Social Attitudes: the 1987 Report*, Gower, Aldershot (1987).
CSO (Central Statistical Office), *Social Trends 19*, HMSO, London (1989).
CLARE, A., *Lovelaw: Love, Sex and Marriage around the World*, BBC Publications, London (1986).
EUROSTAT, *Demographic Statistics 1987*, Statistical Office of the European Communities, Luxembourg (1987).
FAMILY POLICY STUDIES CENTRE, *Bulletin No 7*, London (June 1989).

FOGARTY, M.P., RYAN, L, and LEE, J., *Irish Values and Attitudes,* Dominican Publications, Dublin (1984).

GREELEY, A., *Unsecular Man: the Persistence of Religion,* Schocken Books, New York (1972).

GRICE, E., 'Why divorce spells problems for Britain', *Sunday Times* (18 June, 1989).

HANNAN, D., *Traditional Families?,* Economic and Social Research Institute, Dublin (1977).

HARDING, S. and PHILLIPS, D. (with FOGARTY, M.), *Contrasting Values in Western Europe,* Macmillan, London (1986).

JALLINOJA, R., 'Women between Family and Employment', in Boh, K., Bak, M., Clason, C., Pankratova, M., Qvortrup, J., Sgritta, G.B. and Waerness, K. (eds), *Changing Patterns of European Family Life: A Comparative Analysis of 14 European Countries,* Routledge, London (1989).

NORTON, A.J. and MOORMAN, J.E., 'Current trends in marriage and divorce among American women', *Journal of Marriage and the Family,* no.49 (1987), pp.3–14.

OPCS, (Office of Population Censuses and Surveys), *General Household Survey 1986,* HMSO, London (1989).

RAPOPORT, R. N., FOGARTY, M.P. and RAPOPORT, R. (eds), *Families in Britain,* Routledge and Kegan Paul, London (1982).

REISS, I.L. and LEE, G.R., *Family Systems in America 4th edition,* Holt, Reinhart and Winston, New York (1988).

ROKEACH, M., 'Change and stability in American value systems', *Public Opinion Quarterly,* vol. 38 no. 2 (1974), pp.222–238.

SAPORITI, A., 'Historical changes in the family's reproductive patterns', in Boh, K. *et al* (eds), *Changing Patterns of European Family Life: A Comparative Analysis of 14 European Countries,* Routledge, London (1989).

SAS, J., 'Certain characteristic features of socio-economic development in Hungary', Vienna Centre Background Paper, Vienna (1981).

SIMONS, J., 'Reproductive behaviour or religious practice', in Hohn, C. and Mackensen, R. (eds), *Determinants of Fertility Trend Theories Reexamined,* Ordin, Liège (1989).

SIMONS, J. and HEALD, G., 'Cultural values and fertility', paper presented at EVSSG conference, Oxford (20–22 March, 1987).

WITHERSPOON, S., 'Interim Report: A Woman's Work', in Jowell, R., Witherspoon, S. and Brook, L. (eds), *British Social Attitudes: the 5th Report,* Gower, Aldershot (1988).

Appendix I
Technical details of the surveys

This Appendix describes in brief the various surveys on which the data presented in this Report are based. Fuller details about the 1985, 1986 and 1987 *British Social Attitudes* (BSA) surveys will be found in Appendix I of *The 1986 Report, The 1987 Report,* and *The 5th Report* in this series. Further information about the annual national surveys conducted by the other eight countries participating in the International Social Survey Programme (ISSP) between 1985 and 1988 may be obtained from the respective organisations that mount them, or from the West German *ZentralArchiv* at the University of Cologne (names and addresses are given below); the details provided in this Appendix are derived from the ISSP Codebooks published by the *ZentralArchiv.** Brief technical information is also provided about the Public Understanding of Science survey, carried out jointly by SCPR and the Oxford University Department for External Studies, and about the American survey on which the same questions were asked (see Chapter 6); and about the SCPR/Oxford *1987 British General Election* cross-sectional survey, which included questions on national pride (see Chapter 7).

ISSP surveys

Britain: British Social Attitudes survey series

This annual survey series is now in its seventh year. It is designed and carried out by SCPR, core-funded by the Sainsbury Family Charitable Trusts and financially supported by additional contributions from

---

*1985: Ref. ZA-No.1490; 1986: Ref. ZA-No.1620; 1987: Ref. ZA-No.1680.

government departments, other research bodies and foundations, quasi-government organisations and industry. Data are collected by personal interview, and on a follow-up self-completion questionnaire (on which the ISSP questions are asked).

Each survey is designed to yield a representative sample of adults aged 18 and over living in private households in Britain (south of the Caledonian Canal in Scotland). The sampling frame used is the electoral register, and the sampling method involves a multi-stage design, with four separate stages of selection:

- *parliamentary constituencies* (114 in 1985; 151 in 1986 and 1987), stratified by Standard Region, population density and percentage owner-occupation, and selected systematically with probability proportionate to size of electorate

- *polling districts* (p.d.)

- *addresses* (22 per p.d. in 1985; 30 in 1986 and 29 in 1987) chosen with probability proportionate to their number of listed electors.

- *individuals* – one at each address (or household) chosen by a random selection procedure

In cases where the number of persons listed on the register did not match the number found at the address, corrective weights were applied (see below).

Fieldwork was carried out during the spring of each year, the bulk of interviewing typically taking place in April and May. The questionnaire takes about one hour to administer. Response to the three surveys was as follows:

	1985		1986		1987	
	No	%	No	%	No	%
Addresses issued	2,508		4,530		4,279	
In scope (eligible)	2,450	100	4,454	100	4.240	100
Interview achieved	1,804	74	3,100	70	2,847	67
Self-completion						
questionnaire returned	1,530	62				
(i) Both versions	n/a		2,737	61	2,493	59
(ii) ISSP version	n/a		1,416	64	1,212	57
Proportion of *respondents*						
who returned ISSP						
version		85		91		86

Note. In 1986 and 1987 two (randomly allocated) versions of the questionnaire were fielded, the ISSP questions being carried on one version only.

Where necessary, two postal reminders were sent to respondents in an effort to obtain the self-completion supplement. Since the overall proportion returning the supplement each year is high, no weighting is applied to correct for differential non-response.

Each year the data are weighted to take account of any differences between the number of electors listed on the register, and the number of adults found at the address. Details follow:

	1985	**1986**	**1987**
% of total cases to which weights were applied	20%	19%	27%
ISSP version of the self-completion questionnaire:			
unweighted sample	1,530	1,416	1,212
weighted sample	1,502	1,387	1,181

Users of the *ZentralArchiv* Codebooks should note that the tabulated data presented there are unweighted; for most purposes, analysts should use weighted data.

Full technical details of the three surveys will be found in Witherspoon (1986), Brook and Witherspoon (1987) and Brook and Witherspoon (1988).

All three reports can be obtained from SCPR or from the ESRC Data Archive at the University of Essex where the datasets are publicly available.

United States of America: General Social Survey

The General Social Survey (GSS) has been carried out annually since 1972 by the National Opinion Research Center (NORC), University of Chicago. The project is conducted for the National Data Program for the Social Sciences and is financially supported by the National Science Foundation. Data are collected mainly by face-to-face interview; the ISSP questionnaire modules are in a self-completion supplement, which most respondents fill in immediately after the interview and which is collected by the interviewer.

Each annual survey is designed to be representative of English-speaking persons within the USA, aged 18 years or over and living in non-institutional arrangements. The sample is a multi-stage area probability sample, with three stages of selection:

- *primary sampling units* comprising Standard Metropolitan Statistical Areas; or non-metropolitan counties, stratified before selection by region, age and race

- *block groups and enumeration districts,* stratified before selection by race and income

- *blocks,* selected with probability proportionate to size. (In the absence of block statistics, measures of size are obtained by field counting.)

Corrective weights were applied to the 1985 data (see below) but not in 1986, 1987 or 1988. (The 1987 GSS dataset contains an oversample of black respondents, but this is excluded from the ISSP dataset.)

Fieldwork is carried out between February and April each year. Response to the 1985, 1986 and 1987 surveys was as follows:

	1985		**1986**		**1987**	
	No	%	No	%	No	%
Original sample	2,201		2,192		2,250	
Net sample (eligible)	1,948	100	1,944	100	1,945	100
Interview achieved	1,534	79	1,470	76	1,466	75
Self-administered questionnaire filled in	677	71	1,470	76	1,211	62
Proportion of *respondents* who filled in self-administered questionnaire		90		100		83

Notes. In 1986, 42 of the 1,470 respondents to the ISSP questionnaire did not answer Qs 10–15; full response data for the 1988 GSS have not yet been published.

The 1985 data have been weighted to correct for an unintentional overlap between the respondent selection procedures and form assignment procedures. The weighting compensated for this assignment bias and achieved a random distribution of affected variables (such as age, sex, labour force status and income) across assignments. A discussion of the problem and technical details of its solution will be found in Smith and Petersen (1986).

The GSS data are published annually in a cumulative Codebook produced by NORC and distributed by the Roper Center for Public Opinion Research, University of Connecticut. Further information may be obtained from:

Dr Tom W. Smith
NORC
University of Chicago
115 East 60th Street
Chicago
Illinois 60637, USA

Australia: National Social Science Survey

The National Social Science Survey (NSSS) began in 1984 and is conducted annually by the Research School of Social Sciences, Institute of Advanced Studies, Australian National University (ANU). Other funders include the Australian Research Grants Scheme and the Australian International Development Assistance Bureau. Survey data are collected by a self-completion mail questionnaire.

The NSSS is designed to be representative of Australian citizens in all states and territories, who are aged 18 or over and competent in the English language. Respondents approached in the first round of the NSSS in 1984/1985 were selected either by means of an area probability sample and interviewed face-to-face; or, for the quarter of the population who lived in rural areas, selected at random from the electoral rolls and sent a self-completion questionnaire through the mail. The overall response rate was 67 per cent. The three ISSP modules which the NSSS has carried to date have been fielded as follows:

- *Role of Government.* Respondents to the 1984/1985 NSSS were sent a postal self-completion questionnaire. The survey was in the field from November 1986 to July 1987. From the issued sample of 2,509, 1,528 completed questionnaires were returned (a response rate of 40 per cent).

- *Social Networks and Support Systems.* This ISSP questionnaire was fielded as a supplement to the NSSS 1987 Election Panel, and mailed to all original respondents whose addresses were known and who had not indicated that they were opposed to being contacted again. Data were collected in mid-1987. The completion rate was 60 per cent, yielding 1,250 respondents.*

- *Social Inequality.* The third ISSP questionnaire was fielded as part of the fourth round of the NSSS. The sample was drawn at random from the national electoral rolls, the data collected in late 1987/early 1988, yielding 1,574 cases for the analyses in Chapter 4. Response details are not yet available since further cases will be added to the dataset as a result of telephone reminders.

None of these datasets was weighted.

Additional details about the NSSS sampling and mailing procedures will be found in Kelley *et al* (1987). The NSSS datasets are archived at the Social Science Data Archive at ANU. Further information may be obtained from:

> Dr Jonathan Kelley
> Department of Sociology
> Research School of Social Sciences
> The Australian National University
> Canberra, Australia

West Germany: ALLBUS

ALLBUS (Allgemeinen Bevoelkerungsumfrage der Sozialwissenschaften), conducted biennially since 1980, is the West German general social survey and, like BSA and the GSS, is a replicating time-series. It is the joint responsibility of the *Zentrum für Umfragen, Methoden und Analysen* (ZUMA) in Mannheim and the *ZentralArchiv für Empirische Sozialforschung* (ZA) at the University of Cologne.

Each survey is designed to be a representative sample of adults (aged 18 and over) living in private households in the Federal Republic and West Berlin. A three-stage stratified design is used: selection of sampling points; selection of households within those points by a random route method; and at each household the selection of an eligible West German national. The ISSP data are collected on a self-completion questionnaire, usually

---

*Some additional data on social support systems were collected as part of this study. They are available on request from Dr Clive Bean, Department of Sociology, Research School of Social Sciences, ANU.

filled in following the main ALLBUS interview and returned by post.
    Fieldwork was carried out as follows:

- Role of Government module : May - August 1985

- Social Networks module   : March - May 1986

- Social Inequality module   : September - October 1987

- Women and the family
  module   : April – July 1988

The table below shows the response rates achieved in each year. (The 1985
module was fielded on its own; the 1987 module was carried out as a
supplement to another general social survey, Der Sozialwissenschaften-
Bus.)

	1985		1986		1987		1988	
	No	%	No	%	No	%	No	%
Issued	2,704		5,512		2,896		4,620	
Adjusted sample (eligible)	2,513	100	5,275	100	2,580	100	4,509	100
Achieved interviews	n/a		3,095	59	1,655	64	3,052	68
Completed ISSP questionnaires	1,048	42	2,809	53	1,397	54	2,994	66
% of *respondents* who returned the ISSP questionnaire	n/a	n/a		91		84		98

Note. n/a = not applicable.

Telephone reminders were carried out to maximise response to the ISSP
self-completion questionnaire. The 1985, 1987 and 1988 datasets were not
weighted; the 1986 data were corrected by weighting for non-response.
    Further details are given by Hippler (1986) and Erbslöh and Wiedenbeck
(1987). Further information may be obtained from:
        Dr Peter Ph. Mohler
        ZUMA
        P O Box 5969
        Mannheim
        Federal Republic of Germany

Austria: Sozialer Survey Österreich

The *Sozialer Survey Österreich* (SSOE) was first fielded in 1986, and the
intention is to replicate it regularly in order to provide a time-series. The
SSOE is conducted by the *Institut für Soziologie* (IS) at the University of
Graz and funded from various sources including the Social Science
Foundation, the Austrian National Bank Jubilee Fund, the Ministry for
Science and Research and the State Government of Steiermark.
    The sample, designed to be representative of adults in the Republic of
Austria is three-stage:

- *sampling points* are selected within each *Bundesland* (region) according to the population size of each point

- *households* within each sampling point are selected using addresses drawn randomly from the electoral register

- *individuals* (aged between 16 and 69) are randomly selected for interview in each selected household, using a fixed random number

For details, see IS (1987) and IS (1988).

The main SSOE questionnaires were administered by face-to-face interview; the Role of Government and Social Networks ISSP questionnaires were administered on a self-completion questionnaire (filled in after the interview) during May and June 1986; the Social Inequality module was part of the SSOE questionnaire, conducted by personal interview in June and July 1988. Response rates achieved on each interviewing round are shown below:

	1985 and 1986 modules		1987 module	
	No	%	No	%
Issued addresses	2,820		1,400	
Adjusted sample (eligible)	2,763	*100*	1,361	*100*
Achieved interviews	2,016	*72*	972	*71*
Completed ISSP questionnaires				
(i) Role of Government module*	987 }	*72*		
(ii) Social Networks module*	1,027 }			
(iii) Social Inequality module**			972	*71*

Notes. * = each was administered to a random half of those responding to the main SSOE questionnaire. ** = carried out by personal interview.

The three datasets have been weighted to represent correct population proportions based on an achieved sample of 1,000 adults (IFES-weighting). They are available in *Codenbuch mit Methodenbericht, Variablenliste, Linearauszaehlung, Fragebogen, Listen* (IS, 1987; IS, 1988). Further information may be obtained from:

Prof. Dr Max Haller *or* Dr Franz Höllinger
Sozialer Survey Österreich
Institut für Soziologie der Universität Graz
Mariengasse 24
A-8020 Graz, Austria

Hungary

Each year *Társadalomkutatási Informatikai Egyesülés* (TARKI) carries out a national survey representative of the population of Hungary aged 18 and over. The samples are selected in two stages, the first consisting of a cluster of 'settlements' and the second of individuals. The 1986 module on Social Networks was administered to a subsample of 1,000 adults representative of the population as a whole, and to a further 2,000 younger people (aged 18–39). This booster sample of young people has not been used in any of the analyses in this book.

Technical details of the 1987 TARKI survey on which the module on Social Inequality was administered to 2,606 respondents are not yet published. Similarly the technical details of the 1988 survey are not yet available. This and other information may be obtained from:

> Professor Dr Tamás Kolosi
> TARKI
> 1027 Budapest II
> Frankel Leo U. 11
> Hungary

Italy: Indagine Sociale Italiana

The *Indagine Sociale Italiana* (ISI) is an annual series of surveys, carried out by the *Ricerca Sociale e di Marketing* (EURISKO) Institute in Milan. Since 1985, the surveys have included the ISSP questionnaire modules, administered either as a self-completion supplement to the main ISI interview or as an interviewer-assisted supplement.

The sample for each ISI survey is designed to be respresentative of the population of Italy aged between 18 and 74. A national multi-stage probability sample is used, with quota-selection at the final stages, selecting:

- *at the first stage,* small geographical areas or administrative units to yield a probability sample of primary sampling units (PSUs); areas and units had been pre-stratified according to sex, age and population density

- *at the second stage,* a prespecified number of households (or dwelling units) within each PSU

- *at the third stage,* selection of an adult (aged 18-74) within each selected household according to pre-selected quota criteria.

Response rates are not available from the ZA Codebooks.

Fieldwork on the Role of Government module was carried out in September and October 1985; and in spring 1987 on the Social Networks and Social Inequality modules. Corrective weights were applied to the data for all three surveys to adjust for population size, sex, age and occupation (based on 1981 Census estimates). For details, see ZA (1986). Further information may be obtained from:

> Prof. Gabrieli Calvi *or* Dr Paolo Anselmi
> Ricerca Sociale e di Marketing (EURISKO)
> Via Monte Rosa 15
> 20149 Milano, Italy

Netherlands

The Netherlands has no single annual or biennial national survey on which to field the ISSP module. Instead, the *Sociaal en Cultureel Planbureau* (SCP) at Rijswijk regularly conducts surveys on social and cultural welfare in the Netherlands, as mandated by its terms of reference. (See SCP, 1986.) In 1987, it fielded the Social Inequality module as a self-completion supplement to a nationwide personal interview survey among a full probability sample of Dutch adults aged between 16 and 80. Fieldwork was carried out between September and December 1987; 1,638 interviews were obtained and a response rate of 82 per cent was achieved. No weights were applied to the data.

There are plans to field the 1989 and 1990 questionnaire modules on similar surveys conducted regularly by SCP. Further information may be obtained from:

Dr Carlo van Praag *or* Dr Jos Becker
Sociaal en Cultureel Planbureau
JC van Markenlaan 3
Postbus 37
2280 AA Rijswijk
Netherlands

Switzerland

Switzerland is not one of the ISSP member nations, but in 1987 the *Soziologisches Institut der Universität Zurich* fielded a questionnaire replicating the 1987 Social Inequality module. The Institute used a two-stage stratified random sample designed to be representative of adults (aged 16 and over) resident in Switzerland (including foreign workers). The first selection stage involved selecting 129 'representative Swiss communities'; at the second stage, addresses were selected according to random principles (see Hischier and Zwicky, 1988).

The questionnaire was postal and included some questions repeated from a Swiss survey of 1975. German, French and Italian versions were used, and an incentive payment of SFR50 was made to those returning a completed questionnaire. Returns were received between October and December 1987. Response was as follows:

	1987	
	No	%
Questionnaires mailed	2,046	
(Assumed to be) eligible	1,925	*100*
Completed questionnaires	987	*51*

The dataset was not weighted.

Republic of Ireland

Unlike the majority of ISSP member countries, the Republic of Ireland has no regular national survey on which to field the annual ISSP module. In 1988, however, the Women and the Family module was fielded as part of a nationwide attitude survey dealing with, among other issues, prejudice and tolerance. There are plans to field the next two ISSP modules (on Work Orientation and the repeat of the Role of Government questions) on similar *ad hoc* surveys.

A two-stage probability sample was drawn for the 1988 study, the first stage being District Electoral Divisions and the second, electors aged 18 and over. A total of 1,290 addresses was issued and successful interviews carried out at 1,005 (a gross response rate of 78 per cent). The data were not weighted.

Further information may be obtained from:
Professor Conor K. Ward
Faculty of Philosophy and Sociology
University College Dublin
Dublin 4
Republic of Ireland

Public understanding of science surveys

The surveys described below provided the data which are presented and discussed in Chapter 6.

British survey

The British survey is a joint Oxford University Department for External Studies (OUDES)/SCPR project funded by the Economic and Social Research Council.

The sample was designed to be representative of the adult population of Britain (those aged 18 or over). The sampling method involved four separate stages of selection, using the electoral register as a sampling frame.

The first stage was the selection of 130 parliamentary constituencies with probability proportionate to electorate. Prior to selection, constituencies were allocated to strata according to region and population density. Within each stratum they were then listed, in descending order, according to the proportion of the population with a degree, professional or vocational qualification. The second stage was the selection within each constituency of one polling district, again with probability proportionate to electorate. The third stage was the selection of 23 addresses from the electoral register of each polling district. The selection was made with probability proportionate to the number of electors registered at the address. Thus a total of 2,990 addresses was selected. The fourth and final stage involved the selection of one adult at each address by means of a selection grid.

The design gives equal selection probabilities where the number of electors on the register for an address equals the number of eligible adults found there. As these two numbers are not always equal, a corrective weight is needed (but was not applied to the data presented in Chapter 6).

Fieldwork was carried out by SCPR interviewers during June and July 1988. The response rate, after excluding a small number of ineligible addresses (92) from the base, was 69%. A total of 2,009 interviews was achieved.

American survey

The American survey was conducted by Professor J.D. Miller and his associates at Northern Illinois University and funded by the National Science Foundation.

The national sample frame used was based on a multi-stage cluster design, structured so that each adult in the USA living in a household with a telephone had an equal chance of being selected for the sample. The sample was designed to produce 150 primary sampling units. The largest 33 metropolitan areas in the USA were included in the sample frame on a self-weighting basis. An additional 117 smaller metropolitan areas or counties were selected on a probability proportionate to size basis.

The data were collected by computer-assisted telephone interviewing (CATI) during June and July 1988 by the Public Opinion Laboratories (POL) at Northern Illinois University. A total of 2,829 persons was contacted of whom 237 were ineligible and 529 refused; the net response rate was 73 per cent.

The American sample was weighted to compensate for lower response rates of ethnic minorities and those living in inner city areas. However, unweighted data have been presented in chapter 6.

The decision to use unweighted data for the two countries was taken because the existing weighting schemes for the two surveys are not wholly comparable. A comparison of the weighted American data with the unweighted British data should constitute a strong test of the cross-national differences in attitudes towards science, since weighting the USA data serves to reduce estimates of American interest in, and informedness of, science. Even under these conditions, there remain substantial and statistically significant differences between British and American attitudes towards science. The authors do not believe that their substantive conclusions would thus be affected by using weighted data.

Survey of national pride

In West Germany, the questions on national pride and attitudes to democracy were asked on the 1988 ZUMA ALLBUS survey , details of which are given above. In Britain, they were asked on the SCPR/Oxford *1987 British General Election* survey (technical details of which follow). The research was supported by a grant from the Anglo-German Foundation.

The *1987 British General Election* survey was designed to yield a representative sample of eligible voters living in private households in

Britain. It is not a random sample of all adults; only those registered on the electoral register and eligible to vote in the general election in June 1987 were included in the sampling frame.

As with previous surveys in the election study series, electors living in Northern Ireland and the Scottish Highlands and Islands were excluded from the sampling frame: the former because its party composition and particular concerns would have required a separately designed study, and the latter because the small and scattered population could not be interviewed cost-effectively.

A three-stage selection procedure was used:

- *parliamentary constituencies:* a sample of 250 constituencies was selected, with probability proportionate to size of electorate. Before selection, the constituencies were stratified according to Standard Region, population density and owner-occupation. In order to make the strata more equal in size, the density bandings used varied according to the Standard Region. Constituencies were then systematically sampled, with the probability of selection proportionate to the size of the electorate. In the course of selecting constituencies, a random elector was picked. This selection point was used to identify the polling district within which electors would be selected.

- *polling districts:* all polling districts within the constituencies were ordered in a logical sequence. Any polling district with fewer than 500 electors was combined with the one following it to form one unit.

- *individuals:* within each of the 250 selected polling districts, a systematic random sample of 24 electors was selected with equal probability. Those ineligible to vote were randomly replaced by an eligible elector. Overall, a sample of 6,000 names was selected.

The data were collected by face-to-face interview, followed by a self-completion questionnaire which the interviewer collected later, or the respondent returned by post. The questions on national pride and the questions on democracy were part of the self-completion supplement. Fieldwork took place in the summer of 1987 and was carried out by SCPR's panel of interviewers. Response to the survey was as follows:

1987
British General Election Survey

	No	%
Names issued	6,000	
Total eligible	5,463	*100*
Interview obtained	3,826	*70*
Self-completion supplement returned	3,415	*63*
% of *respondents* returning self-completion supplement		*89*

Since there were differences in the response achieved in different regions, the data were weighted to correct these imbalances. Weights ranged from 0.850 to 1.189. These weights would normally be used in analyses. As the West German data were unweighted, these weights were not, however, applied to the British data presented in Chapter 7.

References

BROOK, L. and WITHERSPOON, S., *British Social Attitudes, 1986 Survey: Technical Report,* SCPR, London (1987).

BROOK, L. and WITHERSPOON, S., *British Social Attitudes, 1987 Survey: Technical Report,* SCPR, London (1988).

ERBSLÖH, B., and WIEDENBECK, M., 'Methodenberichte: Allgemeine Bevoelkerungsumfrage der Sozialwissenschaften, ALLBUS 1986' *ZUMA-Arbeitsbericht,* No. 1987/04, ZUMA, Mannheim, September (1987).

HIPPLER, H.J., 'Methodenforschung im Rahmen des International Social Survey Project (ISSP) 1985', *ZUMA-Nachrichten,* No.19, ZUMA, Mannheim November, (1986) pp.64–75.

HISCHIER, G. and ZWICKY, H., *Die Erhebung der Daten und ihre Bestimmungsgründe,* Soziologisches Institut der Universität Zurich, Zurich (1988).

IS (Institut für Soziologie der Universität Graz), *Codebuch mit Methodenbericht, Variablenliste, Linearauszalung, Fragebogen, Listen 2. Erweiterte und Verbesserte Auflage,* IS, Graz (1987).

IS (Institut für Soziologie der Universität Graz), *Codebuch mit Methodenbericht, Linearauszalung und Fragebogen (ISSP-87 Ungleichneit; ISSP-88 Familie),* IS, Graz (1988).

KELLEY, J., CUSHING, R.G. and HEADLEY, B., *The Australian National Social Science Survey, 1984-1985,* Social Science Data Archive, Australian National University (1987).

SMITH, T.W. and PETERSEN, B.L., 'Problems in Form Randomization on the General Social Surveys', in *GSS Technical Report No.53,* NORC, Chicago (1986).

SCP (Social and Cultural Planning Office), *Social and Cultural Report 1986,* SCP, Rijswijk (1986).

WITHERSPOON, S., *British Social Attitudes, 1985 Survey: Technical Report,* SCPR, London (1986).

ZA (ZentralArchiv für Empirische Sozialforschung), *International Social Survey Programme: Role of Government – 1985,* Codebook ZA-No. 1490, ZA, Mannheim (1986).

ZA (ZentralArchiv für Empirische Sozialforschung), *International Social Survey Programme: Social Networks and Support Systems – 1986,* Codebook ZA-No.1620, ZA, Mannheim (1987).

ZA (ZentralArchiv für Empirische Sozialforschung), *International Social Survey Programme: Social Inequality – 1987,* Codebook ZA-No.1680, ZA, Mannheim (1988).

Appendix II
Notes on the tabulations

1. Tables at the end of chapters are percentaged vertically; tables within the text are percentaged as indicated.

2. In all the tables, whether in the text or at the end of chapters, a percentage of less than 0.5 is indicated by '*', and '-' is used to denote zero.

3. In the great majority of tables, percentages have been rounded up or down to the nearest whole %. Percentages of 0.5 have been rounded up (e.g. 38.5% = 39%).

4. In earlier *British Social Attitudes* reports, percentage bases have included all respondents to the interview questionnaire; or all respondents to the self-completion questionnaire (except in *The 1984 Report*). In this Report, however, following the convention of the *ZentralArchiv* codebooks and datafiles, tables exclude those respondents who answered "don't know" to the relevant question, or who did not answer it at all. For this reason, percentages given in this Report may differ slightly from the British figures reported in earlier volumes in this series.

Appendix III
The questionnaires

The findings which are reported in Chapters 1–5 and Chapter 8 are based on four ISSP (International Social Survey Programme) questionnaire modules, one for each of the years from 1985 to 1988. The English language versions of the questionnaires are reproduced below.

Question numbers of the English language version correspond to the question numbers used in SCPR's *British Social Attitudes* survey. The year in which the British module was fielded is shown in the upper right-hand corner of each page. From 1986, there were two versions of each *British Social Attitudes* questionnaire; the version of which the ISSP module was part is indicated by the suffix 'A' or 'B' following the year.

Chapters 6 and 7 are based on the findings of surveys which were not part of the ISSP. The full questionnaires for these surveys are not reproduced in this Report, but the text of all questions referred to, along with the answer categories, are given in the two chapters.

INTERNATIONAL SOCIAL SURVEY PROGRAMME

1985 MODULE

THE ROLE OF GOVERNMENT

(ENGLISH LANGUAGE VERSION)

1985

- 1 -

201.a) Suppose a newspaper got hold of confidential government papers about defence plans and wanted to publish them.

PLEASE TICK ONE BOX

Should the newspaper be allowed to publish the papers? [1]

OR

Should the government have the power to prevent publication? [2]

Can't choose [8]

b) Now suppose the confidential government papers were about economic plans.

PLEASE TICK ONE BOX

Should the newspaper be allowed to publish the papers? [1]

OR

Should the government have the power to prevent publication? [2]

Can't choose [8]

202. In general, would you say that people should obey the law without exception, or are there exceptional occasions on which people should follow their consciences even if it means breaking the law?

PLEASE TICK ONE BOX

Obey the law without exception [1]

Follow conscience on occasions [2]

Can't choose [8]

OFFICE USE ONLY

CARD 20

20.07

20.08

20.09

- 2 -

203. There are many ways people or organisations can protest against a government action they strongly oppose. Please show which you think should be allowed and which should not be allowed by ticking a box on each line.

PLEASE TICK ONE BOX ON EACH LINE

Should it be allowed?

	Definitely (1)	Probably (2)	Probably not (3)	Definitely not (4)	Can't choose (8)	
A. Organising public meetings to protest against the government						20.10
B. Publishing pamphlets to protest against the government						20.11
C. Organising protest marches and demonstrations						20.12
D. Occupying a government office and stopping work there for several days						20.13
E. Seriously damaging government buildings						20.14
F. Organising a nationwide strike of all workers against the government						20.15

204. There are some people whose views are considered extreme by the majority.

a) First, consider people who want to overthrow the government by revolution. Do you think such people should be allowed to ...

PLEASE TICK ONE BOX ON EACH LINE

	Definitely (1)	Probably (2)	Probably not (3)	Definitely not (4)	Can't choose (8)	
i) ... hold public meetings to express their views?						20.16
ii) ... teach 15 year olds in schools?						20.17
iii) ... publish books expressing their views?						20.18

b) Second, consider people who believe that whites are racially superior to all other races. Do you think such people should be allowed to ...

PLEASE TICK ONE BOX ON EACH LINE

	Definitely (1)	Probably (2)	Probably not (3)	Definitely not (4)	Can't choose (8)	
i) ... hold public meetings to express their views?						20.19
ii) ... teach 15 year olds in schools?						20.20
iii) ... publish books expressing their views?						20.21

1985

OFFICE USE ONLY

- 3 -

205.a) Suppose the police get an anonymous tip that a man with a long criminal record is planning to break into a warehouse.

PLEASE TICK ONE BOX ON EACH LINE

Do you think the police should be allowed, without a Court Order....

	Defin-itely	Proba-bly	Probably not	Definitely not	Can't choose	OFFICE USE ONLY
i) ... to keep the man under surveillance?	1	2	3	4	8	20,22
ii) ... to tap his telephone?	1	2	3	4	8	20,23
iii) ... to open his mail?	1	2	3	4	8	20,24
iv) ... to detain the man overnight for questioning?	1	2	3	4	8	20,25

b) Now, suppose the tip is about a man *without a criminal record*.

PLEASE TICK ONE BOX ON EACH LINE

Do you think the police should be allowed, without a Court Order ...

	Defin-itely	Proba-bly	Probably not	Definitely not	Can't choose	OFFICE USE ONLY
i) ... to keep the man under surveillance?	1	2	3	4	8	20,26
ii) ... to tap his telephone?	1	2	3	4	8	20,27
iii) ... to open his mail?	1	2	3	4	8	20,28
iv) ... to detain the man overnight for questioning?	1	2	3	4	8	20,29

206. All systems of justice make mistakes, but which do you think is worse:

PLEASE TICK ONE BOX

(✓)

to convict an innocent person? [1]

OR

to let a guilty person go free? [2]

Can't choose [8]

20,30

- 4 -

207. The government has a lot of different pieces of information about people which computers can bring together very quickly. Is this ...

PLEASE TICK ONE BOX

(✓)

... a very serious threat to individual privacy, [1]

a fairly serious threat, [2]

not a serious threat, [3]

or - not a threat at all to individual privacy? [4]

Can't choose [8]

20,31

208. Some people think those with high incomes should pay a larger proportion (percentage) of their earnings in taxes than those who earn low incomes. Other people think that those with high incomes and those with low incomes should pay the same proportion (percentage) of their earnings in taxes.

Do you think those with high incomes should ...

PLEASE TICK ONE BOX

(✓)

... pay a much larger proportion, [1]

pay a larger proportion, [2]

pay the same proportion as those who earn low incomes, [3]

pay a smaller proportion, [4]

or - pay a much smaller proportion? [5]

Can't choose [8]

20,32

209. What is your opinion of the following statement: It is the responsibility of the government to reduce the differences in income between people with high incomes and those with low incomes.

PLEASE TICK ONE BOX

(✓)

Agree strongly [1]

Agree [2]

Neither agree nor disagree [3]

Disagree [4]

Disagree strongly [5]

20,33

- 6 -

214. Here are three things the government might do. Some people are in favour of them while other people are against them. Please tick one box for each statement to show how you feel.

PLEASE TICK ONE BOX ON EACH LINE

	Strongly in favour	In favour	Neither in favour nor against	Against	Strongly against	1985 OFFICE USE ONLY
A. The government should increase opportunities for women in business and industry	1	2	3	4	5	20.40
B. The government should increase opportunities for women to go to university	1	2	3	4	5	20.41
C. Women should be given preferential treatment when applying for jobs or promotions	1	2	3	4	5	20.42

215. And now a few questions about education. Here are some things that might be taught in school. How important is it that schools teach each of these to 15 year olds?

PLEASE TICK ON BOX ON EACH LINE

	Essential, must be taught	Very important	Fairly important	Not very important	Not needed, should not be taught	Can't choose	1985 OFFICE USE ONLY
A. Reading, writing and mathematics	1	2	3	4	5	8	20.43
B. Sex education	1	2	3	4	5	8	20.44
C. Respect for authority	1	2	3	4	5	8	20.45
D. History, literature and the arts	1	2	3	4	5	8	20.46
E. Ability to make one's own judgements	1	2	3	4	5	8	20.47
F. Job training	1	2	3	4	5	8	20.48
G. Science and technology	1	2	3	4	5	8	20.49
H. Concern for minorities and the poor	1	2	3	4	5	8	20.50
J. Discipline and orderliness	1	2	3	4	5	8	20.51

- 5 -

210. Please show whether you agree or disagree with each of the following statements.

PLEASE TICK ONE BOX ON EACH LINE

	Agree strongly	Agree	Neither agree nor disagree	Disagree	Disagree strongly	1985 OFFICE USE ONLY
A. A person whose parents are rich has a better chance of earning a lot of money than a person whose parents are poor	1	2	3	4	5	20.34
B. A person whose father is a professional person has a better chance of earning a lot of money than a person whose parents are poor	1	2	3	4	5	20.35
C. In Britain what you achieve in life depends largely on your family background	1	2	3	4	5	20.36

211. Would you say that opportunities for university education are, in general, better or worse, for women than for men?

PLEASE TICK ONE BOX

		1985 OFFICE USE ONLY
Much better for women	1	
Better for women	2	
No difference	3	
Worse for women	4	
Much worse for women	5	
Can't choose	8	20.37

212. How about job opportunities for women: do you think they are, in general, better or worse than job opportunities for men with similar education and experience?

PLEASE TICK ONE BOX

		1985 OFFICE USE ONLY
Much better for women	1	
Better for women	2	
No difference	3	
Worse for women	4	
Much worse for women	5	
Can't choose	8	20.38

213. And how about income and wages: compared with men who have similar education and jobs - are women, in general, paid better or worse than men?

PLEASE TICK ONE BOX

		1985 OFFICE USE ONLY
Women are paid much better	1	
Women are paid better	2	
No difference	3	
Women are paid worse	4	
Women are paid much worse	5	
Can't choose	8	20.39

- 7 -

216. How do you feel about opportunities for young people to go to university?

PLEASE TICK ONE BOX

Should opportunities be ...

... increased a lot,	[1]
increased a little,	[2]
kept the same as now,	[3]
reduced a little,	[4]
or – reduced a lot?	[5]
Can't choose	[8]

(20.52)

217. Some people think the government should provide financial assistance to university students. Others think the government should not provide such aid. In each of the circumstances listed below should the government provide grants that would <u>not</u> have to be paid back, provide loans which the student would have to pay back, or should the government not provide any financial assistance?

PLEASE TICK ONE BOX ON EACH LINE

	Government should give grants	Government should make loans	No Government assistance	Can't choose	
A. For students whose parents have a low income	[1]	[2]	[3]	[8]	20.53
B. For students who have outstanding exam results in secondary school	[1]	[2]	[3]	[8]	20.54
C. For students who have average exam results and middle income parents	[1]	[2]	[3]	[8]	20.55

- 8 -

218. Sometimes public authorities intervene with parents in raising their children. Please show in each of the following cases how far you think public authorities should go in dealing with a <u>10 year old</u> child and his or her parents:

PLEASE TICK ONE BOX ON EACH LINE

Public Authorities should

	Take no action	Give warnings or counselling	Take the child from its parents	Can't choose	
A. The child uses drugs and the parents don't do anything about it.	[1]	[2]	[3]	[8]	20,56
B. The child frequently skips school and the parents don't do anything about it	[1]	[2]	[3]	[8]	20,57
C. The parents regularly let the child stay out late at night without knowing where the child is	[1]	[2]	[3]	[8]	20,58
D. The parents fail to provide the child with proper food and clothing	[1]	[2]	[3]	[8]	20,59
E. The parents regularly beat the child	[1]	[2]	[3]	[8]	20,60
F. The parents refuse essential medical treatment for the child because of their religious beliefs	[1]	[2]	[3]	[8]	20,61
G. The parents refuse to send their child to school because they wish to educate the child at home	[1]	[2]	[3]	[8]	20,62
H. The parents allow the child to watch violent or pornographic films	[1]	[2]	[3]	[8]	20,63

219. Do you think that ......

PLEASE TICK ONE BOX ON EACH LINE

	Agree strongly	Agree	Neither agree nor disagree	Disagree	Disagree strongly	
A. ... the wearing of seat belts in cars should be required by law?	[1]	[2]	[3]	[4]	[5]	20,64
B. ... smoking in public places should be prohibited by law?	[1]	[2]	[3]	[4]	[5]	20,65
C. ... all employees should be required to retire at an age set by law?	[1]	[2]	[3]	[4]	[5]	20,66

1985 OFFICE USE ONLY

- 10 -

222. Listed below are various areas of government spending. Please show whether you would like to see more or less government spending in each area.

Remember that if you say "much more", it might require a tax increase to pay for it.

PLEASE TICK ONE BOX ON EACH LINE

	Spend much more	Spend more	Spend the same as now	Spend less	Spend much less	Can't choose	Office use only 1985
A. The environment	1	2	3	4	5	8	21.15
B. Health	1	2	3	4	5	8	21.16
C. The police and law enforcement	1	2	3	4	5	8	21.17
D. Education	1	2	3	4	5	8	21.18
E. The military and defence	1	2	3	4	5	8	21.19
F. Old age pensions	1	2	3	4	5	8	21.20
G. Unemployment benefits	1	2	3	4	5	8	21.21
H. Culture and the arts	1	2	3	4	5	8	21.22

223. Do you consider the amount of income tax that your household has to pay is...

PLEASE TICK ONE BOX

		Office use only 1985
...much too high,	1	21.23
too high,	2	
about right,	3	
too low,	4	
or - much too low?	5	
Can't choose	8	
Does not apply	6	

- 9 -

220. Please show whether you agree or disagree with each of the following statements.

PLEASE TICK ONE BOX ON EACH LINE

	Agree	Disagree	Can't choose	Office use only 1985
A. The public has little control over what politicians do in office	1	2	8	20.67
B. The average person can get nowhere by talking to public officials	1	2	8	20.68
C. The average citizen has considerable influence on politics	1	2	8	20.69
D. The average person has much to say about running local government	1	2	8	20.70
E. People like me have much to say about government	1	2	8	20.71
F. The average person has a great deal of influence on government decisions	1	2	8	20.72
G. The government is generally responsive to public opinion	1	2	8	20.73
H. I am usually interested in local elections	1	2	8	20.74
J. By taking an active part in political and social affairs the people can control world affairs.	1	2	8	20.75
K. Taking everything into account, the world is getting better	1	2	8	20.76

20.77-80

CARD 21

221. Here are some things the government might do for the economy. Please show which actions you are in favour of and which you are against.

PLEASE TICK ONE BOX ON EACH LINE

	Strongly in favour	In favour	Neither in favour nor against	Against	Strongly against	Office use only 1985
A. Control of wages by legislation	1	2	3	4	5	21.
B. Control of prices by legislation	1	2	3	4	5	21.08
C. Cuts in government spending	1	2	3	4	5	21.09
D. Government financing of projects to create new jobs	1	2	3	4	5	21.10
E. Less government regulation of business	1	2	3	4	5	21.11
F. Support for industry to develop new products and technology	1	2	3	4	5	21.12
G. Supporting declining industries to protect jobs	1	2	3	4	5	21.13
H. Reducing the working week to create more jobs	1	2	3	4	5	21.14

- 11 -

1985

224. Do you consider the amount of tax that business and industry have to pay is too high or too low?

PLEASE TICK ONE BOX

	(✓)	OFFICE USE ONLY
Much too high	1	
Too high	2	
About right	3	21,24
Too low	4	
Much too low	5	
Can't choose	8	

225. If the government had to choose between keeping down inflation or keeping down unemployment to which do you think it should give highest priority?

PLEASE TICK ONE BOX

	(✓)	
Keeping down inflation	1	
Keeping down unemployment	2	21,25
Can't choose	8	

226. Do you think that trade unions in this country have too much power or too little power?

PLEASE TICK ONE BOX

	(✓)	
Far too much power	1	
Too much power	2	
About the right amount of power	3	21,26
Too little power	4	
Far too little power	5	
Can't choose	8	

- 12 -

1985

227. How about business and industry? Do they have too much power or too little power?

PLEASE TICK ONE BOX

	(✓)	OFFICE USE ONLY
Far too much power	1	
Too much power	2	
About the right amount of power	3	21,27
Too little power	4	
Far too little power	5	
Can't choose	8	

228. And what about the government, does it have too much power or too little power?

PLEASE TICK ONE BOX

	(✓)	
Far too much power	1	
Too much power	2	
About the right amount of power	3	21,28
Too little power	4	
Far too little power	5	
Can't choose	8	

229. What do you think the government's role in each of these industries and services should be?

PLEASE TICK ONE BOX ON EACH LINE

The government should

	Own it	Control prices and profits but not own it	Neither own it nor control its prices & profits	Can't choose	
A. Electricity	1	2	3	8	21,29
B. Local public transport	1	2	3	8	21,30
C. The steel industry	1	2	3	8	21,31
D. Banking and insurance	1	2	3	8	21,32
E. The car industry	1	2	3	8	21,33

- 13 -

230. On the whole, do you think it should or should not be the government's responsibility to ....

PLEASE TICK ONE BOX ON EACH LINE

	Definitely should be	Probably should be	Probably should not be	Definitely should not be	Can't choose	1985 OFFICE USE ONLY
A. ... provide a job for everyone who wants one	1	2	3	4	8	21,34
B. ... keep prices under control	1	2	3	4	8	21,35
C. ... provide health care for the sick	1	2	3	4	8	21,36
D. ... provide a decent standard of living for the old	1	2	3	4	8	21,37
E. ... provide industry with the help it needs to grow	1	2	3	4	8	21,38
F. ... provide a decent standard of living for the unemployed	1	2	3	4	8	21,39
G. ... reduce income differences between the rich and poor	1	2	3	4	8	21,40

231. If the government had a choice between reducing taxes and spending more on social services, which should it do?

PLEASE TICK ONE BOX

(✓)

Reduce taxes and spend less on social services   1

OR

Increase taxes and spend more on social services   2

Can't choose   8

21,41

INTERNATIONAL SOCIAL SURVEY PROGRAMME

1986 MODULE

SOCIAL NETWORKS AND SUPPORT SYSTEMS

(ENGLISH LANGUAGE VERSION)

— 1 —

1986 – A

OFFICE USE ONLY

CARD 18

In the first part of this questionnaire, we would like to ask you about your family and friends. For example, about how often you see or visit them, and when you turn to them for help and advice.

MOTHER

201.a) First, your mother, Is she still alive?

Yes → *PLEASE ANSWER Q.1b) BELOW*

No → *GO TO Q.2*

18.08 A = 1

18.09

b) How often do you see or visit your mother?
PLEASE TICK ONE BOX

She lives in the same household
Daily
At least several times a week
At least once a week
At least once a month
Several times a year
Less often

18.10

c) About how long would it take you to get to where your mother lives? Think of the time it usually takes door to door.
PLEASE TICK ONE BOX

Less than 15 minutes
Between 15 and 30 minutes
Between 30 minutes and 1 hour
Between 1 and 2 hours
Between 2 and 3 hours
Between 3 and 5 hours
Between 5 and 12 hours
Over 12 hours

18.11

d) And how often do you have any other contact with your mother, besides visiting, either by telephone or letter?
PLEASE TICK ONE BOX

Daily
At least several times a week
At least once a week
At least once a month
Several times a year
Less often

18.12

— 2 —

1986 – A

OFFICE USE ONLY

FATHER

202.a) Is your father still alive?

Yes → *PLEASE ANSWER Q.2b) BELOW*

No → *GO TO Q.3*

18.13

18.14

b) How often do you see or visit your father?
PLEASE TICK ONE BOX

He lives in the same household
Daily
At least several times a week
At least once a week
At least once a month
Several times a year
Less often

c) About how long would it take you to get to where your father lives? Think of the time it usually takes door to door.
PLEASE TICK ONE BOX

Less than 15 minutes
Between 15 and 30 minutes
Between 30 minutes and 1 hour
Between 1 and 2 hours
Between 2 and 3 hours
Between 3 and 5 hours
Between 5 and 12 hours
Over 12 hours

18.15

d) And how often do you have any other contact with your father, besides visiting, either by telephone or letter?
PLEASE TICK ONE BOX

Daily
At least several times a week
At least once a week
At least once a month
Several times a year
Less often

18.16

- 3 -

SISTERS

1986 - A
OFFICE USE ONLY

203.a) How many sisters aged 18 or older do you have? (We mean sisters who are still alive; please include step-sisters, half sisters and adopted sisters.)

PLEASE TICK ONE BOX

18.17

None   0 → GO TO Q.4
One   1 ⎫
Two   2 ⎪
Three   3 ⎬ PLEASE ANSWER Q.3b) BELOW
Four   4 ⎪
Five or more   5 ⎭

The questions on this page are about your sister. If you have more than one adult sister, please think about the sister you have most contact with.

b) How often do you see or visit your sister?

PLEASE TICK ONE BOX

18.18

She lives in the same household   1
Daily   2
At least several times a week   3
At least once a week   4
At least once a month   5
Several times a year   6
Less often   7

c) About how long would it take you to get to where your sister lives? Think of the time it usually takes door to door.

PLEASE TICK ONE BOX

18.19

Less than 15 minutes   1
Between 15 and 30 minutes   2
Between 30 minutes and 1 hour   3
Between 1 and 2 hours   4
Between 2 and 3 hours   5
Between 3 and 5 hours   6
Between 5 and 12 hours   7
Over 12 hours   8

d) And how often do you have any other contact with your sister, besides visiting, either by telephone or letter?

PLEASE TICK ONE BOX

18.20

Daily   1
At least several times a week   2
At least once a week   3
At least once a month   4
Several times a year   5
Less often   6

- 4 -

BROTHERS

1986 - A
OFFICE USE ONLY

204.a) How many brothers aged 18 or older do you have? (We mean brothers who are still alive; please include step-brothers, half brothers and adopted brothers.)

PLEASE TICK ONE BOX

18.21

None   0 → GO TO Q.5
One   1 ⎫
Two   2 ⎪
Three   3 ⎬ PLEASE ANSWER Q.4b) BELOW
Four   4 ⎪
Five or more   5 ⎭

The questions on this page are about your brother. If you have more than one adult brother, please think about the brother you have most contact with.

b) How often do you see or visit your brother?

PLEASE TICK ONE BOX

18.22

He lives in the same household   1
Daily   2
At least several times a week   3
At least once a week   4
At least once a month   5
Several times a year   6
Less often   7

c) About how long would it take you to get to where your brother lives? Think of the time it usually takes door to door.

PLEASE TICK ONE BOX

18.23

Less than 15 minutes   1
Between 15 and 30 minutes   2
Between 30 minutes and 1 hour   3
Between 1 and 2 hours   4
Between 2 and 3 hours   5
Between 3 and 5 hours   6
Between 5 and 12 hours   7
Over 12 hours   8

d) And how often do you have any other contact with your brother, besides visiting, either by telephone or letter?

PLEASE TICK ONE BOX

18.24

Daily   1
At least several times a week   2
At least once a week   3
At least once a month   4
Several times a year   5
Less often   6

SONS section

- 6 -

	1986 - A OFFICE USE ONLY

SONS

206.a) How many sons aged 18 or older do you have? (We mean sons who are still alive; please include stepsons and adopted sons.)

PLEASE TICK ONE BOX

(✓)

None	0	→ GO TO Q.7
One	1	
Two	2	
Three	3	*PLEASE ANSWER Q.6b BELOW*
Four	4	
Five or more	5	

18.29

The questions on this page are about your son. If you have more than one adult son, please think about the son you have most contact with.

b) How often do you see or visit your son?

PLEASE TICK ONE BOX

(✓)

He lives in the same household	1	→ GO TO Q.7
Daily	2	
At least several times a week	3	
At least once a week	4	
At least once a month	5	
Several times a year	6	
Less often	7	

18.30

c) About how long would it take you to get to where your son lives? Think of the time it usually takes door to door.

PLEASE TICK ONE BOX

(✓)

Less than 15 minutes	1	
Between 15 and 30 minutes	2	
Between 30 minutes and 1 hour	3	
Between 1 and 2 hours	4	
Between 2 and 3 hours	5	
Between 3 and 5 hours	6	
Between 5 and 12 hours	7	
Over 12 hours	8	

18.31

d) And how often do you have any other contact with your son, besides visiting, either by telephone or letter?

PLEASE TICK ONE BOX

(✓)

Daily	1	
At least several times a week	2	
At least once a week	3	
At least once a month	4	
Several times a year	5	
Less often	6	

18.32

DAUGHTERS section

- 5 -

	1986 - A OFFICE USE ONLY

DAUGHTERS

205.a) How many daughters aged 18 or older do you have? (We mean daughters who are still alive; please include step-daughters and adopted daughters.)

PLEASE TICK ONE BOX

(✓)

None	0	→ GO TO Q.6
One	1	
Two	2	
Three	3	*PLEASE ANSWER Q.5b) BELOW*
Four	4	
Five or more	5	

18.25

The questions on this page are about your daughter. If you have more than one adult daughter, please think about the daughter you have most contact with.

b) How often do you see or visit your daughter?

PLEASE TICK ONE BOX

(✓)

She lives in the same household	1	→ GO TO Q.6
Daily	2	
At least several times a week	3	
At least once a week	4	
At least once a month	5	
Several times a year	6	
Less often	7	

18.26

c) About how long would it take you to get to where your daughter lives? Think of the time it usually takes door to door.

PLEASE TICK ONE BOX

(✓)

Less than 15 minutes	1	
Between 15 and 30 minutes	2	
Between 30 minutes and 1 hour	3	
Between 1 and 2 hours	4	
Between 2 and 3 hours	5	
Between 3 and 5 hours	6	
Between 5 and 12 hours	7	
Over 12 hours	8	

18.27

d) And how often do you have any other contact with your daughter, besides visiting, either by telephone or letter?

PLEASE TICK ONE BOX

(✓)

Daily	1	
At least several times a week	2	
At least once a week	3	
At least once a month	4	
Several times a year	5	
Less often	6	

18.28

- 7 -

207. Which of these statements applies to you?

PLEASE TICK ONE BOX

- I am married and living in the same household as my husband or wife
- I am living as married and my partner and I live together in the same household
- I have a husband or wife or steady partner but we don't live in the same household
- I don't have a steady partner

18.33

208.a) Now thinking of all your other adult relatives - those still living and aged 18 or older. How many of each do you have?

(Begin with your grandparents. Please write in a number to show how many grandparents you have. If you have none, tick 'NONE', and then go on to the next relative.)

NUMBER OR NONE

- Grandmother, grandfather ——— OR 0
- Adult grandchildren ——— OR
- Aunts, uncles ——— OR
- Parents-in-law and adult brothers-in-law and sisters-in-law ——— OR
- Adult nieces, nephews, cousins and other relatives (AN APPROXIMATE NUMBER WILL DO) ——— OR

18.34
18,35-36
18,37-38
18,39-40
18,41-42

b) Thinking of all these adult relatives, which one do you have most contact with?

PLEASE TICK ONE BOX

- Grandmother
- Grandfather
- Granddaughter
- Grandson
- Aunt
- Uncle
- Mother-in-law
- Father-in-law
- Sister-in-law
- Brother-in-law
- Other adult female relative
- Other adult male relative
- None of these

PLEASE ANSWER Q.8c OPPOSITE

GO TO Q.9 ON PAGE 10

18,43-44

- 8 -

The questions on this page are about the adult relative you have just ticked, that is the one you have most contact with.

208.c) How often do you see or visit this relative?

PLEASE TICK ONE BOX

- He/she lives in the same household → GO TO Q.9
- Daily
- At least several times a week
- At least once a week
- At least once a month
- Several times a year } PLEASE ANSWER Q.8d BELOW
- Less often

18,45

d) About how long would it take you to get to where this relative lives? Think of the time it usually takes door to door.

PLEASE TICK ONE BOX

- Less than 15 minutes
- Between 15 and 30 minutes
- Between 30 minutes and 1 hour
- Between 1 and 2 hours
- Between 2 and 3 hours
- Between 3 and 5 hours
- Between 5 and 12 hours
- Over 12 hours

18,46

e) And how often do you have any other contact with this relative, besides visiting, either by telephone or letter?

PLEASE TICK ONE BOX

- Daily
- At least several times a week
- At least once a week
- At least once a month
- Several times a year
- Less often

18,47

- 9 -

1986 - A

OFFICE USE ONLY

209. Thinking now of close friends – not your husband, or wife, or partner, or family members – but people you feel fairly close to.

a) How many close friends would you say you have?

PLEASE WRITE IN NUMBER (✓) OR NONE ☐

18.48

b) How many of these friends are people you work with now?

PLEASE WRITE IN NUMBER (✓) OR NONE ☐

18.49

c) How many of these friends are your close neighbours?

PLEASE WRITE IN NUMBER (✓) OR NONE ☐

18.50

d) Now thinking of your best friend, or the friend you feel closest to. Is this friend a man or a woman?

PLEASE TICK ONE BOX (✓)

Man ☐ 1
Woman ☐ 2

18.51

e) How often do you see or visit this friend?

He/she lives in the same household → *GO TO Q.10* ☐ 1

PLEASE TICK ONE BOX

Daily ☐ 2
At least several times a week ☐ 3
At least once a week ☐ 4
At least once a month ☐ 5
Several times a year ☐ 6
Less often ☐ 7

18.52

f) About how long would it take you to get to where this friend lives? Think of the time it *usually* takes door to door.

PLEASE TICK ONE BOX (✓)

Less than 15 minutes ☐ 1
Between 15 and 30 minutes ☐ 2
Between 30 minutes and 1 hour ☐ 3
Between 1 and 2 hours ☐ 4
Between 2 and 3 hours ☐ 5
Between 3 and 5 hours ☐ 6
Between 5 and 12 hours ☐ 7
Over 12 hours ☐ 8

18.53

g) And how often do you have any other contact with this friend, besides visiting, either by telephone or letter?

PLEASE TICK ONE BOX (✓)

Daily ☐ 1
At least several times a week ☐ 2
At least once a week ☐ 3
At least once a month ☐ 4
Several times a year ☐ 5
Less often ☐ 6

18.54

- 10 -

1986 - A

OFFICE USE ONLY

20. Now we'd like to ask you about some problems that can happen to anyone.

First, there are some household and garden jobs you really can't do alone – for example, you may need someone to hold a ladder, or to help you move furniture.

a) Who would you turn to first for help?

b) And who would you turn to second?

PLEASE TICK ONLY ONE AS YOUR FIRST CHOICE AND ONE AS YOUR SECOND CHOICE

	a) FIRST (✓)	b) SECOND (✓)
Husband/wife/partner	01	01
Mother	02	02
Father	03	03
Daughter	04	04
Son	05	05
Sister	06	06
Brother	07	07
Other relative, including in-laws	08	08
Closest friend	09	09
Other friend	10	10
Neighbour	11	11
Someone you work with	12	12
Social services, or home help	13	13
Someone you pay to help	14	14

Other (PLEASE WRITE IN) FIRST _____ 97

Other (PLEASE WRITE IN) SECOND _____ 97

No-one 00 00

BEFORE GOING ON TO THE NEXT QUESTION, PLEASE CHECK TO SEE THAT YOU HAVE ONLY ONE FIRST CHOICE AND ONE SECOND CHOICE

18.55-56 /
18.57-58

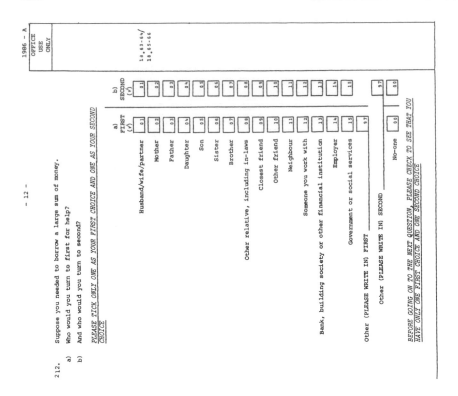

212.

a)   Suppose you needed to borrow a large sum of money.
     Who would you turn to first for help?

b)   And who would you turn to second?

PLEASE TICK ONLY ONE AS YOUR FIRST CHOICE AND ONE AS YOUR SECOND CHOICE

	a) FIRST (✓)	b) SECOND (✓)
Husband/wife/partner	01	01
Mother	02	02
Father	03	03
Daughter	04	04
Son	05	05
Sister	06	06
Brother	07	07
Other relative, including in-laws	08	08
Closest friend	09	09
Other friend	10	10
Neighbour	11	11
Someone you work with	12	12
Bank, building society or other financial institution	13	13
Employer	14	14
Government or social services	15	15
Other (PLEASE WRITE IN) FIRST _____	97	
Other (PLEASE WRITE IN) SECOND _____		97
No-one	00	00

1986 - A
OFFICE
USE
ONLY

18,63-64/
18,65-66

BEFORE GOING ON TO THE NEXT QUESTION, PLEASE CHECK TO SEE THAT YOU HAVE ONLY ONE FIRST CHOICE AND ONE SECOND CHOICE

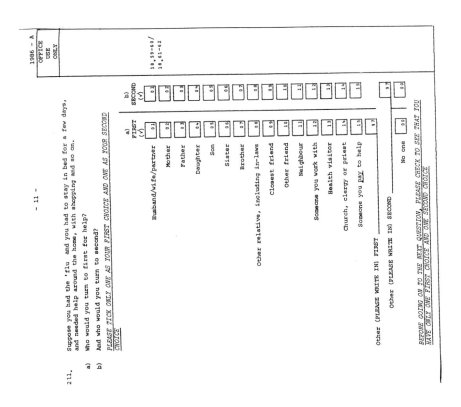

211.

     Suppose you had the 'flu and you had to stay in bed for a few days,
     and needed help around the home, with shopping and so on.

a)   Who would you turn to first for help?

b)   And who would you turn to second?

PLEASE TICK ONLY ONE AS YOUR FIRST CHOICE AND ONE AS YOUR SECOND CHOICE

	a) FIRST (✓)	b) SECOND (✓)
Husband/wife/partner	01	01
Mother	02	02
Father	03	03
Daughter	04	04
Son	05	05
Sister	06	06
Brother	07	07
Other relative, including in-laws	08	08
Closest friend	09	09
Other friend	10	10
Neighbour	11	11
Someone you work with	12	12
Health visitor	13	13
Church, clergy or priest	14	14
Someone you pay to help	15	15
Other (PLEASE WRITE IN) FIRST _____	97	
Other (PLEASE WRITE IN) SECOND _____		97
No one	00	00

1986 - A
OFFICE
USE
ONLY

18,59-60/
18,61-62

BEFORE GOING ON TO THE NEXT QUESTION, PLEASE CHECK TO SEE THAT YOU HAVE ONLY ONE FIRST CHOICE AND ONE SECOND CHOICE

Question 214 (page - 14 -)

1986 - A

OFFICE
USE
ONLY

18,71-72/
18,73-74

214.

Now suppose you felt just a bit down or depressed, and you wanted to talk about it.

a) Who would you turn to first for help?

b) And who would you turn to second?

PLEASE TICK ONLY ONE AS YOUR FIRST CHOICE AND ONE AS YOUR SECOND CHOICE

	a) FIRST (√)	b) SECOND (√)
Husband/wife/partner	01	01
Mother	02	02
Father	03	03
Daughter	04	04
Son	05	05
Sister	06	06
Brother	07	07
Other relative, including in-laws	08	08
Closest friend	09	09
Other friend	10	10
Neighbour	11	11
Someone you work with	12	12
Church, clergy or priest	13	13
Family doctor (GP)	14	14
Psychologist, psychiatrist, or other professional counsellor	15	15
Other (PLEASE WRITE IN) FIRST	97	
Other (PLEASE WRITE IN) SECOND		97
No-one	00	00

BEFORE GOING ON TO THE NEXT QUESTION, PLEASE CHECK TO SEE THAT YOU HAVE ONLY ONE FIRST CHOICE AND ONE SECOND CHOICE

Question 213 (page - 13 -)

OFFICE
USE
ONLY

18,67-68/
18,69-70

213.

Suppose you were very upset about a problem with your husband, wife or partner, and haven't been able to sort it out with them.

Even if you are not married or have no partner, what would you do if you were?

a) Who would you turn to first for help?

b) And who would you turn to second?

PLEASE TICK ONLY ONE AS YOUR FIRST CHOICE AND ONE AS YOUR SECOND CHOICE

	a) FIRST (√)	b) SECOND (√)
Husband/wife/partner	01	01
Mother	02	02
Father	03	03
Daughter	04	04
Son	05	05
Sister	06	06
Brother	07	07
Other relative, including in-laws	08	08
Closest friend	09	09
Other friend	10	10
Neighbour	11	11
Someone you work with	12	12
Church, clergy or priest	13	13
Family doctor (GP)	14	14
Psychologist, psychiatrist, marriage guidance or other professional counsellor	15	15
Other (PLEASE WRITE IN) FIRST	97	
Other (PLEASE WRITE IN) SECOND		97
No-one	00	00

BEFORE GOING ON TO THE NEXT QUESTION, PLEASE CHECK TO SEE THAT YOU HAVE ONLY ONE FIRST CHOICE AND ONE SECOND CHOICE

- 15 -

215. And suppose you needed advice about an important change in your life - for example about a job, or moving to another part of the country.

a) Who would you turn to first for help?

b) And who would you turn to second?

PLEASE TICK ONE ONLY AS YOUR FIRST CHOICE AND ONE ONLY AS YOUR SECOND CHOICE

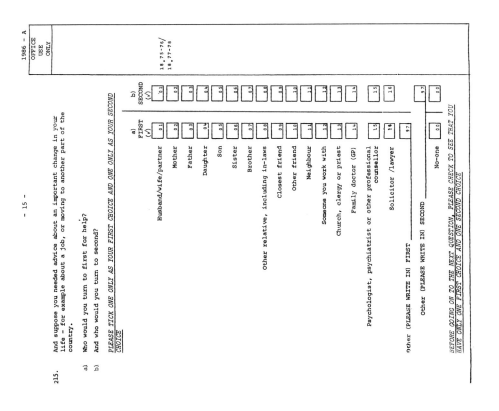

	a) FIRST (✓)	b) SECOND (✓)
Husband/wife/partner	01	01
Mother	02	02
Father	03	03
Daughter	04	04
Son	05	05
Sister	06	06
Brother	07	07
Other relative, including in-laws	08	08
Closest friend	09	09
Other friend	10	10
Neighbour	11	11
Someone you work with	12	12
Church, clergy or priest	13	13
Family doctor (GP)	14	14
Psychologist, psychiatrist or other professional counsellor	15	15
Solicitor /lawyer	16	16
Other (PLEASE WRITE IN) FIRST	97	
Other (PLEASE WRITE IN) SECOND		97
No-one	00	00

18.75-76/
18.77-78

BEFORE GOING ON TO THE NEXT QUESTION, PLEASE CHECK TO SEE THAT YOU HAVE ONLY ONE FIRST CHOICE AND ONE SECOND CHOICE

INTERNATIONAL SOCIAL SURVEY PROGRAMME

1987 MODULE

SOCIAL INEQUALITY

(ENGLISH LANGUAGE VERSION)

1987 - B

- 1 -

201. To begin, we have some questions about opportunities for getting ahead ...

Please tick one box for each of these to show how important you think it is for getting ahead in life ...

a) First, how important is coming from a wealthy family?
PLEASE TICK ONE BOX

Essential	1
Very important	2
Fairly important	3
Not very important	4
Not important at all	5
Can't choose	8

OFFICE USE ONLY: 17.09

b) Having well-educated parents?
PLEASE TICK ONE BOX

Essential	1
Very important	2
Fairly important	3
Not very important	4
Not important at all	5
Can't choose	8

OFFICE USE ONLY: 17.10

c) Having a good education yourself?
PLEASE TICK ONE BOX

Essential	1
Very important	2
Fairly important	3
Not very important	4
Not important at all	5
Can't choose	8

OFFICE USE ONLY: 17.11

d) Ambition?
PLEASE TICK ONE BOX

Essential	1
Very important	2
Fairly important	3
Not very important	4
Not important at all	5
Can't choose	8

OFFICE USE ONLY: 17.12

1987 - B

- 2 -

e) Natural ability - how important is that for getting ahead in life?
PLEASE TICK ONE BOX

Essential	1
Very important	2
Fairly important	3
Not very important	4
Not important at all	5
Can't choose	8

OFFICE USE ONLY: 17.13

f) Hard work - how important is that?
PLEASE TICK ONE BOX

Essential	1
Very important	2
Fairly important	3
Not very important	4
Not important at all	5
Can't choose	8

OFFICE USE ONLY: 17.14

g) Knowing the right people?
PLEASE TICK ONE BOX

Essential	1
Very important	2
Fairly important	3
Not very important	4
Not important at all	5
Can't choose	8

OFFICE USE ONLY: 17.15

h) Having political connections?
PLEASE TICK ONE BOX

Essential	1
Very important	2
Fairly important	3
Not very important	4
Not important at all	5
Can't choose	8

OFFICE USE ONLY: 17.16

- 4 -

1987 – B

m) A person's political beliefs, how important
are they for getting ahead in life?
PLEASE TICK ONE BOX

	(✓)	
Essential	☐	1
Very important	☐	2
Fairly important	☐	3
Not very important	☐	4
Not important at all	☐	5
Can't choose	☐	8

OFFICE USE ONLY: 17,21

202. Please tick a box to show how much you agree or
disagree with the following statement:

The way things are in Britain, people like
me and my family have a good chance of
improving our standard of living.

PLEASE TICK ONE BOX

	(✓)	
Strongly agree	☐	1
Agree	☐	2
Neither agree nor disagree	☐	3
Disagree	☐	4
Strongly disagree	☐	5
Can't choose	☐	8

OFFICE USE ONLY: 17 22

203. Some people earn a lot of money while others
do not earn very much at all ...

In order to get people to work hard, do you
think large differences in pay are ...

PLEASE TICK ONE BOX

	(✓)	
Absolutely necessary	☐	1
Probably necessary	☐	2
Probably not necessary	☐	3
Definitely not necessary	☐	4
Can't choose	☐	8

OFFICE USE ONLY: 17,23

17,24-25

- 3 -

1987 – B

i) A person's race - how important is that
for getting ahead in life?
PLEASE TICK ONE BOX

	(✓)	
Essential	☐	1
Very important	☐	2
Fairly important	☐	3
Not very important	☐	4
Not important at all	☐	5
Can't choose	☐	8

OFFICE USE ONLY: 17,17

j) A person's religion?
PLEASE TICK ONE BOX

	(✓)	
Essential	☐	1
Very important	☐	2
Fairly important	☐	3
Not very important	☐	4
Not important at all	☐	5
Can't choose	☐	8

OFFICE USE ONLY: 17,18

k) The part of the country a person comes from?
PLEASE TICK ONE BOX

	(✓)	
Essential	☐	1
Very important	☐	2
Fairly important	☐	3
Not very important	☐	4
Not important at all	☐	5
Can't choose	☐	8

OFFICE USE ONLY: 17,19

l) Being born a man or a woman - how important
is that?
PLEASE TICK ONE BOX

	(✓)	
Essential	☐	1
Very important	☐	2
Fairly important	☐	3
Not very important	☐	4
Not important at all	☐	5
Can't choose	☐	8

OFFICE USE ONLY: 17,20

- 5 -

204. Do you agree or disagree with each of these statements?

PLEASE TICK ONE BOX ON EACH LINE

	Strongly agree	Agree	Neither agree nor disagree	Disagree	Strongly disagree	Can't choose	
a) People would not want to take extra responsibility at work unless they were paid extra for it.	1	2	3	4	5	8	17.26
b) Workers would not bother to get skills and qualifications unless they were paid extra for having them.	1	2	3	4	5	8	17.27
c) Inequality continues because it benefits the rich and powerful.	1	2	3	4	5	8	17.28
d) No-one would study for years to become a lawyer or doctor unless they expected to earn a lot more than ordinary workers.	1	2	3	4	5	8	17.29
e) Large differences in income are necessary for Britain's prosperity.	1	2	3	4	5	8	17.30
f) Allowing business to make good profits is the best way to improve everyone's standard of living.	1	2	3	4	5	8	17.31
g) Inequality continues to exist because ordinary people don't join together to get rid of it.	1	2	3	4	5	8	17.32

- 6 -

205. We would like to know what **you** think people in these jobs actually earn.

Please write in how much you think they **usually earn each year, before taxes.**

(Many people are not exactly sure about this, but your best guess will be close enough. This may be difficult, but it is important, so please try.)

Please write in how much they actually earn each year, before tax

		OFFICE USE ONLY
a) First, about how much do **you** think a bricklayer earns?	£	17.33-38
b) A doctor in general practice?	£	17.39-44
c) A bank clerk?	£	17.45-50
d) The owner of a small shop?	£	17.51-56
e) The chairman of a large national company?	£	17.57-63
f) A skilled worker in a factory?	£	17.64-69
g) A farm worker?	£	17.70-75
h) A secretary?	£	18.09-14
i) A city bus driver?	£	18.15-20
j) An unskilled worker in a factory?	£	18.21-26
k) A cabinet minister in the national government?	£	18.27-33

- 8 -

1987 - B
OFFICE USE ONLY

207. Please show how much you agree or disagree with each statement....

PLEASE TICK ONE BOX ON EACH LINE

	Agree strongly	Agree	Neither agree nor disagree	Disagree	Disagree strongly	Can't choose	
a) Differences in income in Britain are too large.	1	2	3	4	5	8	19.34
b) It is the responsibility of the government to reduce the differences in income between people with high incomes and those with low incomes.	1	2	3	4	5	8	19.35
c) The government should provide more chances for children from poor families to go to university.	1	2	3	4	5	8	19.36
d) The government should provide a job for everyone who wants one.	1	2	3	4	5	8	19.37
e) The government should spend less on benefits for the poor.	1	2	3	4	5	8	19.38
f) The government should provide a decent standard of living for the unemployed.	1	2	3	4	5	8	19.39
g) The government should provide everyone with a guaranteed basic income.	1	2	3	4	5	8	19.40

- 7 -

1987 - B
OFFICE USE ONLY

206. Next, **what do you think** people in these jobs **ought** to be paid - how much do you think they **should** earn **each** year **before** taxes, regardless of what they actually get?

Please write in how much they should earn each year, before tax

		OFFICE USE ONLY
a) First, about how much do **you** think a bricklayer should earn?	£ -------	18.34-39
b) A doctor in general practice?	£ -------	18.40-45
c) A bank clerk, how much should s/he earn? ..	£ -------	18.46-51
d) The owner of a small shop?	£ -------	18.52-57
e) The chairman of a large national company?	£ -------	18.58-64
f) A skilled worker in a factory?	£ -------	18.65-70
g) A farm worker?	£ -------	18.71-76
h) A secretary?	£ -------	19.09-14
i) A city bus driver?	£ -------	19.15-20
j) An unskilled worker in a factory? ...	£ -------	19.21-26
k) A cabinet minister in the national government?	£ -------	19.27-33

- 9 -

208. Generally, how would you describe taxes in Britain today ...

(We mean all taxes together, including national insurance, income tax, VAT and all the rest.)

a) First, for those with high incomes, are taxes ...

PLEASE TICK ONE BOX

Much too high	1	
Too high	2	
About right	3	
Too low	4	
Much too low	5	
Can't choose	8	

19.41

b) Next, for those with middle incomes, are taxes ...

PLEASE TICK ONE BOX

Much too high	1	
Too high	2	
About right	3	
Too low	4	
Much too low	5	
Can't choose	8	

19.42

c) Lastly, for those with low incomes, are taxes ...

PLEASE TICK ONE BOX

Much too high	1	
Too high	2	
About right	3	
Too low	4	
Much too low	5	
Can't choose	8	

19.43

209. Do you think that people with high incomes should pay a larger share of their income in taxes than those with low incomes, the same share, or a smaller share?

PLEASE TICK ONE BOX

Much larger share	1	
Larger	2	
The same share	3	
Smaller	4	
Much smaller share	5	
Can't choose	8	

19.44

- 10 -

210. In all countries there are differences or even conflicts between different social groups. In your opinion, in Britain how much conflict is there between ...

PLEASE TICK ONE BOX ON EACH LINE

	Very strong conflicts	Strong conflicts	Not very strong conflicts	There are no conflicts	Can't choose	
a) Poor people and rich people?	1	2	3	4	8	19.45
b) The working class and the middle class?	1	2	3	4	8	19.46
c) The unemployed and people with jobs?	1	2	3	4	8	19.47
d) Management and workers?	1	2	3	4	8	19.48
e) Farmers and city people?	1	2	3	4	8	19.49
f) Young people and older people?	1	2	3	4	8	19.50

211. In our society there are groups which tend to be towards the top and groups which tend to be towards the bottom. Below is a scale that runs from top to bottom. Where would you put yourself on this scale?

PLEASE TICK ONE BOX

Top	01	
	02	
	03	
	04	
	05	
	06	
	07	
	08	
	09	
Bottom	10	

19.51-52

212. Please think of your present job (or your last one if you don't have one now). If you compare this job with the job your father had when you were 16, would you say that the level or status of your job is (or was) ...

Much higher than your father's	1	
Higher	2	
About equal	3	
Lower	4	
Much lower than your father's	5	
(I never had a job)	6	
(Never knew father/father never had a job)	7	

19.53

- 11 -

1987 - B
OFFICE USE ONLY

213.a) Here is a list of different types of jobs. Which type did your father have when you were 16?
(If your father did not have a job then, please give the job he used to have.)
PLEASE TICK ONE BOX   (✓)

Professional and technical (for example: doctor, teacher, engineer, artist, accountant)	01
Higher administrator (for example: banker, executive in big business, high government official, union official)	02
Clerical (for example: secretary, clerk, office manager, bookkeeper)	03
Sales (for example: sales manager, shop owner, shop assistant, insurance agent)	04
Service (for example: restaurant owner, police officer, waiter, barber, caretaker)	05
Skilled worker (for example: foreman, motor mechanic, printer, tool and die maker, electrician)	06
Semi-Skilled worker (for example: bricklayer, bus driver, cannery worker, carpenter, sheet metal worker, baker)	07
Unskilled worker (for example: labourer, porter, unskilled factory worker)	08
Farm (for example: farmer, farm labourer, tractor driver)	09
(Never knew father/father never had job)	10

19,54-55

b) Was your father self-employed, or did he work for someone else?
PLEASE TICK ONE BOX   (✓)

Self-employed, had own business or farm	1
Worked for someone else	2
(Never knew father/father never had job)	3

19,56

19,57

- 12 -

1987 - B
OFFICE USE ONLY

214.a) And how about your first job - the first job you had after you finished full-time education?
(Even if that was many years ago, we would still like to know about it.)
PLEASE TICK ONE BOX   (✓)

Professional and technical (for example: doctor, teacher, engineer, artist, accountant)	01
Higher administrator (for example: banker, executive in big business, high government official, union official)	02
Clerical (for example: secretary, clerk, office manager, bookkeeper)	03
Sales (for example: sales manager, shop owner, shop assistant, insurance agent)	04
Service (for example: restaurant owner, police officer, barber, waitress, caretaker)	05
Skilled worker (for example: foreman, motor mechanic, printer, seamstress, electrician)	06
Semi-skilled worker (for example: bricklayer, bus driver, cannery worker, carpenter, sheet metal worker, baker)	07
Unskilled worker (for example: labourer, porter, unskilled factory worker)	08
Farm (for example: farmer, farm labourer, tractor driver)	09
(Never had a job)	10

19,58-59

b) Were you self-employed, or did you work for someone else?
PLEASE TICK ONE BOX   (✓)

Self-employed, had own business or farm	1
Worked for someone else	2
(Never had a job)	3

19,60

19,61-62

- 13 -

215.a) And how about your job now?

(If you are not working now, please tell us about your last job.)

PLEASE TICK ONE BOX

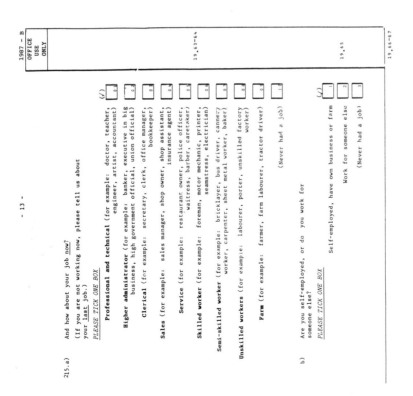

	(✓)	
Professional and technical (for example: doctor, teacher, engineer, artist, accountant)		☐ 01
Higher administrator (for example: banker, executive in big business, high government official, union official)		☐ 02
Clerical (for example: secretary, clerk, office manager, bookkeeper)		☐ 03
Sales (for example: sales manager, shop owner, shop assistant, insurance agent)		☐ 04
Service (for example: restaurant owner, police officer, waitress, barber, caretaker)		☐ 05
Skilled worker (for example: foreman, motor mechanic, printer, seamstress, electrician)		☐ 06
Semi-skilled worker (for example: bricklayer, bus driver, cannery worker, carpenter, sheet metal worker, baker)		☐ 07
Unskilled workers (for example: labourer, porter, unskilled factory worker)		☐ 08
Farm (for example: farmer, farm labourer, tractor driver)		☐ 09
(Never had a job)		☐ 10

b) Are you self-employed, or do you work for someone else?

PLEASE TICK ONE BOX

	(✓)	
Self-employed, have own business or farm		☐ 1
Work for someone else		☐ 2
(Never had a job)		☐ 3

1987 - B

OFFICE
USE
ONLY

19.63-64

19.65

19.66-67

INTERNATIONAL SOCIAL SURVEY PROGRAMME

1988 MODULE

WOMEN AND THE FAMILY

(ENGLISH LANGUAGE VERSION)

— 1 —

1989 - A
OFFICE USE ONLY
CARD 18

201. To begin, we have some questions about women.
Do you agree or disagree ...?

PLEASE TICK ONE BOX ON EACH LINE

	Strongly agree	Agree	Neither agree nor disagree	Disagree	Strongly disagree	Can't choose	
a. A working mother can establish just as warm and secure a relationship with her children as a mother who does not work.	1	2	3	4	5	8	1808
b. A pre-school child is likely to suffer if his or her mother works.	1	2	3	4	5	8	1809
c. All in all, family life suffers when the woman has a full-time job.	1	2	3	4	5	8	1810
d. A woman and her family will all be happier if she goes out to work.	1	2	3	4	5	8	1811
e. A job is all right, but what most women really want is a home and children.	1	2	3	4	5	8	1812
f. Being a housewife is just as fulfilling as working for pay.	1	2	3	4	5	8	1813
g. Having a job is the best way for a woman to be an independent person.	1	2	3	4	5	8	1814
h. Both the husband and wife should contribute to the household income.	1	2	3	4	5	8	1815
i. A husband's job is to earn money; a wife's job is to look after the home and family.	1	2	3	4	5	8	1816

Do you agree or disagree ...

	Strongly agree	Agree	Neither agree nor disagree	Disagree	Strongly disagree	Can't choose	
j. I would enjoy having a job even if I didn't need the money.	1	2	3	4	5	8	1817

— 2 —

1989 - A
OFFICE USE ONLY

202. Do you think that women should work outside the home full-time, part-time or not at all under these circumstances?

PLEASE TICK ONE BOX ON EACH LINE

	Work full-time	Work part-time	Stay at home	Can't choose	
a. After marrying and before there are children?	1	2	3	8	1818
b. When there is a child under school age?	1	2	3	8	1819
c. After the youngest child starts school?	1	2	3	8	1820
d. After the children leave home?	1	2	3	8	1821

203. Think of a child under 3 years old whose parents both have full-time jobs.

How suitable do you think each of these childcare arrangements would be for the child?

	Very suitable	Somewhat suitable	Not very suitable	Not at all suitable	Can't choose	
a. A state or local authority nursery?	1	2	3	4	8	1822
b. A private creche or nursery?	1	2	3	4	8	1823
c. A childminder or babysitter?	1	2	3	4	8	1824
d. A neighbour or friend?	1	2	3	4	8	1825
e. A relative?	1	2	3	4	8	1826

204.a) If you were advising a **young woman**, which of the following ways of life would you recommend?

PLEASE TICK ONE BOX ONLY

	(✓)	
To live alone, without a steady partner?	1	1827
To live with a steady partner, without marrying?	2	
To live with a steady partner for a while, and then marry?	3	
To marry without living together first?	4	
Can't choose	8	

- 3 -

1989 - A
OFFICE USE ONLY

204.b) If you were advising a young man, which of the following ways of life would you recommend?

PLEASE TICK ONE BOX ONLY

	(✓)
To live alone, without a steady partner?	[1]
To live with a steady partner, without marrying?	[2]
To live with a steady partner for a while, and then marry?	[3]
To marry without living together first?	[4]
Can't choose	[8]

1828

205. Do you agree or disagree ...?
PLEASE TICK ONE BOX ON EACH LINE

	Strongly agree	Agree	Neither agree nor disagree	Disagree	Disagree strongly	Can't choose	OFFICE USE ONLY
a. Married people are generally happier than unmarried people.	[1]	[2]	[3]	[4]	[5]	[8]	1829
b. Personal freedom is more important than the companionship of marriage.	[1]	[2]	[3]	[4]	[5]	[8]	1830
c. The main advantage of marriage is that it gives financial security.	[1]	[2]	[3]	[4]	[5]	[8]	1831
d. The main purpose of marriage these days is to have children.	[1]	[2]	[3]	[4]	[5]	[8]	1832
e. It is better to have a bad marriage than no marriage at all.	[1]	[2]	[3]	[4]	[5]	[8]	1833
f. People who want children ought to get married.	[1]	[2]	[3]	[4]	[5]	[8]	1834
g. A single mother can bring up her child as well as a married couple.	[1]	[2]	[3]	[4]	[5]	[8]	1835
h. A single father can bring up his child as well as a married couple.	[1]	[2]	[3]	[4]	[5]	[8]	1836
i. Couples don't take marriage seriously enough when divorce is easily available.	[1]	[2]	[3]	[4]	[5]	[8]	1837
j. Homosexual couples should have the right to marry one another.	[1]	[2]	[3]	[4]	[5]	[8]	1838

- 4 -

1989 - A
OFFICE USE ONLY
1839-40

206. All in all, what do you think is the ideal number of children for a family to have?

PLEASE WRITE THE NUMBER IN THE BOX [ ]

207. In general, what do you feel about each of these family sizes?

PLEASE TICK ONE BOX ON EACH LINE

A family with: It is ...

	Very desirable	Desirable	Neither desirable nor undesirable	Un-desirable	Very un-desirable	Can't choose	OFFICE USE ONLY
a. No children?	[1]	[2]	[3]	[4]	[5]	[8]	1841
b. One child?	[1]	[2]	[3]	[4]	[5]	[8]	1842
c. Two children?	[1]	[2]	[3]	[4]	[5]	[8]	1843
d. Three children?	[1]	[2]	[3]	[4]	[5]	[8]	1844
e. Four children or more?	[1]	[2]	[3]	[4]	[5]	[8]	1845

208. Do you agree or disagree ...?
PLEASE TICK ONE BOX ON EACH LINE

	Strongly agree	Agree	Neither agree nor disagree	Disagree	Strongly disagree	Can't choose	OFFICE USE ONLY
a. Children are more trouble than they are worth.	[1]	[2]	[3]	[4]	[5]	[8]	1846
b. Watching children grow up is life's greatest joy.	[1]	[2]	[3]	[4]	[5]	[8]	1847
c. Having children interferes too much with the freedom of parents.	[1]	[2]	[3]	[4]	[5]	[8]	1848
d. A marriage without children is not fully complete.	[1]	[2]	[3]	[4]	[5]	[8]	1849
e. It is better not to have children because they are such a heavy burden.	[1]	[2]	[3]	[4]	[5]	[8]	1850
f. People who have never had children lead empty lives.	[1]	[2]	[3]	[4]	[5]	[8]	1851

- 5 -

1989 - A

209. In general, would you say that the law now makes it easy or difficult for people who want to get divorced?
PLEASE TICK ONE BOX ONLY

Very easy	1
Fairly easy	2
Neither easy nor difficult	3
Fairly difficult	4
Very difficult	5
Impossible	6
Can't choose	8

OFFICE USE ONLY 1852

210. And in general, how easy or difficult do you think the law **should** make it for **couples without young children** to get a divorced?
PLEASE TICK ONE BOX ONLY

Very easy	1
Fairly easy	2
Neither easy nor difficult	3
Fairly difficult	4
Very difficult	5
Impossible	6
Can't choose	8

1853

211. And what about **couples with young children**? How easy or difficult should the law make it for them to get a divorce?
PLEASE TICK ONE BOX ONLY

Very easy	1
Fairly easy	2
Neither easy nor difficult	3
Fairly difficult	4
Very difficult	5
Impossible	6
Can't choose	8

1854

- 6 -

1989 - A

212. When a marriage is troubled and unhappy do you think it is generally better for the **children** if the couple stays together or gets divorced?
PLEASE TICK ONE BOX ONLY

Much better to divorce	1
Better to divorce	2
Worse to divorce	3
Much worse to divorce	4
Can't choose	8

OFFICE USE ONLY 1855

213. And when a marriage is troubled and unhappy, is it generally better for the **wife** if the couple stays together or gets divorced?
PLEASE TICK ONE BOX ONLY

Much better to divorce	1
Better to divorce	2
Worse to divorce	3
Much worse to divorce	4
Can't choose	8

1856

214. And when a marriage is troubled and unhappy, is it generally better for the **husband** if the couple stays together or gets divorced?
PLEASE TICK ONE BOX ONLY

Much better to divorce	1
Better to divorce	2
Worse to divorce	3
Much worse to divorce	4
Can't choose	8

1857

215. Did your mother ever work for pay for as long as **one year after** you were born and **before** you were 14?
PLEASE TICK ONE BOX ONLY

Yes, she worked	1
No	2
Did not live with mother	3

1858

1859

ASKED ON PAGE 41A OF THE INTERVIEW QUESTIONNAIRE

		Col./Code	Skip to
A903a)	INTERVIEWER TO COMPLETE :	1471	
	RESPONDENT IS: Man	1 →	Q.904
	Woman	2 →	b)
	IF WOMAN:	1472	
	b) RESPONDENT IS: (SEE CODE 1, Q.900) Married	1 →	c)
	Not married	2	Q.904
	IF MARRIED WOMAN:	1473	
	c) RESPONDENT: Has children (SEE H/H GRID Q.901)	1 →	d)
	OR Has had children (CODE 1 AT Q,902)		
	Has not	2 →	Q.904

IF MARRIED WOMAN WITH CHILDREN (CODE 1 AT Q.903c)

CARD FF

d) Please use this card to say whether you worked full-time, part-time or not at all ...

READ a)-d) BELOW AND CODE ONE FOR EACH

		Worked full-time	Worked part-time	Stayed at home	Does not apply		
a)	... after marrying and before you had children?	1	2	3	8		1474
b)	... and what about when a child was under school age?	1	2	3	8		1475
c)	... after the youngest child started school?	1	2	3	8		1476
d)	... and how about after the children left home?	1	2	3	8		1477
					1478-80	SPARE	
					1506-07	CARD 15	

- 7 -

1989 - A

		OFFICE USE ONLY
216.	Have you ever been divorced?	
	PLEASE TICK ONE BOX ONLY	1860
	(✓)	
	Yes [ ] 1 ⎫ PLEASE ANSWER Q.17	
	No [ ] 2 ⎬ BELOW	
	Never married [ ] 3 → GO TO Q.20, PAGE 8	
217.	Are you married or living as married now?	1861
	PLEASE TICK ONE BOX ONLY	
	(✓)	
	Yes [ ] 1 → PLEASE ANSWER Q.18-19 BELOW	
	No [ ] 2 → GO TO Q.20, PAGE 8	
218.a)	Has your husband or wife or partner ever been divorced?	1862
	PLEASE TICK ONE BOX ONLY	
	(✓)	
	Yes [ ] 1	
	No [ ] 2	
b)	Did you live with your husband or wife or partner before you got married?	1863
	PLEASE TICK ONE BOX	
	(✓)	
	Yes [ ] 1	
	No [ ] 2	
	Not married [ ] 3	
219,a)	Do you and your husband or wife or partner both have paid work at the moment?	1864
	PLEASE TICK ONE BOX	
	(✓)	
	Yes [ ] 1 → ANSWER b), BELOW	
	No [ ] 2 → GO TO Q.20, PAGE 8	
b)	Who earns more money?	1865
	PLEASE TICK ONE BOX ONLY	
	(✓)	
	Husband earns **much** more [ ] 1	
	Husband earns a **bit** more [ ] 2	
	We earn about the **same** amount [ ] 3	
	Wife earns a **bit** more [ ] 4	
	Wife earns **much** more [ ] 5	

Subject index

A

ALLBUS (West Germany), technical details of 161-162
Australia 3, 5, 8, 11, 12, 35–58 *passim*, 59–86 *passim*, 87–103 *passim*
Austria 5, 8, 12, 15–34 *passim*, 35–58 *passim*, 87–103 *passim*

B

Banks, borrowing from 97
Basic Law, pride in 124-131, 136–137
British Social Attitudes, technical details of survey 157–159
Bundestag, see Parliament

C

Children
    and ease of divorce 152–153
    and working mothers 144–147
    borrowing money from adult 97
    choice of having 150–151
    contact with adult 98–100
    desirable and ideal number of 148–149
    sharing household with adult 89–90
    state intervention for welfare of 44–45
    also see Family; Parents; Relatives; Siblings

Civil liberties 9, 46–47
Class, *see* Social class
Class conflict as explanation of inequality 69–70
Cross-national surveys,
    benefits of data from 6–11
    difficulties of measurements from 4–6

D

Democracy, working of 133–134
Divorce,
    and children 152–153
    availability of 151–153

E

Earnings,
    coefficient of variation of 23
    factors affecting 24–25
    trade union membership and 23–26
    also see Income inequalities; Wage rates
Education,
    influence of on earnings 25
    support for spending on 41
    also see Higher education
Egalitarianism 61–63, 74
Employment,
    government role in providing 38–39

part-time 18
women in 18, 19–20, 144–147
also see Workforce; Unemployment
Environment, support for state
       spending on 41

F

Family,
    contact with 92–94, 100–101
    government intervention in 44–45
    help and support from 95–96
    living with members of 89–91
    models of attitudes to 150–151
    proximity to 91–92
    also see Children; Parents; Relatives;
        Siblings; 'Symmetrical Family'
Family networks 89–103 *passim*
Family size 148–149
Fieldwork 157–169 *passim*
Freedom of speech 8–9, 46–47, 49
Friends,
    contact with 94–95, 100–101
    gender of 'best friend' 94
    help and support from 95–98

G

Gender,
    and contact with relatives 98–100
    and help and support from spouse
        96, 102
    and inequality of opportunity 47–49
    and levels of earnings 25
    also see Women
General Social Survey (GSS) (USA)
    and ISSP 3, 12
    technical details of 159–160
Government intervention,
    in industry 37–38
    in price levels 38–39
    in providing employment 38–39
    in wage levels 38–39, 61–62
    models of 36–37
    also see Government responsibility;
        Welfare state
Government responsibility,
    and class inequality 48–49
    and gender inequality 47–49
    for children 44–45
    for economy 37–40
    for welfare 40–41
    also see Government intervention;
        Welfare state

H

Health, knowledge of risks to 112–113

Health care, state spending on 42–43,
    49–50
Higher education,
    and mobility of students 90
    and state assistance for children of
        poor families to go on to 62–63
Household,
    income 147
    sharing with relatives 89–91
    size 89
Housing, effect of shortages of 90–91
Hungary,
    and participation in ISSP 5, 8, 12
    technical details of surveys 163–164
    also see 15–34 *passim*, 59–86 *passim*,
        87–103 *passim*, 143–155 *passim*

I

Income inequalities,
    as incentives to working hard 69, 71
    perceptions of and support for
        reductions in 65–67, 73–74
    role of in national prosperity 70–71
Income redistribution 50–51, 61, 64–65,
    73, 74–75
Indagine Sociale Italiana (ISI), technical
    details of survey 164
Individualism 60, 74
Industry,
    government intervention in 37–38
    state ownership of 39–40
Inequality,
    class 48–49
    in opportunities for women 47–49
    perceived reasons for 69–71
    support for government action to
        redress 47–49
    also see 59–73 *passim*; Income
        inequalities
Inequality and welfare 59–86
**Interim report: the changing family
    143–155**
International patterns of work 15–34
International Social Survey Programme
    (ISSP),
    character of member nations 5–6
    current membership of 12
    modules fielded 12
    origins of 2–3
    technical details of surveys 157–169
Ireland, Republic of 5, 12, 143–155
    passim, 166
Italy,
    and participation in ISSP 5, 8, 12
    and technical details of surveys 164
    also see 15–34 *passim*, 35–58 *passim*,
        59–86 *passim*, 87–103 *passim*

K

Kinship and friendship 87–103

L

Libertarianism 9

M

Marriage,
    and help and support from spouse
      96–97
    and sharing with relatives 90
    nature of relationship 101–102
Measuring national differences 1–13
Mobility, socio-economic,
    chances for 10–11, 66–67
    factors influencing 68–69
Monarchy, pride in 124–130, 136–137

N

National pride,
    and political participation 134–136
    lack of 127, 132
    objects of 125–128
    significance of 122–123
    also see 121–142 *passim*
National pride surveys, technical
details of 167–169
National Social Science Survey (NSSS)
    (Australia),
    and ISSP 3, 12
    technical details of 160–161
Netherlands,
    and participation in ISSP 5, 8, 12
    technical details of survey 165
    also see 59–86 *passim*
Notes on tabulations 170

O

Opportunity, perceptions of 67–69

P

Parents,
    and ease of divorce 152–153
    borrowing money from 97
    contact with 92–94, 98–100
    help and support from 95–96
    interests *versus* children's 150–151
    living with 89–91

    proximity to 91–92
    also see Children; Family; Relatives
Parliament, pride in 124–128, 130–131
Pensions, state spending on 42–43,
    49–51
Political participation, and national
    pride 134–136
Political systems,
    and welfare programmes 61–63
    models of 59–61
Poverty, support for state spending to
    alleviate 61–62
    also see Inequality; Welfare state
Prices, role of state in controlling 38–39
**Pride in one's country: Britain and West
    Germany 121–142**
Probabilistic reasoning, public
    understanding of 112
Protest, political 46–47
Public expenditure 37–44, 59–62,
    117–118
    also see Government intervention;
      Government responsibility;
      Welfare state
Public understanding of science,
    technical details of surveys 166–167
    also see 105–119 *passim*

Q

The questionnaires 173–203

R

Regional variations in pride in
    monarchy 128–130
Relatives,
    contact with 92–94
    help and support from 95–96
    living with 89–91
    proximity to 91–92
    also see Children; Family; Parents;
      Siblings
Religion
    and acceptance of scientific theories
      114–116
    and attitudes to cohabitation 90
    and divorce 151–153
    and family size 151
Religious attendance 7–8
'Retired' persons in the labour market
    19–20
The role of the state 35–58

S

Sampling 157–169 *passim*

Science,
    informedness about 107, 108
    interest in 106–107, 108
    knowledge of 109-112
    national pride in achievements of
        125–127
    perceived relevance of 108–109
    state spending on 117–118
Scientific theories, acceptance of
    114–116
Self-employment 17, 18–19, 26
Siblings,
    contact with 98–101
    living with 89–90
    also see Family; Relatives
Social class 10–11, 49–51, 72–73
Social conflict, assessments of 71–72
Social support systems 89–103 *passim*
Sozialer Survey Österreich (SSOE),
    technical details of survey 162–163
State ownership of industry 39–40
Switzerland,
    technical details of survey 165
    also see 15–34 *passim*
'Symmetrical family' 98–100

T

Taxation,
    of different income groups 63–64
    support for progressive 64–65, 73
Technical details of surveys 157–169
Trade unions,
    influence of on members' wages
        23–26
    membership levels 21–22
    membership profiles 22–23
    strength of 17, 23–26

U

**Understanding of science in Britain and
    the USA 105–119**
Unemployment,
    rates 20–21

state spending on benefits 43–44,
    49–51
also see Employment; ,Workforce
USA,
    and participation in ISSP 3, 5, 12
    public understanding of science in
        105–119 *passim*
    technical details of surveys 159–160
    also see 15–34 *passim*, 35–'58 *passim*,
        59–87 *passim*, 87–103 *passim*,
        143–155 *passim*

W

Wage rates,
    government intervention to control
        38–39, 61–62
    also see Earnings
'Welfare capitalism' 35–37
Welfare state,
    pride in 125–127
    support for 61–63, 72–75
    also see Government responsibility;
        Public expenditure
West Germany,
    and participation in ISSP 3, 5, 12
    and national pride 121–142 *passim*
    also see 15–34 *passim*, 35–58 *passim*,
        59–86 *passim*, 87–103 *passim*,
        143–155 *passim*
Women,
    and participation in the labour
        market 18–20, 144–147
    contact with relatives among 98–100
    earnings levels of 25
    inequalities in opportunities for
        47–49
    trade union membership among 21–
        22
    unemployment rates among 21
    also see Gender
Workforce,
    composition 18–19
    participation rates 19–20
Working week, length of 27

BEDFORDSHIRE
LEISURE
SERVICES
COUNTY COUNCIL